BLACKED OUT

In 1966, the U.S. Congress passed the landmark Freedom of Information Act (FOIA), giving the public the right to government documents. This "right to know" has been used over four decades to challenge overreaching Presidents and secretive government agencies. FOIA has also become a model for other nations, spawning similar laws in sixty other countries. Nonetheless, the struggle for openness is far from over. This book describes the tactics that politicians and bureaucrats around the world have used to preserve government secrecy. It explains how profound changes in the structure of government – privatization of public services, the rise of powerful international organizations, the growth of tightly knit networks of security agencies – are complicating campaigns for openness. The complex effects of new information technologies – sometimes enhancing openness, sometimes creating new barriers to transparency – are also described. *Blacked Out* provides an invaluable overview of the challenges confronting the new global movement for open government.

Alasdair Roberts is an associate professor of public administration in the Maxwell School of Citizenship and Public Affairs at Syracuse University. He is also Director of the Campbell Public Affairs Institute at Syracuse University, and an Honorary Senior Research Fellow of the Constitution Unit, University College London. He received a law degree from the University of Toronto and a PhD in Public Policy from Harvard University. His research focuses on two areas: public sector restructuring and transparency in government. His web address is http://www.aroberts.us.

BLACKED OUT

GOVERNMENT SECRECY IN THE INFORMATION AGE

Alasdair Roberts

The Maxwell School of Syracuse University

CAMBRIDGE
UNIVERSITY PRESS

CAMBRIDGE UNIVERSITY PRESS
Cambridge, New York, Melbourne, Madrid, Cape Town, Singapore, São Paulo

Cambridge University Press
40 West 20th Street, New York, NY 10011-4211, USA

www.cambridge.org
Information on this title: www.cambridge.org/9780521858700

First published 2006
Reprinted 2006 (twice)

Printed in the United States of America

A catalog record for this publication is available from the British Library.

ISBN-13   978-0-521-85870-0 hardback
ISBN-10   0-521-85870-4 hardback

The eye of the public makes the statesman virtuous. The multitude of the audience multiplies for disintegrity the chances of detection.

Jeremy Bentham, 1785

Our country has forgotten how to keep a secret.

Donald Rumsfeld, U.S. Secretary of Defense, 2004

CONTENTS

ACKNOWLEDGEMENTS

This is a book about transparency, so let me make a full disclosure of the debts I owe to the people and organizations who have helped to bring it to fruition.

I am Canadian, and began using Canada's Access to Information Act when I started teaching at the School of Policy Studies at Queen's University in 1989. (My first request, for a copy of the instruction manual given to newly appointed Canadian cabinet ministers, was denied in full.) But I did not begin conducting research on the subject until 1997, when the Canadian Newspaper Association asked me to write a survey on the state of Canada's federal and provincial disclosure laws. It has been a pleasure to work over the last eight years with the CNA and its President Anne Kothawala, an articulate proponent of the right to information in Canada.

In 1999, a fellowship at the Woodrow Wilson International Center for Scholars allowed me to contrast Canadian experience with the United States' track record under its older Freedom of Information Act. I also had the privilege of working with Laura Neuman and other staff at the Carter Center, learning more about efforts to improve transparency in the Caribbean and Latin America.

In 2000, the Open Society Institute awarded a fellowship that provided a wonderful opportunity to travel and study struggles over openness in other countries. In 2003 the Open Society Justice Initiative, an operational program of the Institute, provided support for an international workshop on national security and open government that was organized by the Campbell Public Affairs Institute, a research center of the Maxwell School of Syracuse University, which I currently direct. I have benefited on many occasions from conversations with

Acknowledgements

Helen Darbishire, Senior Program Manager of the Justice Initiative's Freedom of Information and Expression Program.

I have also been honored to work with the ten other members of the Transparency Task Force, an international committee of scholars and activists established in 2002 by Professor Joseph Stiglitz's Initiative for Policy Dialogue, to improve understanding of transparency as a tool for advancing human rights and economic development. Chaired by Shekhar Singh and Ann Florini, the Task Force includes Tom Blanton, Richard Calland, Jamie Horsley, Laura Neuman, Ayo Obe, Elena Petkova, Vivek Ramkumar, Ivan Szekely, and Hanhua Zhou.

The last decade has witnessed the emergence of a remarkable international community of scholars, advocates, and public servants interested in open government. The members of this group correspond regularly and rely on each other for advice and support in their campaigns for transparency. The extent to which this network has grown over a few short years – in breadth, in depth of interconnectedness, and in sophistication of dialogue – has been extraordinary. I have learned a great deal from the members of this community. I am particularly indebted to David Banisar, who has for several years done an extraordinary job of tracking international developments in this field; to Toby Mendel, Law Programme Director of ARTICLE 19; and to David Goldberg, for his manuscript comments.

I am also grateful for the assistance of the staff of the Campbell Public Affairs Institute, Bethany Walawender and Kelley Coleman, and the support of six graduate assistants who have worked with me while completing their master's degrees in public administration at the Maxwell School: Lillian Foo, Sarah Holsen, Kevin Lo, Michael N'dolo, Katherine Younker, and Andrea Stenhoff. Thanks are due as well to John Berger, Senior Editor at Cambridge University Press, for his enthusiasm and advice.

Over the years, I have filed hundreds of requests for information, using disclosure laws in several countries. In most cases, these requests have been handled by disclosure officers who have done their best to honor the spirit of the law. It is a difficult job, which often requires career public servants to mediate between dissatisfied citizens and balky higher-level officials. I'm indebted to this group of civil servants, as well as to the investigators who have dealt with my complaints and appeals, for their professionalism and patience with sometimes complex requests.

Finally, I must thank my parents, James and Nancy Roberts, who have passed down their own love of knowledge and a measured skepticism of authority. My wife, Sandra, has listened patiently to many stories on arcane points of law; and my children, John and Constance, now know what I have been doing down in our basement all these months.

The massive glass cupola of the renovated German Parliament, opened in 1999. The British architect Norman Foster said that he intended the Parliament to be "transparent, its activities on view." The cupola contains an observation platform "allowing the people to ascend above the heads of their political representatives." Photograph by Hendrik Brixius.

1

THE GLASS CASE

Hoy todos estamos en una caja de cristal, porque hoy todo se ve, todo se lee y todo se escucha.

— Vicente Fox, President of Mexico, March 2004[1]

The village of Kelwara sits in the arid folds of the Aravalli mountains in the southern part of the Indian state of Rajasthan. Above the village are Kumbalgarh Fort, half a millennium old, and luxury hotels for tourists who visit the Fort. The villagers are very poor; the price of a night's stay in one of the hotels, 3000 rupees, is more than many earn in a year. The villagers rely on wheat, sugar, and kerosene that is distributed by the government for sale by local ration dealers at reduced prices. But many ration dealers are corrupt. They falsify their registers to show that they have sold rations to poor villagers and then sell the supplies on the black market.

In January 2004, 400 villagers from Kelwara and neighboring *panchayats* gathered on a mango-shaded flat below the check dam that gathers Kelwara's water. The *jan sunwai* – Hindi for public hearing – was organized by an activist group, Mazdoor Kisan Shakti Sangathan (MKSS), which had worked with the poor of southern Rajasthan for fifteen years. The ration dealers were there as well, standing at the edge of the meeting; at the front was a table at which sat the leaders of MKSS, the local magistrate, and visitors from Delhi. A banner behind the table, in Hindi, said: "Democracy Is Transparency with Accountability to the People."[2]

This was perhaps the twentieth *jan sunwai* that MKSS had organized, and by now the dramatic arc of the meeting was well established. Shankar Singh, one of MKSS's leaders, led the villagers in a

1

song that he had composed, and that had become the organization's anthem:

> *A Hero Honda*
> > *I don't demand*
> *A new Maruti*
> > *I don't demand*
> *Pepsi Cola*
> > *I don't demand*
> *Full wages*
> > *We demand!*
> *Food security*
> > *We demand!*
> *The right to information*
> > *We demand!*[3]

Next came a report on MKSS's recent work, and then the highlight of the meeting: public testimony. MKSS organizers had acquired the registers in which ration dealers recorded the sale of rationed goods. "Did you buy thirty-five kilograms of wheat from your ration shop on the fourth of January?" an organizer asked Lal Singh Rawat, a red-turbaned quarry worker, after reading from the register. "I did not," said Rawat. "I was told that there was no wheat available." Quickly the meeting fell apart. Ration dealers surrounded Rawat, the generator that supplied power to the microphone suddenly shut off, and for twenty minutes the meeting fell into tempered anarchy. The disruption was expected. The villagers stayed, order was restored, and the truth came out. Nikhil Dey, another MKSS leader, read the list of alleged disbursements from the registers, while Shankar Singh checked entries in the villagers' ration books. In eight *panchayats*, at least thirty ration dealers had defrauded the poor by making false entries in their registers.

This was theatre (agreed Aruna Roy, the former civil servant who with Dey and Singh had set up MKSS) – but with the very serious purpose of helping the poor. An earlier public hearing in nearby Janawad *panchayat* had revealed the depth of corruption in public works projects. Engineers recorded measurements for "ghost works" that did not exist, and muster rolls showed the payment of wages to villagers who had never worked on a project. Almost five million rupees could not be accounted for. The state government appointed a commission that concluded that only one out of seven projects in the *panchayat* had actually been completed, and twenty-six government officials were charged with corruption. In other meetings, village leaders faced with evidence of their fraud apologized, returned money to the *panchayat*, and promised to mend their ways.

In Janawad, and again in Kelwara, it had been bureaucratic routine – paperwork – that proved the undoing of officials and ration dealers. The revelation of a damning document was the highlight of a *jan sunwai*. The MKSS, realizing the power of this moment of revelation, made the right to documents the centerpiece of its work. "The right to information," its slogan said, "is the right to life." The MKSS began a campaign for adoption of a state law that would provide citizens with a right to obtain copies of documents, such as ration registers and muster rolls, held in government offices. Rajasthan's Right to Information Act, adopted in 2000, entitles citizens to ask for such documents, outlines the circumstances in which officials are entitled to withhold them, and provides methods for enforcing the law against recalcitrant bureaucrats. The law does not always lead to ready access to documents – in Kelwara, the ration registers were not released until shortly before the *jan sunwai* – but it establishes the principle of transparency.[4]

By 2004, nine state governments in the world's most populous democracy had adopted laws like Rajasthan's Right to Information Act.[5] Inspired by MKSS's example, the advocacy group Parivartan used Delhi's new disclosure law to obtain information about public works allegedly completed in two of the city's poorest neighborhoods; a *jan sunwai* in one community revealed pervasive fraud and allowed Parivartan's leaders to eke out a promise from local officials that notice of new projects would be publicly posted.[6] Another group, Satark Nagrik Sangathan, exposed abuses by ration dealers in Delhi slums, leading the city government to offer tighter inspection of ration shops.[7]

The state of Maharashtra – home to one of the world's largest cities, Mumbai – adopted a Right to Information Act in 2003, prodded by the hunger strike of a prominent activist, Anna Hazare. ("All corruption can end only if there is freedom of information," said Hazare, who resumed his strike in February 2004 to push for better enforcement of the Act.[8]) Within months, residents of Mumbai seized on the law to learn how many city employees had been suspended with pay, what fees contractors were allowed to collect in city parking lots, how frequently politicians had interfered in transfers of police officers, and how often leaky sewer pipes were inspected. In Maharashtra's second-largest city, Pune, activists obtained logbooks that showed civic leaders had taken frequent vacations in official cars.[9]

Elsewhere there were similar rebellions against official secretiveness. In Bangkok, Thailand, Sumalee Limpa-ovart was troubled after her daughter Nattanit was denied admission to the first grade of the prestigious Kasetsart University Demonstration School. In 1998, school officials told Limpa-ovart that Nattanit had failed the admission exam, taken by over 2000 children. Limpa-ovart, frustrated after two years of test preparation, asked the school to provide the test results for her daughter and the 120 successful applicants. The school refused. However, Limpa-ovart had a new recourse: As part of a constitutional reform program undertaken the preceding year, Thailand had adopted the Official Information Act, which operated much like Rajasthan's Right to Information Act. Limpa-ovart, a public prosecutor, appealed to Thailand's Official Information Board for an order that would oblige the school to release the test results.

Midway through her two-year struggle, school officials offered Limpa-ovart a compromise: a list of test results for the first grade class, with student names removed. The list showed that one-third of the newly admitted students had also received a failing grade. Limpa-ovart suspected that these students were *dek sen* – children from privileged families who used social connections or payments of "tea money" to gain access to the publicly funded school. In 2000, Thailand's Supreme Court finally ordered the disclosure of the names of these students, revealing that many were the sons and daughters of leading political and business families. The wide press coverage of Limpa-ovart's case prodded other parents to make similar demands for the release of information about admission tests. The Thai State Council ruled that the Kasetsart University Demonstration School's admission policy violated a constitutional guarantee against discrimination on social or economic grounds, and Thailand's Ministry of University Affairs ordered schools to reform their admission procedures – an "historic ruling," said *Asiaweek*, that undercut "nepotism and cronyism" in the nation's school system.[10]

In Japan, most local governments had adopted ordinances to implement *shiru kenri* – the right to know – by the mid-1990s. Promoted by a coalition of consumer groups, civil libertarians, and progressive legislators, the laws were modeled on the U.S. Freedom of Information Act. In 1995, an extraordinary group of lawyers volunteered for a nationwide campaign to uncover spending abuses by local officials. Calling themselves the *Zenkoku Shimin Ombudsmen* (the Citizens' Ombudsmen Association), the lawyers filed simultaneous requests for information about spending on travel and entertainment across the country, and discovered that in one year officials had spent at least one-quarter of a billion dollars, largely aimed at currying favor with bureaucrats in the national government. A new phrase, *kan-kan settai* – "official-to-official entertainment" – entered the popular lexicon. Soon it was joined by another – *kara shutcho*, the "empty business trip" – as investigators found that expense vouchers had often been forged to hide embezzlement. (In one government, even the auditors had falsified expense reports to create a private slush fund.) The ombudsmen's study led to dramatic changes in the spending and accounting practices of local government.[11]

Japan's national government adopted its own Information Disclosure Law, also patterned on American legislation, in 1999. (To a degree, the law was also the result of American prodding: U.S. trade negotiators argued that the lack of a disclosure law constituted a barrier to free trade in Japan.[12]) When it went into effect in April 2001, Japanese ministries received 4,000 information requests in the first week.[13] In 2003 the Cabinet Secretariat was ordered to provide Tokyo's *Daily Yomiuri* with documents showing that the chief cabinet secretary controlled a secret $13 million fund; critics alleged that the money was used to "smooth business" in the legislature.[14] Sometimes the consequences of disclosure were more profound. In February 2004, the Health Ministry was ordered to release the names of 500 hospitals that had been supplied with blood products contaminated with the hepatitis C virus over the last two decades. The information was sought by Japanese legislator Satoru Ienishi, a hemophiliac who was infected with AIDS and hepatitis C through tainted blood products in the 1990s. It was estimated that thousands of other Japanese might have fallen ill in the same way.[15]

Uganda did not have a disclosure law until early 2005.[16] However its 1995 constitution, drafted in an effort to restore democratic control of government, recognizes that citizens have "a right of access to information in the possession of the State."[17] In 2001 the Ugandan environmental group Greenwatch, backed by the California-based

5

International Rivers Network, invoked the constitutional guarantee to obtain a confidential agreement between the Ugandan government and AES Nile Power Limited to build a major hydroelectric dam. (Greenwatch claimed that the dam would unnecessarily ruin the culturally important Bujagali Falls.) The government refused to disclose the agreement, but in 2002 the Ugandan High Court ruled that there was no valid reason to withhold the document.[18] Greenwatch and the International Rivers Network claimed that the agreement showed the Ugandan government had agreed to excessive payments of almost $300 million.[19] A month later, AES withdrew from the project.[20]

In Mexico, the reformist National Action Party led by Vicente Fox promised a right to information law as part of a program to transform government into "una caja de cristal, donde todo lo que hacemos, absolutamente todo, puede ser sujeto de hacerse público": a glass case, in which "absolutely everything" officials do would be laid open to public view.[21] Adopted in 2002, the law soon proved to be a useful tool for scrutinizing political parties themselves. Parties registered with Mexico's Federal Electoral Institute are generously supported by public funds, but critics have complained that party leaders face little accountability for their use of public money. (In 2003, one minor party was fined $18 million for embezzlement and other abuses of public funds.[22]) A journalist with Mexico City's *El Universal*, Arturo Zárate Vite, asked the Electoral Institute to release information it had collected on the salaries of senior party officials; in November 2003, the Institute refused. With the aid of a nongovernmental organization, Libertad de Información-México, Zárate appealed to a federal tribunal, which ruled in 2004 that the salary data should be released. Within a week, Mexico's major parties published salary details on their websites, adding fuel to the debate over federal policy on the funding of political parties.[23] (Libertad de Información-México scored a second victory in early 2005, when the Mexican attorney general's office was compelled to release parts of an indictment against former President Luis Echeverría relating to the murder of student protesters by paramilitary troops in 1971.[24])

Around the world, stories about the large and small victories attained by the use of new right to information laws continued to tumble out. On September 28, 2004 – the date selected by transparency advocates in 2003 as the global Right to Know Day – an American nongovernmental organization catalogued other disclosures: in

Romania, statistics about domestic surveillance by the intelligence service; in South Africa, information about apartheid-era deals between the government-owned arms corporation and foreign weapons manufacturers; in Ireland, documents showing weaknesses in a new electronic voting scheme; and in the Slovak Republic, details about the privatization of state-owned industries.[25]

The British Labour Party led by Prime Minister Tony Blair promised a new Freedom of Information Act as part of its own reform platform in 1997, and the Blair government eventually adopted the law in 2000. However, time in office had dulled Blair's enthusiasm for transparency, and his government delayed implementation until New Year's Day of 2005. The public's appetite for information was not diminished: In the first four weeks, major government departments received 4,000 requests.[26] Newly released documents showed that the British royal family received more than £1 million in farm subsidies from the European Union in the previous two years,[27] and that the government's financial losses from the 1992 "Black Wednesday" debacle (a failed effort to defend the pound against attacks by currency speculators) had actually been only a fraction of earlier public estimates.[28]

Records also exposed the sordid corners of British history, such as the torture of detainees during the Kenyan Mau Mau rebellion of the 1950's, and governmental complicity in the bribery of foreign officials by British arms dealers before the practice was outlawed in 2002. One confidential memorandum contained the reply of a British army chief to a query from Britain's ambassador in Venezuela as to whether the government was prepared to tolerate such bribery:

> I am completely mystified by just what your problem is. . . . People who deal with the arms trade, even if they are sitting in a government office . . . day by day carry out transactions knowing that at some point bribery is involved. Obviously I and my colleagues in this office do not ourselves engage in it, but we believe that various people who are somewhere along the train of our transactions do. They do not tell us what they are doing and we do not inquire. We are interested in the end result.[29]

Most surprising, perhaps, was the extent to which the rhetoric of transparency had permeated China – one of the most secretive regimes in the world and notorious for its persecution of journalists and official whistleblowers who reveal details of government policy. Ministries of the central government took limited (but nonetheless unprecedented) steps to release crime reports, documents from diplomatic archives, and details about procurement procedures. "China's progress in the area of transparency is irreversible," claimed the state-run *People's Daily* in 2003.[30] The *Economist* reported that the Chinese State Council was contemplating the adoption of a regulation that would acknowledge a citizen's right of access to government information and affirm the principle that government information should be publicly available except in enumerated circumstances.[31]

The Chinese government had good reason to improve access to government information. Some of its actions were mandated in trade agreements that China signed as part of the process of joining the World Trade Organization. The country had also been embarrassed by its mishandling of its SARS epidemic, which was rooted principally in official recalcitrance in providing details about the spread of the disease. As well, China's leaders hoped that transparency would curb official corruption and quell growing public restlessness evidenced, ironically, in newly released statistics showing a dramatic increase in "mass group incidents."[32] And even Chinese policy makers were sensible of the extent to which the "right to information" was becoming entrenched in the laws of other countries.

Lower levels of Chinese government actually raced ahead of central government. In 2002 the government of Guangzhou, a metropolis of ten million people on China's south coast, announced a "revolutionary" change in policy on access to government information.[33] Guangzhou's Provisions on Open Government Information acknowledge the "right to know of citizens and organizations," establish a "general principle" that government information should be made public, and promise that a detailed list of documents will be published on the government's own initiative. In 2004, the municipality of Shanghai – home to another seventeen million – adopted a similar code. Like the Guangzhou law, the Shanghai code requires officials to release information within fifteen days or provide reasons for refusal.[34]

Whether the Guangzhou and Shanghai codes can be effectively enforced by citizens remains a critical question. No citizen of Guangzhou attempted to sue the municipality over a refusal to comply with the disclosure rules during the first two years in which they were in force. In Shanghai, however, an attorney quickly filed a suit after local officials declined to provide documents that might have shown whether his client was the true owner of a home taken during the Cultural Revolution. "This is a pre-conceived legal test," said He Guoping, who conceded that he was surprised when the Xuhui District Court agreed to hear the case in August 2004.[35] (By spring 2005 the case still had not been decided.) Municipal officials in Shanghai claimed at the end of 2004 that they had already received 3000 requests for information and approved almost 70 percent of the applications. At the same time, however, officials warned that they would "stand firm on holding back information that has a strong bearing on state security and social stability."[36]

From arcani imperii to data smog

Central to this global "right to information" movement is the presumption that information held by government should be publicly available, unless government officials can make a good case that legitimate interests – perhaps the public interest in preserving national security, or the need to protect another citizen's privacy – would be harmed by releasing information. By the end of the 1990s there were many people who believed that the "right to know" – and the presumption of openness – had finally become entrenched as a basic principle of democratic governance. If so, this would mark the final overthrow of a much older proposition: that the business of government should, as a rule, be done in secret.

The tussle over access to information has always been closely tied to struggles over the distribution of political power. In pre-revolutionary France, the absolute authority of the King was bolstered by a practice of strict secrecy in public affairs, extending even to a ban on the distribution of friendly commentaries on government policy.[37] As a practical matter, secrecy was easily preserved at a time when the only method of distributing information was by manuscript (that is, handwritten) texts. A dramatic advance in information technology – the printing press – triggered a government crackdown, culminating in the "law of silence" of 1764, which prohibited public discussion of matters of state.

This technological transformation, and the challenges to state authority it encouraged, also forced supporters of the King's prerogatives to articulate an explicit defense of the practice of secrecy. The political philosopher Jean Bodin revived the term used by the Roman historian Tacitus to describe the "secrets of imperial policy" that had to be protected against senatorial prying: the *arcana imperii*. Following Tacitus, Bodin and other supporters of absolutist rule argued that the King's ability to maintain the integrity of the state would be undercut if *arcana imperii* were not protected: With publicity, the King's plans "would be as effective as an exploded mine."[38] In seventeenth-century England, the political theorist Robert Filmer wrote a defense of kingly authority that also accepted the presumption of secrecy:

> I have nothing to do to meddle with Mysteries of State: such *Arcana Imperii*, or Cabinet Counsels, the Vulgar may not pry into. An implicite Faith is given to the meanest Artificer in his own Craft, how much more is it then due to a Prince in the profound Secrets of Government. The Causes and Ends of the greatest politique Actions and Motions of State dazle the Eyes, and exceed the Capacities of all men, save only those that are hourly versed in the managing of Publique Affairs.[39]

Revolutions in England (in 1688) and France (in 1789) led to an abandonment of the absolutist conception of state secrecy. The right to free speech was gradually entrenched, legislatures improved their capacity to monitor taxing and spending, and the process of lawmaking was itself opened to public scrutiny. The pace of reform should not be over-estimated. It was not until 1803 that the British House of Commons acknowledged the right of the press to sit in the public gallery and record its debates; the now-familiar *Hansard*, the daily record of British parliamentary debates, did not begin publication until 1829. Elaine Scarry has recently noted the lengths to which the drafters of the U.S. Constitution went to emphasize the need for open lawmaking – for example, by requiring publication of a "regular statement of Account of the Receipts and Expenditures of all public Money," as well as a journal of Congressional proceedings.[40] In 1789, these matters could not be taken for granted.

By the end of the nineteenth century, the Western democracies had achieved what we might call a level of basic transparency: The rule of law was established, the process of lawmaking (including the business of taxing and spending) was open to public view, and the right to speak freely about governmental affairs was protected. This was a great achievement, but it was very far from a repudiation of the presumption of official secrecy. Within the bowels of the bureaucracy, secrecy was still very much the rule. Writing shortly before the Great War, the German sociologist Max Weber argued that secretiveness was a hallmark of bureaucratic life:

> Every bureaucracy seeks to increase the superiority of the professionally informed by keeping their knowledge and intentions secret. Bureaucratic administration always tends to be an administration of "secret sessions"; in so far as it can, it hides its knowledge and action from criticism.... The concept of the "official secret" is the specific invention of bureaucracy, and nothing is so fanatically defended by the bureaucracy as this attitude.... In facing a parliament, the bureaucracy, out of a sure power instinct, fights every attempt of the parliament to gain knowledge by means of its own experts or from interest groups.... Bureaucracy naturally welcomes a poorly informed and hence a powerless parliament – at least in so far as ignorance somehow agrees with the bureaucracy's interests.[41]

The extent to which bureaucratic secrecy was to be regarded as a problem depended upon the perceived power of bureaucrats. In the early part of the twentieth century, the bureaucracies of Western governments were still comparatively small. This was particularly true in the United States, where the central government had a modest role in national affairs. Even in the 1920s it was typical for high-level officials to be titled "clerks" – a reflection of the extent to which they were thought able to shape the content of government policy.

Perceptions about the power of bureaucrats changed dramatically in the 1930s. In the United States this was partly a result of the expansion of the federal role in commissioning public works, providing social insurance, and regulating business activity – which was manifested in the "alphabet soup" of new agencies such as the SEC, TVA, AAA, PWA, NLRB, CCC, and NRA. As important, however, was a change in the *kind* of work done by federal bureaucrats. Increasingly, officials were given broad mandates in legislation passed by Congress, and expected to craft regulations that gave concrete expression to those mandates. Senior federal employees were no longer clerks: Now they were lawmakers, with the capacity to formulate rules that could have a profound effect on the economic interests of American businesses and citizens.

It is difficult, in retrospect, to appreciate the anxiety with which a large part of the American public viewed the accretion of power by the federal bureaucracy in the Depression years. Many cheered the Supreme Court when it struck down laws that gave federal agencies broad authority to make rules governing the American economy. (After a 1935 decision in which the Court ruled unconstitutional a key New Deal statute because it gave President Franklin Delano Roosevelt unchecked power, the *New York Herald Tribune* celebrated "a tyranny overthrown." An American Bar Association report warned that the growth of federal agencies might lead to a state of "administrative absolutism."[42]) In 1937, Roosevelt tried to expand the Supreme Court to circumvent its obstructive majority, but his "court-packing" scheme failed, defeated by a coalition of Republicans and conservative Democrats. In 1938, the same coalition defeated another Roosevelt plan to expand the White House and consolidate its control over federal departments and agencies. Critics called it a scheme for "one-man rule" and "authoritarian government" and handed Roosevelt the worst rebuff of his presidency.[43]

In broad terms, the complaints made in the 1930s by opponents of the Roosevelt administration would sound familiar to contemporary critics of institutions such as the World Trade Organization or the International Monetary Fund. Power had clearly shifted from Congress to a newly enlarged bureaucracy; matters once resolved in legislation were now disposed of in regulations crafted by officials who, only ten years earlier, had been regarded as clerks. (Today, the parallel complaint is about the shift of power from national bureaucracies to new supranational organizations.) This extraordinary new power was often exercised secretly and capriciously, critics said: New rules suddenly would be announced, without the opportunity to challenge the grounds on which they had been adopted. "The rise of administrative bodies probably has been the most significant legal trend of the last century," said one distinguished jurist. "They have become a veritable fourth branch of the Government, which has deranged our three-branch legal theories much as the concept of a fourth dimension unsettles our three-dimensional thinking."[44] A

British jurist put the problem more bluntly, calling rule by bureaucrats the "new despotism."[45]

Even progressive reformers recognized the need for steps to regulate and legitimize bureaucratic power, and in 1946 Congress adopted the Administrative Procedure Act.[46] The APA imposed three constraints on the "fourth branch" of government. It required federal officials to provide notice about proposed new rules in the recently created Federal Register, and provide "interested parties" an opportunity to comment. It also gave citizens a right to fair treatment and a right to appeal unfair decisions. The third element was least appreciated at the time: a rough guarantee of access to information. Each federal department was expected to publish basic information about its organization, the rules it enforced, policy statements and procedures that guided its work, and its decisions. Furthermore, any other "matters of official record" were to "be made available to persons properly and directly concerned except information held confidential for good cause." Officials were expected to accept requests for documents, but the Justice Department quickly made clear that it would construe the law narrowly. The APA was not intended "to open up Government files for general inspection," the Attorney General warned in 1947. "The great mass of material relating to the internal operation of an agency is not a matter of official record."[47]

The APA was the progenitor of two contemporary species of disclosure rule. One (as I note in Chapter 8) comprises a host of disclosure requirements now imposed on countries through World Trade Organization agreements. The other consists of contemporary disclosure laws such as the American Freedom of Information Act, or FOIA. The idea of an FOIA was conceived by Harold Cross, the former counsel of the *New York Herald Tribune*, which had so harshly criticized Roosevelt's reach for power during the New Deal. In 1950, Cross was commissioned by the American Society of Newspaper Editors to write a report on the problem of government secrecy. Cross tallied the weaknesses of the APA and proposed a new law that would acknowledge the "right to know" and create a presumption that *all* citizens should have access to *all* government records.[48]

Ironically, an idea that had been born out of conservative frustration with the New Deal quickly gained favor with the press and with Democrats and progressives. Journalists led by the ASNE seized on

Cross's idea as the Truman and Eisenhower administrations tightened secrecy rules in the early years of the Cold War.[49] For the first two years of his presidency, Eisenhower had the support of a Republican-dominated Senate and House of Representatives, but Democrats regained control of the House in 1954 and had both the motive and the opportunity to push for tougher disclosure rules.[50] And by the earlier 1960s, a growing number of environmental and consumer rights groups also advocated for a right to information, to scrutinize federal agencies they claimed had been co-opted by industry.[51]

This was a remarkable turnabout. In 1940, Franklin Roosevelt vetoed an early version of the APA, decrying it as a tool crafted by "powerful and concentrated interests" to stymie reforms aimed at improving the welfare of "a diversified mass of individuals."[52] When the Freedom of Information Act was finally adopted in 1966, one of its most vocal proponents was Ralph Nader's Center for Study of Responsive Law, which exercised the right to information in an effort to unmask instances in which government regulators had bent to pressure from business lobbies. The Center also provided support to NBC reporter Carl Stern in FOIA litigation that provided early evidence of the Federal Bureau of Investigation's surveillance and harassment of protest groups.[53] Other groups in the emerging "public interest movement" also used the law, and in 1974 they seized the opportunity created by the resignation of President Richard Nixon to have the FOIA considerably strengthened.

The Freedom of Information Act of 1966 established a right to information held by government agencies, articulated a presumption that government documents should be publicly accessible, and provided methods for compelling officials to comply with its requirements. It was also, by international standards, an oddity. (Sweden and Finland, for example, had older laws affirming a right to official documents; however, many documents that are subject to FOIA would not be considered "official" as the term is defined in Swedish or Finnish law.) While the FOIA served as a model for advocates and legislators in other countries, their governments were not quick to replicate the law. Twenty years later, only eleven countries had comparable statutes. It was assumed that FOIA-style laws were a luxury, only likely to be adopted by wealthy, politically stable democracies – perhaps as a way of appeasing disaffected voters as the advanced economies stagnated in the late 1970s and early 1980s.

This assumption was shattered after 1989, as countries began to emulate American practice at a remarkable pace. Dominant states such as Japan and the United Kingdom within the club of affluent democracies adopted disclosure laws; so did states in Central and Eastern Europe recently liberated from Soviet domination. Other countries "transitioning" to democratic rule in Latin America, Asia, and Africa also passed FOIA-style statutes. By the end of 2004, *fifty-nine* countries had adopted right to information laws (See Chart[54]). Even this figure was understated: Some countries acknowledged a right to information in their newly adopted constitutions but had not yet adopted legislation to elaborate how the right would work in practice. There were also federal states such as Germany whose subnational governments had adopted disclosure laws even though the national government had not. Furthermore the pace of adoption showed no indication of slackening. (Germany, for example, finally adopted a national law in July 2005.)

Obviously this trend was a product of profound changes in the international political order in the 1990s. In many instances, nations sought a dramatic way to repudiate the secrecy of collapsed authoritarian regimes and signal their new alliance with the remaining superpower, and the constitutional or statutory recognition of a right to information was an effective way of doing this. In many countries, governments also took special measures to open the archives of their secret services. Even in the United States, new programs were established to declassify Cold War-era documents, and the Clinton administration promised to reform policies that governed the classification of records in the future. By the end of the 1990s, nongovernmental organizations that lobbied for disclosure in different countries had been knitted together into a robust, global movement. Many international organizations – nongovernmental and governmental both – had endorsed the right to information and advocated "model laws" that were built on principles articulated (if not always respected) in the U.S. FOIA.

It was difficult, in such circumstances, not to believe that the world was on the cusp of an unprecedented era of openness. "Secrecy is in retreat," said the influential British sociologist Anthony Giddens in 2000, heralding public demands for increased transparency as part of a global "second wave of democratization."[55] Another British scholar suggested that transparency should be regarded as one of the basic

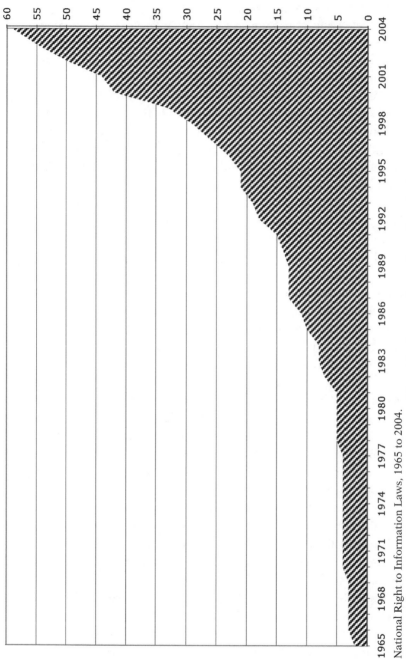

National Right to Information Laws, 1965 to 2004.

After 1989, the number of countries that had adopted laws like the United States' Freedom of Information Act increased rapidly. By 2004, fifty-nine countries had similar laws.

"constitutive principles" that must be respected by institutions if they expected to retain legitimacy in the eyes of the public.[56] Writing in the American journal *Foreign Policy* in 2002, the head of an influential American public interest group suggested that "the international freedom-of-information movement stands on the verge of changing the definition of democratic governance. The movement is creating a new norm, a new expectation, and a new threshold requirement for any government to be considered a democracy. . . . The ideal openness regime would have governments publishing so much that the formal request for specific information . . . would become almost unnecessary."[57]

The very idea that a government might publish this much information would have seemed ludicrous were it not for technological advances that radically reduced the cost of collecting, distributing, and accessing data. The "internet bubble" was as evident in discussions about public access to information as it was in the stock market. Technological evangelists foresaw a world in which "anyone with a modem can gather nearly as much intelligence as the CIA."[58] (In the pre-9/11 era, this was an homage to technology, not a slight on the CIA.) In 1999 the Canadian government, which took pride in its leadership in the new field of "e-government," said its goal was to allow Canadians to "access all government information . . . on-line at the time and place of their choosing" by 2004.[59] Active use of information technology by government (the G8 countries said in a 2000 statement) would move us toward "a truly Global Information Society."[60]

Some commentators even suggested that the main difficulty confronting citizens in the future would be their inability to exploit the vast amounts of information that soon would be available. A 2003 study by researchers at the University of California calculated that the rate of production of "new stored information" produced globally had doubled in just three years: In 2002, 800 megabytes of recorded information – roughly equal to 30 feet of books – were produced for every person on the planet.[61] In 1969, one study estimated that the U.S. government maintained "roughly 70 billion sheets of paper in the equivalent of five million four-drawer filing cabinets."[62] In digital form, this is roughly 340 terabytes of data – probably less, as I note in Chapter 9, than the amount of data that is now exchanged daily in e-mail within the federal bureaucracy; and all of it subject to potential scrutiny under the U.S. FOIA.

The technology columnist David Shenk, alarmed by our inability to keep up with this sprawling mass of information, suggested that citizens might become lost in "data smog" – a phenomenon exacerbated by the indiscriminate release of government information. Shenk criticized the "disclosure mania" typified by the release, in 1998, of 60,000 pages of material from the Starr inquiry's investigation of President Clinton. "An unrestricted flood of information can sometimes be more onerous than beneficial," he said. "One of the dangers is that we will be exposed to so much data so quickly that we'll lose perspective on what it means."[63] Shenk was not alone in thinking that the real question was how citizens would deal with the looming "information glut."[64]

The limits to transparency

Has the old presumption of secrecy really been overthrown in favor of a new presumption of openness? In this book I present a series of essays to argue that – notwithstanding the real gains that have been attained over the last three decades – there are still important limits to the principle of governmental transparency. In part this is because there are enclaves within government in which the "right to know" has made little headway. There are also substantial changes in the conditions of governance – in the context in which governments operate, in the structure of institutions that formulate and execute policy, and in the technology that is used to produce and distribute information – that may constrain the ability to obtain government information.

As I will argue in Chapter 2, the security sector of government – the collection of departments and agencies responsible for defense, intelligence, and policing – is one in which the right to information has gained only a tenuous hold. It will seem odd to say this in light of the remarkable revelations over the past decade about the conduct of security services in former communist states, in the military-dominated countries of Latin America, and during the years of apartheid government in South Africa. However, we must distinguish between the standards of transparency applied to the security services of collapsed regimes and the standards applied to security services today: In many countries, disclosure laws have been carefully tailored to ensure that the security sector survives as an enclave of secrecy.

In the United States, the "decade of openness"[65] came to an abrupt end with a dramatic change in the context of governance, triggered by the terror attacks of September 11, 2001. New worries about vulnerability to terror attacks led to an expansion of secrecy as government agencies reconsidered the wisdom of disclosing information that once had been made routinely available. New threats are leading us to craft new understandings about the limits to transparency: Some facts that once were readily acquired might now need to be more carefully controlled. However, there is a danger in taking this too far – and a danger, too, in not recognizing that the best way to deal with new threats is sometimes to pull down old constraints on transparency.

The Bush administration's attempt to reverse openness policies in its first term was not simply a reaction to the events of 9/11. (For convenience, references to the Bush administration relate to presidency of George W. Bush and not that of his father, George H. W. Bush.) In Chapter 3, I observe that senior members of the Bush administration – such as Vice President Dick Cheney and Defense Secretary Donald Rumsfeld – share an antipathy toward open government rules that is three decades old. This antipathy may be unreasonable, but it is not irrational: Distaste for openness is part of a larger concern about the proliferation of constraints on executive authority since the early 1970s. Indeed, there is good evidence that a combination of factors (more aggressive advocacy groups, broader media competition, public distrust, and the advent of the internet) have created an environment that is, from the point of view of Presidents and their advisors, much more complex and tumultuous.

The Bush administration's retreat from openness can be regarded as an attempt to address executive anxiety about the capacity to govern effectively in this new environment. Rumsfeld, the most vocal critic of the restrictions put on policy makers in the executive branch, sometimes sounded like a latter-day Jean Bodin, the political philosopher remembered for his attempt to defend the *arcana imperii* as kingly authority was challenged by technological and social change. To be fair, Rumsfeld is not an absolutist – but he, too, is attempting to defend an *ancien regime*. Whether the Bush administration's attempts to reverse openness rules will ultimately be effective in restoring governability remains an open question. Although the administration was routinely damned for excessive secrecy during its first term, its efforts at rollback were limited and often unsuccessful, and the term was marked by some remarkable revelations about its inner workings.

Anxiety over the erosion of executive power is not unique to the United States, nor to the conservative end of the political spectrum. In many countries, leaders of different political hues express the same concerns about the challenges of governing in a policy environment that is more thickly settled with journalists and advocacy groups and more fast-paced and unpredictable. As I note in Chapter 4, these concerns have often lead to open assaults on disclosure rules. Governments have also been resourceful in developing internal procedures designed to ensure that their control of the affairs of state is not shaken by the disclosure of sensitive documents. Because these procedures are buried in administrative practice, they can be difficult to detect and counter. Nevertheless, they are important: Internal rules crafted to impose order on the disclosure process – to minimize the disruptive potential of openness rules – essentially constitute a "hidden law" designed to restrict access to government information.

Much of this story is about the debate over transparency in countries of the First World – nations that are, by global standards, rich, democratic, politically stable, and technologically advanced. There was a time when it was thought that disclosure laws would only be adopted in countries such as these. In the last decade this idea has been decisively refuted. The countries that are now rushing to adopt right-to-information laws are often poor, sometimes weakly democratic or authoritarian, politically unstable, and technologically limited. Nevertheless, the governments and citizens of these countries expect their new right-to-information laws to do great things – to legitimize rulers, reduce corruption, and heighten popular participation in governance. In Chapter 5, I suggest that there is good reason to doubt whether these high ambitions will be quickly realized. Advanced democracies spend millions of dollars to operate their laws, which depend as well upon a professional civil service and modern record-keeping systems. A repressive political system could also mean that citizens are able to do little with information even when it is made available.

As I noted earlier, openness rules developed in Western democracies were crafted to deal with problems of control and legitimacy as modern states emerged and consolidated their power. These rules are built on certain assumptions about the structure of power – that it is exercised by autonomous and sovereign governments and implemented through public bureaucracies controlled by those governments. The rapid diffusion of FOIA-style laws could be regarded as a sort of triumph, a definitive statement about the subordination of executives and bureaucracies to the principle of transparency. Obviously, for reasons I have just described, I am skeptical about the extent of this triumph. But even if none of these reservations held merit, there would be a another problem: The very *structure* of governing institutions is changing, subverting the effectiveness of newly adopted disclosure rules. In the second part of this book, I canvass three of these structural changes.

One of these changes, discussed in Chapter 6, is the emergence of "networked" forms of governance, through which agencies in different governments cooperate to achieve a common goal. It will seem odd to think of networking as a threat to transparency – after all, one of the aims in network building is to break down impediments to the flow of information among agencies within the network. However, this sort of information sharing often comes at a steep price: the construction of barriers designed to ensure that shared information is never disclosed to people or organizations outside the network, including citizens, journalists, and legislators. The results can be a decline in external accountability for every agency in the network. Efforts to promote information sharing among law enforcement agencies in the United States after 9/11 are a prominent form of networking, raising exactly these sorts of accountability concerns. But the trend toward tighter networking of agencies in different countries – particularly in the security sector – was already well-advanced before 9/11. This is one instance in which the effect of American policy has been to compel other governments to adopt more restrictive policies on access to information.

A second structural change is the transfer of government functions to the private sector. Most right-to-information laws are drafted to apply exclusively to government agencies, an approach that may have made sense when government responsibilities were clearly demarcated and expansive. Privatization requires us to consider fundamental questions, as I note in Chapter 7. Why does the right of access to information expire when work is transferred from a government agency to a private organization? Should the right expire if the character of the work itself has not changed? Countries such as South Africa have adopted right-to-information laws that accommodate the realities of privatization and that may provide a better way of thinking about the boundaries of the right to information in an age when government itself has a shrinking role in the production of critical services.

This is not the only way in which power has shifted out of familiar institutions of government. Increasingly, basic questions of national policy are negotiated in supranational forums, such as the World Trade Organization, the International Monetary Fund, or the World Bank. These organizations actively promote transparency as a tool for improving governance. However, transparency is a malleable concept that can be bent to many different purposes, and the particular kind of openness promoted by these organizations is often designed to protect the interests of the financial and commercial enterprises of the First World. As I show in Chapter 8, holding supranational organizations to the principle of transparency in their own operations is another matter entirely. Long protected by the cloak of diplomatic confidentiality, these institutions have steadily resisted openness policies like those in force in the advanced democratic states.

There is, finally, a critical change in the *technology* of governance, which will also radically transform debates over governmental openness. In popular consciousness, we think of bureaucracy as a world of paper memoranda, manila folders, and steel file cabinets. In reality, this view is already archaic. The stockpile of government information is increasingly digitized, held within massive databases or as a variety of forms of electronic "unstructured data." In Chapter 9, I acknowledge that the process of digitization has revealed opportunities for substantial – and sometimes alarming – increases in governmental transparency. On the other hand, many stakeholders – industry, private citizens, and bureaucrats themselves – now have strong incentives to push for new restrictions on the release of digitized data. Digitization will also introduce new complexities for stakeholders interested in monitoring government. Oversight will now require technical sophistication and the resources to interpret a deepening pool of digitized data.

This, then, is the terrain covered by much of the book. On the one hand, it acknowledges that the idea of transparency has gained considerable ground over the last half century. On the other hand, there are changes in context – new fears of terrorism or the increasing complexity of the policy environment or the new challenges in implementation that arise in "soft states" – that can still thwart the drive for openness. There are also changes in the structure of government – networking, privatization, internationalization of policy making – that undermine traditional methods for assuring openness. And finally there is change in the technology of governance, whose effects on transparency are complex and not fully realized.

The reader will recognize that I am, on the whole, an advocate for transparency, although I am more prepared than some to acknowledge the contrary point of view – for example, in recognizing the increasing pressures put on policy makers and the threat to privacy posed by the bulk release of personal data. The commitment to openness comes from a recognition of the harm that unchecked power can do to basic rights, and the power of collective deliberation as a tool for solving complex problems. It also comes from a recognition of the essential frailty of our governing arrangements. Every form of governance is an experiment – a concrete elaboration of hypotheses about the best way to govern. These hypotheses might be wrong, and the experiment might fail, doing great damage to society as a whole. "There is a public interest," says the political philosopher Charles Anderson, "in assuring that established practice is always open to challenge, reconsideration, and change."[66] That is what transparency does.

I CONTEXT

2

SECRECY AND SECURITY

Even at the end, the secret police thought they would survive. The most feared security service in the Communist bloc, the *Ministerium für Staatssicherheit* – commonly known as the Stasi – had constructed a surveillance apparatus that penetrated every corner of East German society. With 93,000 employees, it was larger even than the East German army; another 173,000 East Germans collaborated as Stasi informers. The Stasi's surveillance records, stored in its sprawling complex on Normannestrasse in Lichtenberg, a suburb of East Berlin, were massive. Put end-to-end, the shelves of files would have stretched for 120 miles.[1]

An equally massive catalog of index cards, organized within an array of mechanized cabinets and known internally as the F22 index, allowed Stasi workers to access this mass of information. However, the Stasi had taken a precautionary step to ensure the security of the information in its files. Pseudonyms were used in place of the real names of informants and victims, in the files themselves and also in the F22 index. To decode the files – to know who had been spying on whom – a select group of Stasi workers were given access to a second card catalog, the F16 index, which matched pseudonyms to real names. Without the F16 index, the meaning of the files would have been practically impenetrable.

By fall 1989, the East German government was tottering. The communist regimes of Hungary and Poland had already collapsed, and there were growing street protests in East Germany itself. On October 16, East German leader Erich Honecker was replaced by another Politburo member, Egon Krenz. The Krenz government opened the border to West Germany, made futile attempts to negotiate with the regime's domestic opposition, and collapsed on December 6. On December 10, Czechoslovakia's communist government also fell. Finally, on December 16, a special Congress of the Communist Party promised free elections in East Germany.

Throughout these weeks, the Stasi became a special object of the protesters' enmity. Its regional offices were surrounded, and in November the Krenz government promised that the security service would be reformed. On November 6, the Minister of State Security, Erich Mielke, gave orders for sensitive documents to be destroyed. The shredding began, and continued until a hundred Stasi shredders had burned out. Then documents were ripped by hand. By the time that protestors stormed the Stasi's Normannestrasse headquarters in January 1990, about one-tenth of its files had been torn apart. (Torn, but not disposed of: Later, archivists began slowly reconstructing the 17,000 bags of shredded and torn documents.[2]) Strangely, though, the F16 index remained intact. By destroying it, the Stasi leadership might have made the entire file system unintelligible. Their aim, however, was not to destroy the system: The aim was to scrub the files, not ruin them. Stasi officials assumed that the organization would survive in some form, and that their files would continue as the heart of its operations. Even at the end, the intelligence service underestimated the intensity of popular anger.

The Stasi itself was finally buried in 1990, but its filing system lived on – and even thrived, in a sense. In August 1990, the newly elected East German legislature voted to preserve the records and to allow victims of the old regime access to their files. A new Stasi File Authority was established to preserve the files, and over the years it made improvements to ease access to their contents. In the four years following reunification, the authority received two million inquiries from German citizens. The results were often shocking: "A story of deceit and betrayal on a national scale," said one observer, "with husbands spying on wives, children sneaking on their parents and priests reporting on their parishioners."[3] Prominent politicians – including the minister-presidents of Thuringia and Brandenburg and a mayoral candidate in Berlin – were called to account for their relationship to the security service. More than a decade later, Germany's bid to host the 2012 Olympic games was thrown into turmoil when two officials organizing the bid were compelled to resign following the revelation of their past links to the Stasi.

The disclosures were painful, and sometimes strongly resisted. While negotiating the terms for unification in 1990, the West German government proposed that the Stasi files be given over to its archives, where they might be sealed for decades; the proposals were abandoned only after a hunger strike by civil rights campaigners at Normannestrasse. The chancellor of the newly united state, Helmut Kohl, later launched his own litigation against the File Authority, hoping to block disclosure of records that commentators said might reveal Stasi meddling in West German politics in the 1980s. Kohl claimed that the release of the documents would violate his "human dignity," but in 2004 a federal court disagreed.[4] The Stasi files revealed "monstrous things," said Joachim Gauck, the East German pastor and dissident who served as the authority's first head. And yet the process of revelation seemed an essential step in coming to terms with the past. "We didn't want to say a friendly goodbye to another dictatorship," Gauck said in 1996. "Only with knowledge, perhaps with some mourning, will we ever become a democratic country."[5]

The power of the official file

Other nations in the former Communist Bloc later emulated, with varying degrees of rigor, the German policy of opening secret police files. Hungary adopted a law in 1994 allowing access to secret police files; the law was strengthened in 2003 following an admission by Prime Minister Medgysessy that he had worked as a counterintelligence officer in the secret police during the Communist era.[6] The Czech Republic followed in 1996, and expanded its law again in 2002; later, it published a list of 75,000 former collaborators on a government website. Legislators in Bulgaria, Poland, Romania, and Slovakia also sought to open old records, although the post-communist intelligence services that inherited the files sometimes proved reluctant to cooperate in exposing them to public scrutiny.[7]

Russia itself did not follow the model of the Communist Bloc countries; the secret files of the former Communist Party and the KGB were transferred to state archives, subject to rules that permitted only limited access to the oldest documents.[8] But the truth came out in other ways. In 1992 a dissident KGB archivist, Vasili Mitrokhin, smuggled to the West thousands of documents that revealed how

Soviet leaders had wielded power over seven decades. The "Mitrokhin Archive" provided evidence of Moscow's attempts to liquidate "enemies of the people," its disinformation campaigns against Western leaders and its own dissidents, and its infiltration of Western governments, political parties, and media.[9]

Whether divulged as a matter of state policy or not, these newly public documents helped to advance the process of democratic reform. The very act of disclosing police files constituted a repudiation of the secrecy that had been one of the main tools of repression, employed to foster a crippling fear of state authorities. Once disclosed, the files allowed a reconstruction of official history, which had denied the reality that the communist governments systematically abused the human rights of their citizens. Victims were able to identify and hold accountable the perpetrators of abuses and ensure they were removed from positions of influence.

The official files had a special power. It was one thing for victims to give testimony about their persecution by the state; testimony could be bent by imperfect memory or long-held grievances. It was another thing to see the files – tangible, contemporaneous, coldly bureaucratic records of state employees' complicity in the persecution of citizens.[10]

The same rituals of revelation were undertaken as military regimes collapsed throughout Latin America. In Argentina, the military leaders who seized power in 1976 and waged a "dirty war" against alleged domestic subversion were compelled to transfer power to civilian leaders in 1983. Newly elected President Raul Alfonsin established a commission that produced a 1984 report, *Nunca Más* (*Never Again*), that documented the abduction, torture, and killing of almost 10,000 Argentinians. Although military leaders had tried to destroy the evidence, they could not be thorough. Systematic abuses required bureaucratic action, which in turn produced a documentary record of the procedures employed by security services. The files gave concrete proof of crimes that the commission itself conceded were otherwise hard to believe.[11] The Brazilian military also attempted to avoid accountability for abuses, but were undone by official files. In 1985 the Catholic Church's Archdiocese in São Paolo published a report – also titled *Never Again* – that documented the habitual use of torture against thousands of political dissidents over two decades. The

Archdiocese relied on documents from military court proceedings that had been secretly photocopied by lawyers associated with the church.[12]

In 1989, the Chilean junta led by General Augusto Pinochet yielded power following elections to a civilian President, Patricio Aylwin, who created a commission based on the Argentine model, but with significant limitations: The commission could not investigate abuses that did not lead to death or disappearance, and its access to military records was restricted. Nevertheless, the commission found documentary evidence of at least 2,000 deaths.[13] Other records also surfaced to incriminate the Pinochet regime. In Buenos Aires, the investigative journalist Mónica González found a cache of files that revealed the Chilean-led effort to coordinate "anti-subversion" activities by the security services of several military regimes, eventually known as Operation Condor. In Paraguay, activists uncovered tons of intelligence documents that laid open Condor's breadth and the role of Paraguayan security forces in the torture and execution of dissidents. It became known as the *Archivo del Terror* – the Archive of Terror.[14] (In 2003, Chilean President Ricardo Lagos appointed a second commission to document abuses under the military dictatorship; the commission issued its report in November 2004, describing the indiscriminate detention and torture of thousands of Chileans.[15])

Many other Latin American countries marked the transition to democratic rule with inquiries to reveal the past abuses of security services.[16] After Mexico ended seventy years of rule by the Institutional Revolutionary Party in 2000, the government of President Vicente Fox appointed a special prosecutor to investigate hundreds of cases of "forced disappearances" by security services that had been documented by the National Human Rights Commission. The government also opened 60,000 files that detailed an extensive spying and disinformation campaign against opponents of the state from the 1960s to the 1980s. The files also contain:

> ...records of an even dirtier war, which chronicle the state's attempt to eliminate the radical left: army counterinsurgency plans; cables from Guerrero [state] describing the hunt for guerillas, the mass detentions of families of rebel leaders. Reports on interrogation sessions. Photographs of detainees with visible signs

of torture. Photographs of dead people . . . [The] records have all
the hallmarks of an efficient intelligence bureaucracy: perfectly
organized, pristine, arranged chronologically.[17]

Similar experiments with post-transition openness were undertaken in Africa, most prominently in South Africa after the end of
the apartheid government in 1994.[18] Secrecy had been a way of life
under the apartheid regime, bolstered by strict laws that prevented the
release and distribution of information about the activity of security
forces.[19] A post-apartheid Truth and Reconciliation Commission was
given the power to compel the release of documents on the suppres-
sion of political dissent, and found many papers that demonstrated
the breadth and intensity of the government's effort.

But the commission also determined that its investigation had
been thwarted by a concerted effort to destroy incriminating records
in the waning years of the apartheid government. The apartheid state
(the commission concluded in 1998) had sought to impose "a selective
amnesia" on the nation through "a massive deletion of state documentary memory within the security establishment."[20] That the commission could take this view – when thousands of victims remained to
testify to the conduct of the security services – was itself a testament
to the symbolic power of the official file.

The new attitude of openness was evident in the 1990s in the
United States, where sensitive projects that had been hidden in the
name of national security were laid open for public scrutiny. In 1995,
a special commission reported on a decades-long series of radiation
experiments secretly undertaken by government scientists on unwit-
ting American citizens.[21] A 1998 law compelled the declassification
of files that showed the support secretly given by the CIA and FBI to
former Nazi officials, including suspected war criminals, in the earliest years of the Cold War.[22] In 1999 the Clinton administration also
ordered a review of documents that revealed the U.S. government's
role in the Pinochet coup of 1973, and its knowledge of human rights
abuses by Chilean and other South American security forces.[23]

The enclave survives

Throughout the Cold War, the security establishments of most
nations – the national communities of defense, intelligence and

counterintelligence, and internal security agencies – successfully resisted demands for increased openness. In authoritarian states, this secretiveness was justified under the "doctrine of national security," which said that openness and the other democratic virtues would have to be subordinated in the drive to suppress imminent and substantial threats to the state.[24] Even democratic states had their own, more benign version of the national security doctrine, which said that the power to address security threats ought to be concentrated in the hands of well-meaning but secretive elites. In any case, the effect was to transform the security establishment into an enclave of secrecy – a realm in which the usual logic of transparency (a calculus of the benefits and risks of openness) did not apply. Security was an absolute trump over any demand for openness.

The two decades that followed Argentina's 1984 *Nunca Más* report were years of horrible revelation. The walls that had protected many security establishments from outside scrutiny collapsed, providing proof of terrible abuses done by military, intelligence, and police forces. The disclosure of official files was often justified as a method of achieving justice for the victims of security agencies, but it also constituted a repudiation of the logic that had allowed security establishments to survive as enclaves of secrecy. The dangers of allowing security to act as an absolute trump had become too clear.

As a matter of policy, the implication was that security establishments could not be allowed to survive as enclaves of secrecy. Throughout the 1990s, many human rights advocates asserted a new norm – "a right to know the truth," validated in international law, that had to be weighed against security concerns.[25] Many countries emerging from authoritarian rule attempted to entrench this proposition by adopting constitutional or statutory provisions that affirmed, in general terms, a right to information. These actions, one observer suggested, reflected a "critical transformation" of the terms in which citizens related to the state, which would limit the potential for abuses of state power in the future.[26]

But had there really been a fundamental shift in thinking about transparency in the security sector? In reality, the security establishment in many nations appeared to be more resilient than expected. In Argentina, the activities of the national intelligence service, SIDE, were still broadly defined as state secrets, and SIDE became the principal force opposing the adoption of a national disclosure law.[27]

Brazilian policy makers also resisted adopting a disclosure law, thereby thwarting public demands for access to the dictatorship-era archives of its security forces.[28] Chile lacked a disclosure law as well; meanwhile, a statute creating Chile's new National Intelligence Agency contained provisions designed to preserve the secrecy of the information it collected.[29] And countries that had adopted disclosure laws took special precautions to protect security organizations. The Peruvian law adopted in 2002 does not include the armed forces or national police.[30] Similarly, the Ecuadorian law adopted in 2004 prohibits the disclosure of classified national security information except with the approval of the military-dominated Consejo de Seguridad Nacional. The law's adoption was delayed for a year because of resistance from the country's Armed Forces.[31]

Most countries in Central and Eastern Europe also adopted broader constitutional and legislative guarantees of a right to government documents. But by the late 1990s, the region had also been affected by a second and contrary trend: the adoption of new state secrecy laws. (I examine the reasons for this trend in more detail in Chapter 6.) In 2002, the head of Slovakia's National Security Office, rebutting criticisms of the country's new state secrecy law, explained: "The right to access classified information is not a human right."[32] This was correct, in the narrow sense that there was no irrefutable right to classified information – but it also would not be saying anything at all, as there is no irrefutable right to any kind of information, even unclassified. More likely the security official was resisting pressure to extend the logic of transparency – the balancing of harms and benefits from disclosure – into the security sphere. The Latvian Supreme Court reached the same conclusion in 2003, insisting, in a case that challenged the Latvian state secrecy law, that the "human right to freedom of information" did not include the "right of requiring access to state secrets."[33]

In fact, many new disclosure laws include special protections for security organizations. India's 2002 law did not apply to nineteen of the country's security and intelligence organizations. This, as activists have noted, created a philosophical contradiction: On the one hand, the law mandated the immediate disclosure of information when it concerned the "life and liberty of a person"; on the other, it did not impose this mandate on the agencies most often accused of violating civil liberties.[34] In 2005, the Indian government amended the law to accommodate this criticism, providing a limited right to information from security and intelligence agencies in cases of alleged human rights abuses. In 2003, South African intelligence authorities persuaded the government to delay the full application of the country's disclosure law, and lobbied for a permanent exemption from its requirements. Human rights advocates have complained that security agencies destroyed or hid records for several years after the transition to majority rule.[35]

Even established democracies have proved reluctant to press transparency in the security sector, as the United Kingdom recently demonstrated. In 1997, Britain's newly elected Labour government published a discussion paper on their plans for the country's first Freedom of Information Act. Although the paper was widely hailed for its progressive attitude on openness, its liberality had sharp limits: Several key security organizations were totally excluded from the law.[36] As added protection, the new law also excludes any information held by other parts of government that is supplied by these agencies, or even relates to them. For other parts of the security establishment, British cabinet ministers are allowed to sign certificates to prevent independent review bodies from overruling their judgment about whether national security interests are at stake.[37]

Other Commonwealth countries take a similar approach. For example, Australia's Freedom of Information Act – one of the oldest outside the United States – also excludes key intelligence and counterintelligence services, and gives ministers the power to block courts from questioning their claim that disclosure of information would harm national security.[38] Governments in New Zealand and Canada may also issue such certificates. In Western Europe, some countries simply exclude information from their disclosure laws if it has been classified by government officials for national security reasons.[39]

Even in the United States, the security establishment enjoys a special level of protection against demands for openness. The Freedom of Information Act denies a right of access to information that is properly classified. The critical question is whether courts are prepared to challenge official decisions about the application of classification rules; even though the law was modified in 1974 to encourage closer scrutiny, it remains true that courts are very reluctant to challenge executive branch judgments on the classification of documents.[40] Other programs to declassify documents, while important, affect only a small and diminishing proportion of the total stock of classified documents. (The government's 2005 statistics suggest that the pace at which new classified information is created is increasing, while the volume of information being declassified through special review programs has declined to its lowest point in a decade.[41]) Despite the protection already given to national security information under the Act, four intelligence agencies have also lobbied successfully to have their "operational files" completely excluded from the law.[42]

By 2004 it was clear that the lesson drawn from these two decades of revelation was largely a lesson about history. The proposition that transparency could be used as a tool for controlling human rights abuses within the security sector was not carried forward; on the contrary, security organizations continued to exist in enclaves where the logic of transparency did not apply. The "right to know the truth" was a right that applied to collapsed regimes or historical records of fading relevance; openness served as a tool for achieving "transitional justice," to use a phrase widely applied by legal scholars.[43] Jon Elster characterized access to the files of security organizations as one way of "closing the books" – an unfortunate turn of phrase, perhaps, as the difficulty lay largely in the fact that the books had never been open.[44] But it conveys the reality: Once accounts were settled, security organizations began rebuilding the walls of the enclave.

New threats, new secrets

In the United States, the process of rebuilding these walls of secrecy had begun even before the terror attacks of September 11, 2001. In the early 1990s, defense and intelligence agencies resisted initiatives to reform classification rules and declassify Cold War records, only to be overruled by the White House and Congress; by the end of the decade, however, the political climate in Washington had shifted. Declassification efforts were underfunded, while conservatives' fears about the threat of espionage by agents of the Chinese government undermined efforts to develop less onerous classification policies.[45] "The vast secrecy system," Senator Daniel Patrick Moynihan complained, "shows no signs of receding."[46]

After September 11, secrecy became even more deeply entrenched, once again raising fears about the harm being done to civil and political rights behind closed doors. Hundreds of aliens were detained by the U.S. government, which refused to reveal their names or their place of detention; many were subsequently deported following hearings that were closed to the public. Hundreds of alleged "enemy combatants" – many held on slight evidence and having little or no value as sources of intelligence value – were hidden at a Defense Department facility in Guantanamo Bay. The Central Intelligence Agency ran its own network of secret detention facilities, as well as a secret program to seize suspected terrorists covertly from other nations.[47] Much of this was deeply disturbing, but nonetheless familiar: It was the sort of behavior one expected to see from the regimes that had allowed security concerns to overwhelm concern for human rights. However, Americans also saw a new form of secrecy emerging after September 11, as organizations not typically counted within the security establishment began to restrict access to information already in the public domain.

The withdrawn material was of two types. The first was information about so-called "critical infrastructure" – such as refineries, pipelines, dams, nuclear plants, power lines, and other physical assets, as well as less tangible assets such as computer systems – that seemed vulnerable to terror attacks. In the months following 9/11, several federal agencies – hoping to avoid providing a "road map for terrorists" – restricted or eliminated access to maps that showed the location of critical infrastructure, or reports that assessed the risks that these facilities posed to neighboring communities.[48] For example, the Federal Energy Regulatory Commission, which regulates key components of the nation's energy infrastructure such as hydroelectric dams and natural gas terminals and pipelines, withdrew a substantial amount of material from its web-accessible docket, instead making the information available to selected individuals subject to restrictions on its use.[49] The Department of Homeland Security also adopted new rules that allowed it to deny requests for "critical infrastructure information" provided to it by industry.[50]

A second type of now-restricted information related to the monitoring and inspection work of federal agencies. Two weeks after the 9/11 attacks, the Federal Aviation Administration blocked public access to its database of enforcement actions, which journalists had used to identify security lapses by airlines and airports.[51] Federal officials also denied access to the results of "detection tests" undertaken to check whether weapons would be discovered at airport security checkpoints.[52] The Transportation Safety Administration, formed in the aftermath of 9/11, later received broader statutory authority to withhold "sensitive security information" without regard to the requirements of the Freedom of Information Act.[53] The Customs Service refused to release information about its inspection practices for incoming shipping containers,[54] while the Nuclear Regulatory Commission decided that it would no longer release scorecards showing the results of its inspections of the physical security of nuclear plants or information about enforcement actions on matters relating to plant security.[55]

These new policies reflected a fundamental shift in perceptions about the character of the security threat confronting the United States. In the era of the Cold War, security policy had been premised on the assumption that the principal threat to national security would be posed by other states, and that those threats would be manifested through overt military confrontations rather than sporadic acts of terror or sabotage within national borders. The 9/11 attacks compelled a reconsideration of this view, weakening the concept of the "impenetrable nation state"[56] and inducing "a level of vulnerability that Americans have not seen since they were living on the edge of a dangerous frontier 150 years ago."[57]

Fears about the United States' susceptibility to domestic attack, already stoked by the attacks, were further heightened in the following months. Bush administration officials said that documents found in al Qaeda's Tora Bora cave complex in eastern Afghanistan in December 2001 gave evidence of further plotting: maps of the Washington subway system, blueprints of nuclear power plants and water distribution systems, photographs of the Seattle waterfront, and trade publications of the American chemical industry.[58] In January 2002, the computer of a suspected al Qaeda member was found to contain detailed information about dams and water systems in the United States.[59]

The attempt to restrict access to information that might reveal domestic vulnerabilities was subject to three main criticisms. The first was a fatalistic view about the likely effectiveness of such efforts in a world of "information abundance."[60] In 2002, a George Washington

University Law student, Air Force Major Joseph Jacobson, demonstrated that information comparable to that contained in the EPA's now-inaccessible risk-management plans could be compiled from other sources on the internet. Producing a list of chemical plants that could be potential targets was straightforward, and enough information on production processes for specific plants could be obtained to reach conclusions about the "off-site consequences" of an accident that were roughly comparable to the conclusions provided by plant owners to the EPA. "Not posting this information on the Internet," Jacobson concluded, "simply forces a would-be terrorist to spend a few extra minutes on the computer researching available 'target' data that would otherwise be conveniently assembled by the EPA."[61]

A 2004 RAND study reached a similar conclusion, observing that in many cases information similar to that provided by government sources was available from "a diverse set of non-federal sources" – and that in any case "direct access or observation" of potential targets was more likely to be the first choice for collecting information needed to plan an attack. A survey of hundreds of federal data-sets revealed none whose contents were "critical to meeting attacker needs." The study also noted that attackers had the advantage of a "broad range" of targets: If access to information about one potential target was blocked, another could easily be found.[62]

A second criticism of these new restrictions emphasized the harm done to citizens, because of their undermined capacity to monitor government or business actions that would have an important impact on their well-being. In the three years following the September 11th attacks, complaints about the erosion of these rights were common, although the evidence was still inchoate. In one prominent case, a Utah-based environmental group, Living Rivers, challenged the Interior Department's refusal to provide maps that showed the likely impact of a failure of the Glen Canyon Dam on the Colorado River, the second highest concrete-arch dam in the United States. Government officials justified their refusal by arguing that the maps would reveal that the dam could be turned into a "weapon of mass destruction," threatening down-river communities.[63] Living Rivers retorted that residents were being kept "in the dark" about risks posed by the dam; however, the group conceded that it had been able – through other sources – to document those risks.[64]

Critics complained that new rules to protect "critical infrastructure information" also undercut their rights. Community organizers in Virginia said that FERC's new rules to protect energy infrastructure had compromised their ability to learn the proposed route of a new natural gas pipeline, constraining residents' ability to mobilize against a route that crossed their property and created a significant safety risk.[65] At the same time, activists in Alabama claimed that FERC's rules would restrict access to information about the safety of a liquid natural gas terminal proposed for the Port of Mobile.[66] Many journalists also protested over FERC's insistence that they sign agreements before receiving information that allowed FERC staff to undertake a pre-publication review of stories based on that information.[67] On the other hand, FERC asserted in 2004 that it had not received any complaints that a participant in a Commission proceeding had been denied access to information needed to participate in the proceeding.[68]

Early decisions to withhold information sometimes failed to recognize the distinction between information that revealed previously unknown vulnerabilities and information that merely confirmed the magnitude of known risks. The failure of the Glen Canyon Dam was a known risk, particularly after a government official affirmed under oath that its failure could cause "mass destruction"; the security interest in withholding details about the precise dimensions of the likely destruction was less clear. It was similarly obvious that a substantial risk would be posed by a liquid natural gas terminal located in a populated area. The case for withholding information about hidden weaknesses – for example, about the location of airports or nuclear plants that frequently failed security tests – seemed clearer.

There were many critics who were prepared to challenge even this position, however. This was the third criticism made against the new pattern of secrecy: Rather than promoting security, the unwillingness to disclose information about vulnerabilities actually weakened it. The decision to withhold details about gaps in security was predicated on the assumption that officials or businesses that held the information would take steps to remedy the problems. But here was the fundamental question: Could large bureaucracies – public or private – be trusted to act vigorously without being prodded by journalists or advocacy groups who shared knowledge of security defects?

Skepticism about the public's ability to rely on the vigilance of officials in fixing security problems pervaded the post-9/11 debate over the withholding of information. Rena Steinzor, a sharp critic of rules to protect "critical infrastructure information" collected by the Department of Homeland Security, warned:

> Disclosure leads to accountability not just for information but for eliminating the vulnerability the information describes. As a matter of human nature, the absence of this powerful incentive for action will lead to failures to address security problems, ultimately making people less safe, not more. These outcomes will occur even if the individuals who know about a vulnerability are well-meaning and patriotic because it is very difficult for Americans to combat institutional inertia from a wide variety of sources.... The dilemma is not whether information will fall into terrorist hands, but rather whether suppression of such information, ... will lead to even graver outcomes.[69]

As if to validate Steinzor's complaint, the Department of Homeland Security announced in 2004 that it had sharply reduced the number of chemical plants it regarded as serious terror risks, a decision that limited plant owners' obligation to invest in new security measures.[70]

The Nuclear Regulatory Commission's restrictions on access were challenged for similar reasons. Advocacy groups that had long complained about industry influence over the regulator argued that the NRC's decision to withhold new security standards would simply hide its unwillingness to set rigorous rules on the protection of nuclear plants against terror attacks.[71] "Without public pressure," a Greenpeace spokesman said in August 2004, when the Commission announced further restrictions on inspection data, "these guys go back to sleep."[72] A month later, federal auditors validated that complaint: A report by the independent Government Accountability Office criticized the Commission for its slowness in improving security, suggesting that its efforts had been compromised by close relationships with plant owners.[73] A few months later, the Commission was chastised again, this time for withholding data from a National Academy of Sciences panel charged with assessing the vulnerability to terrorist attack of spent-fuel cooling pools at some reactor sites. The panel ultimately concluded that the Commission had not taken adequate measures to limit risks.[74]

Transparency and security

Criticisms such as these pose a challenge to a precept that has, for many years, sustained the security establishment as an enclave in which the right to information has little hold: the presumed identity of *security* and *secrecy*. The assumption that the defense of national security demands strict controls on the flow of information is deeply embedded in bureaucratic – and popular – culture. But events following the 2001 terror attacks give reason for holding an alternative view: that in robust democracies, the path to improved security may actually lie in a policy that encourages the free flow of information.

The 9/11 Commission, like the earlier Joint Congressional Inquiry into 9/11, concluded that informational blockages contributed to the failure of federal agencies to anticipate the terror attacks. Most of the ten "operational opportunities" to deter the attacks that the Commission identified in its 2004 report involved the failures to share information within or between agencies.[75] By the summer of 2001, CIA Director George Tenet told the Commission, senior officials responsible for counterterrorism had deep concern about an impending attack: In Tenet's words, "the system was blinking red." But no warning was distributed to lower-level officials responsible for dealing with attacks within the United States, and investigators working on late-emerging leads on potential threats did not connect them to broader concerns about impending attacks.[76]

For the Commission, one of the essential steps in reform following the 9/11 attacks was overcoming the bureaucratic and technical hurdles to the sharing of information within the federal government. In its final report, the Commission urged abandoning the "'need-to-know' culture of information protection" in favor of a "'need-to-share' culture" that rewards information sharing. By doing this, the Commission argued, analysts and investigators would have a better chance of "connecting the dots" to anticipate impending threats.[77] Other commentators reached the same conclusion. "Today," says Bruce Berkowitz, "effective warning often means getting information in front of as many people as possible so as to improve the odds that someone will see a telltale pattern."[78]

This approach to reform can be regarded as a combination of an old problem with new technology. The problem of "connecting the dots" was described forty years ago in a classic study of the intelligence failure before the attack on Pearl Harbor. The United States had ample signs of an impending attack in 1941, Roberta Wohlstetter argued, but the critical signals were lost in a "buzzing and blooming confusion" of irrelevant information, or "noise."[79] The task of distinguishing signals from noise constituted the intelligence analysts' key challenge. Then – as now – it was complicated by limited organizational resources. (The FBI's counterterrorism head told the 9/11 Commission that he wished he had had "500 analysts looking at Bin Ladin threat information" in the summer of 2001 – "instead of two."[80])

The most extreme example of an attempt to distinguish signals from noise may be the University of California's SETI project – an attempt to discern evidence of extraterrestrial intelligence from an overwhelming amount of data collected by the world's largest radio telescope. The task of analysis requires enormous computing power, which as a practical matter would be unavailable if investigators were compelled to rely on a single computer. Instead, SETI researchers developed an alternative approach, in which analytic tasks are undertaken by a network of over three million personal computers that receive data from SETI and process it using otherwise idle capacity. Researchers estimated that the approach had yielded the computing power equivalent to a $300 million supercomputer.[81]

This "distributed-computing" model has become an increasingly popular approach for handling complex analytic problems. The post-9/11 investigations recommended what is essentially the bureaucratic equivalent, proposing a network in which data is widely shared and that harnesses the analytic capacity of a much larger group of specialists. A prerequisite, according to the Commission, is the loosening of Cold War-era rules that gave greater weight to the risks of inadvertent disclosure than it did to the benefits of broad dissemination. The approach to reform is liberal but still limited: It proposes better information sharing principally *inside* the community of government agencies.

Nevertheless, a similar logic could be used to justify broader information sharing to stakeholders *outside* government as well. Like many officials inside government, the general public remained unaware of high-level concern about impending attacks in the summer of 2001. An informed public might have observed actions that gave evidence of looming threats: It was an attentive citizen, after all, who alerted the FBI to the suspicious behavior of the alleged "twentieth hijacker," Zacarias Moussaoui.[82] (A few weeks before the September 11th attacks, actor James Woods also observed suspicious behavior by four Middle Eastern men on a transcontinental flight; he later identified two as 9/11 hijackers.[83]) Representatives of the victims' families later suggested that the public might have made sense of events on the morning of September 11 more quickly – perhaps taking steps to minimize the effect of the attacks – if they had been told about the intelligence community's assessment of the risk of attack.[84] Before September 11, the congressional inquiry concluded in 2003, "the U.S. Intelligence Community was involved in fighting a 'war' against Bin Ladin largely without the benefit of what some would call its most potent weapon in that effort: an alert and committed American public."[85]

The Bush administration's post-9/11 decision to invade Iraq provided further evidence of the ways in which excessive secrecy could undermine, rather than enhance, national security. By fall 2004, it had become clear that the war in Iraq had been justified on the basis of intelligence that was badly flawed and twisted in its representation to the public, and that planning for the post-combat occupation of Iraq had also been inadequate. A policy of secrecy had aggravated the weaknesses in analysis and planning, and created the possibility of misrepresentation – resulting in a prolonged and bloody campaign of pacification.

Public opinion polls conducted in early 2003 showed that American public opinion was overwhelmingly in favor of war with Iraq.[86] Research found that support for the war was closely tied to popular beliefs about Iraqi complicity in the September 11th attacks and the threat that Iraq posed to American security. In a succession of polls, a majority of Americans said that they believed there was clear evidence of Iraqi involvement in the September 11th attacks; a near-majority said that Saddam Hussein had been "personally involved" in the attacks. Overwhelming majorities also believed that Iraq had weapons of mass destruction.[87] In a CBS poll conducted on the eve of war in March 2003, 45 percent of Americans said that Iraq posed a threat requiring immediate military action, and a similar proportion expected that war would be "fairly quick and successful."[88]

These assessments were later repudiated. In July 2004 the Senate Committee on Intelligence, reviewing the evidence available to the U.S. intelligence community, concluded that there was no evidence that Saddam Hussein had tried to employ al Qaeda to conduct terrorist attacks, and "no evidence proving Iraqi complicity or assistance in an al-Qaida attack."[89] A CIA reappraisal in October 2004 also questioned earlier evidence linking the Hussein government to an alleged al Qaeda leader, Abu Musab al-Zarqawi.[90] In the same month, the CIA's Iraq Survey Group – a team of experts given the responsibility of searching for weapons of mass destruction in post-occupation Iraq – reported that the Iraqi government did not possess such weapons at the time of the invasion, and was not actively seeking to produce them.[91] The head of the occupational authority also said in October 2004 that the American government had underestimated the number of troops that would be needed to preserve order in Iraq after the invasion.[92] A leaked CIA report concluded that Iraq faced a significant risk of civil war.[93]

How had the American public come to hold opinions about Iraq that proved to be so badly misguided? One reason was the Bush administration's public misrepresentation of the evidence available to American intelligence agencies in the months before the war – a tactic that was feasible because of the secrecy that prevented a more complete view of the available evidence. For example, a National Intelligence Estimate produced by the CIA in October 2002 noted important disagreements within the intelligence community about the threat posed by Iraq, and its links to al Qaeda. However, the Estimate itself remained classified and inaccessible to the general public. Legislators with access to the Estimate and other intelligence summaries were compelled to sign agreements pledging not to release classified information, and the CIA resisted declassification requests.[94] After the completion of the Estimate, however, senior administration spokesmen repeatedly made public statements about the Iraqi threat and its connection to al Qaeda that ignored internal disputes over the interpretation of evidence that had been recorded in the classified document.[95]

Some commentators suggested that public misperceptions were also a reflection of misperceptions within the intelligence community about the threat posed by Iraq before invasion. Borrowing a term coined by psychologist Irving Janis,[96] the Senate Intelligence Committee suggested in July 2004 that intelligence analysts had fallen into a "collective groupthink" that led them to ignore evidence that was inconsistent with their preconceptions about the Iraqi threat.[97] One of the prerequisites for groupthink is the insulation of a group from external forces that would challenge prevailing views.[98] In fact, the intelligence community has developed mechanisms – such as internal "red teams" tasked with contesting the dominant interpretation of evidence – designed to mimic the role played by such external forces. But the Senate Committee says that the intelligence community's collective predisposition was so strong that these internal mechanisms were not deployed. (The strain of events may have contributed to the corrosion of critical analysis: According to another report, at a critical moment in 2003, CIA head George Tenet dismissed a dissenting view about the reliability of intelligence on the Iraqi threat "with words to the effect of 'yeah, yeah,' and that he was 'exhausted.'"[99])

In August 2004, an internal CIA study concluded that its capacity to analyze intelligence may have been compromised in other ways. The leaked report suggested that the agency's analytic branch had "never been more junior and inexperienced" and that its ability to assess intelligence was compromised by "tradecraft weaknesses."[100] If either view – groupthink or limited analytic capacity – is right,[101] then it creates a powerful case for greater openness – so that other stakeholders can perform the essential function of weighing evidence and challenging preconceptions about its meaning.

The British government became immersed in a similar controversy over its handling of intelligence on the Iraqi threat. In 2003, a parliamentary committee criticized the government for publicly exaggerating the evidence of an imminent threat, and for its unwillingness to provide access to intelligence papers and personnel.[102] In one instance, Prime Minister Tony Blair unwittingly relied on material that was found to have been plagiarized from a decade-old graduate student thesis.[103] Blair eventually conceded that the pre-war evidence on Iraq had been largely wrong.[104]

The American government's approach to post-war planning suffered from the same weaknesses. In 2004, it was reported that classified pre-war assessments had warned of the possibility of prolonged and intense internal conflict in Iraq.[105] Before the invasion, however, the Bush administration had publicly rebuffed pessimistic assessments about the occupation; at the same time, it refused to release details about its post-war planning. Pressed by reporters in February

2003, Defense Secretary Donald Rumsfeld said that "it's not useful" to release details on post-war planning for public discussion.[106] Two weeks before the invasion, a Council on Foreign Relations report criticized the Bush administration for its failure to "fully describe to Congress and the American people the magnitude of the resources that will be required to meet post-conflict needs...[or] their perspectives on the structure of post-conflict governance."[107] The complaint was shared by humanitarian groups who hoped to participate in reconstruction efforts.[108] Journalist James Fallows later concluded that key planners within the Bush administration had developed their own "groupthink" on the question of occupation – a blindness to evidence of potential difficulties in reconstruction. "Everyone had that 'Stalingrad stare'," a senior administrator told Fallows. "People had been doing stuff under pressure for too long and hadn't had enough sleep."[109]

The weaknesses in decision making that preceded the Iraqi war have been seen before. In 1968, Professor James C. Thomson, Jr., wrote a widely acclaimed article in *The Atlantic* magazine that attempted to explain the weaknesses in the United States government's policy toward Vietnam. Thomson, who had served in the Kennedy and Johnson administrations, predicted that historians would look back at the Vietnam years and wonder how "men of superior ability, sound training, and high ideals" could have made decisions that were "regularly and repeatedly wrong." The answer, thought Thomson, could be found largely in the process of decision making itself. The concentration of responsibility at the top led to executive fatigue and an inability to respond to new and dissonant information. This was compounded by a lack of expertise within key agencies and "closed politics" of policy making on sensitive issues.[110]

(Ironically, Defense Secretary Robert McNamara understood the weaknesses of the process by which decisions on Vietnam were being made. Unknown to Thomson, McNamara had taken the unusual step a few months earlier of commissioning a large study of American decision making on Vietnam. Unfortunately, the Pentagon Papers – as they were eventually known – did little to improve the quality of government policy. Classified as TOP SECRET, the papers were largely inaccessible inside government until they were leaked by Daniel Ellsberg in 1971.)

47

The problems observed by Thompson during the Vietnam conflict, and experienced again in the months before the Iraq war, are likely typical of large public bureaucracies. The concentration of authority at the top of the bureaucratic pyramid means that leaders and their advisors are overwhelmed with information, juggling problems that are often outside their area of expertise. Fatigue, confusion, and ignorance about key facts are commonplace. In most circumstances, a policy of openness helps to check the damage that might arise because of these bureaucratic pathologies. Transparency allows outside actors to challenge evidence and present their own – to assess the merits of proposed policies and present alternatives. The analytic capacity of a few bureaucracies is aided by the vastly larger analytic capacity of the public sphere as a whole. It is, in a metaphorical sense, another application of the distributed computing model used in the SETI project.

But this does not hold true in the security sector, where long tradition – and an instinctive reaction against disclosure of sensitive information – militate against transparency. This is justified in the name of national security. Perversely, however, the security sector is probably the one area where the consequences of poor analysis are most severe, and where the more substantial analytic capacity of the public sphere is most badly needed. In the long run, it may be a policy of openness, rather than secrecy, that best promotes security, by avoiding the tremendous costs that can follow from poor bureaucratic decision making.

Hardened targets

There is another powerful argument for greater openness on questions such as the threat posed by Iraq: the protection of basic political rights. A decision to go to war is arguably one of the most important choices that a nation can be expected to make, because it involves an explicit gamble with human lives. Citizens are entitled to expect that they will be given an opportunity to make an informed judgment about the need for war. In the case of preventative rather than defensive war, this expectation cannot be dismissed on the grounds of urgency. Respect for the fundamental right to self-determination demands greater openness.[111] Secrecy, by contrast, compels the public to defer to the judgment of a narrow elite.[112]

Unfortunately, good arguments alone have done little to overturn habits of secrecy within the security establishment. Openness may help to avoid human rights abuses; it may protect political participation rights; it may even help to improve national security itself. All this may be true, but the security establishment nonetheless has remained (to use the military's own jargon) a hardened target – a sector that has largely succeeded in resisting the trend toward greater openness in government.

There are several reasons for this. One is the ease with which bureaucratic self-interest can be cloaked in the mantle of the public interest. In moments of great insecurity – when the public fears significant threats to public order – it is also least likely to challenge claims about the need to keep secrets. We saw this in the months following the September 2001 attacks, when the public's willingness to defer to government leaders soared to levels not seen in the past thirty years and opinion polls showed that a large majority of Americans were prepared to weaken civil rights to ensure public security.[113] Furthermore, the basic equation that is essential to the maintenance of the security establishment as an enclave of secrecy – the presumed equivalence of security and secrecy – is deeply embedded in popular culture. ("It's classified," says Maverick in the movie *Top Gun*. "I could tell you, but then I would have to kill you.")

The bureaucratic interest in keeping secrets is also very strong. Rules on access to information perform the function of preserving hierarchy within public bureaucracies. If lower strata of workers within public agencies have better access to information, they are more likely to challenge their superiors, either directly or by mobilizing constituencies outside the bureaucracy to challenge the agency leadership. Liberalization of access rules also challenges hierarchy in a less tangible way, by undermining status distinctions within public bureaucracies. Within the security establishment, rank is signaled by security clearance: To put it roughly, who you are (in terms of social status) depends on what you know. (Access to "the inside dope," Daniel Ellsberg recalls in a memoir of his early years in the Defense Department, "made you feel important."[114]) An attempt to remove restrictions on access to information is, therefore, a challenge to social hierarchy within public agencies.

The system is also deeply entrenched in bureaucratic routine. The work life of the vast federal bureaucracy consists, in large part, in the handling of information; a change in rules about information management – such as rules about the making and keeping of secrets – can have fundamental and broad consequences. The current system of secret keeping has had more than a half-century to embed itself in bureaucratic practice. In addition there are other, less easily observed constraints on reform, as I will note in Chapter 6: the growing web of intergovernmental agreements that compel agencies in the American government – and other governments as well – to retain traditional methods of controlling sensitive information.

3

REGIME CHANGE

On April 22, 2004, U.S. Defense Secretary Donald Rumsfeld gave a luncheon address to the annual convention of the American Society of Newspaper Editors, meeting at the J. W. Marriott Hotel on Washington's Pennsylvania Avenue. Fifty years earlier, it had been the ASNE that first lobbied for adoption of a federal Freedom of Information Act, and so it was perhaps natural for Rumsfeld to begin with an encomium on the virtues of open government:

> Our republic was founded on the notion that an unchecked government is a major obstacle to human freedom and to progress, and that our leaders need to be challenged, internally through the complex constitutional system of checks and balances, and externally by a free and energetic press. This is a notion I've supported throughout my adult life. As a matter of fact, as a young member of Congress back in the 1960s, still in my 30s, I was a co-sponsor of the Freedom of Information Act. Now we all recognize that that Act causes government officials occasional pain, but in my view, it has been a valuable Act in helping to get the facts to the American people. . . . Our great political system needs information to be self-correcting. While excesses and imbalances will inevitably exist for a time, fortunately they tend not to last. Ultimately truth prevails.[1]

The depth of Secretary Rumsfeld's commitment to transparency was, at that moment, open to question. Ten days before Rumsfeld's ASNE speech, Defense Department officials had learned that the CBS news program *60 Minutes II* was about to broadcast a story on abuse of Iraqi detainees at Abu Ghraib prison, west of Baghdad. The CBS story, based on a leaked copy of an internal report by Major General Antonio Taguba, was damning. While Rumsfeld and other senior officials boasted publicly that the torture of Iraqi citizens had ended with the fall of Saddam Hussein,[2] Taguba had collected "extremely graphic photographic evidence . . . [of] sadistic, blatant, and wanton criminal abuses . . . intentionally perpetrated" by American troops.[3]

Although Taguba's report, completed in early March, had leaked to CBS and other journalists, the Defense Department did its best to keep the lid on the story. The report had been classified as SECRET – a decision that was later challenged as an abuse of classification rules but restricted its circulation and would have blocked disclosure under the Freedom of Information Act.[4] The Chairman of the Joint Chiefs of Staff, General Richard Myers, called CBS news anchor Dan Rather on April 14, and again on April 21, twice persuading him to delay the network's report on Abu Ghraib.[5]

On April 28, CBS refused to wait any longer. But Rumsfeld said nothing to members of Congress about the report in a briefing on Capitol Hill only hours before the CBS broadcast.[6] Interviewed by MSNBC's Chris Matthews the next evening, Rumsfeld refused to discuss Taguba's investigation, denying that he knew anything more than what CBS had reported:

> **MATTHEWS**: You've seen these photos from CBS of the treatment of some of the prisoners over there. **RUMSFELD**: Yes, I have. . . . **MATTHEWS**: You're a good man, but what is your reaction to – when you see that? Are these bad apples, or is there something in the pressure on these troops over there, the heat? What is it that brings to – these guys are being paraded around, made to do all these things naked and these weird kind of things to humiliate themselves. What's that about? **RUMSFELD**: I watched the program, is all I have seen on it.[7]

"He did display a lot of candor today," said Matthews after the interview, thinking that he knew enough to make that judgment.

As controversy grew in the following days, Rumsfeld maintained his silence, refusing to meet with reporters on the subject. Rumsfeld's press chief, Lawrence Di Rita, also declined to "talk about the specifics of a report which (a), remains classified, and (b), remains under review."[8] When portions of the Taguba report were posted on the internet, some in the Defense Department still fought the tide. An internal e-mail from security staff warned:

> Fox News and other media outlets are distributing the [Taguba] report.... Someone has given the news media classified information and they are distributing it.... This leakage will be investigated for criminal prosecution. If you don't have the document and have never had legitimate access, please do not complicate the investigative processes by seeking information.... THE INFORMATION CONTAINED IN THIS REPORT IS CLASSIFIED; DO NOT GO TO FOX NEWS TO READ OR OBTAIN A COPY.[9]

The e-mail was promptly leaked to *Time* magazine. Within days, efforts to contain the scandal collapsed. In *The New Yorker*, journalist Seymour Hersh published a second story on Abu Ghraib, based not only on his own leaked copy of the Taguba report, but on military hearing transcripts and soldiers' correspondence as well.[10] The former commander of Abu Ghraib, Brigadier General Janis Karpinski, appeared on ABC's *Good Morning America*, *Nightline*, and CNN's *American Morning* to rebut claims that she bore much of the responsibility for the abuses. The CIA acknowledged that its Inspector General was also investigating misconduct by its officers at Abu Ghraib,[11] and the Army conceded that it had begun over thirty criminal investigations into suspicious deaths and other abuses in Iraq and Afghanistan, finding at least two criminal homicides.[12]

Finally, a week after the *60 Minutes II* broadcast, Rumsfeld held a news conference to discuss the controversy, and two days later he was called before House and Senate committees. His frustration was palpable. "The system works," Rumsfeld told reporters on May 4. "I understand the appetite of people for instant information and instant conclusions. These things are complicated. They take some time."[13] The controversy, he almost suggested to legislators on May 6, was fueled by an excess of openness: "Someone took that secret report and gave it to the press" before senior officials had the chance to properly consider it. The problem, he told senators, was this:

> We're functioning in a – with peacetime restraints, with legal requirements in a war-time situation, in the information age, where people are running around with digital cameras and taking these unbelievable photographs and then passing them off, against the law, to the media, to our surprise, when they had not even arrived in the Pentagon.[14]

The controversy over the Taguba report, which metastasized in the following weeks into a broader scandal about use of torture as a tool in the war on terror, perfectly illustrated the Bush administration's attitude toward open government. As the etiquette of public discourse required, the administration expressed its general commitment to the principle of openness. In practice, however, it did what it could to restrict access to government records.

The Bush administration did this because it feared the consequence of excessive openness – the corrosion of its ability to maintain a decent degree of control over the business of government. The vortex into which the Bush administration had been drawn after the *60 Minutes II* report could be regarded, by advocates of openness, as the high price that is paid for excessive secretiveness. But for people like Rumsfeld, concerned mainly with the executive's capacity to govern, the following week might well have illustrated the basic problem that preoccupied their days: the irrationality and chaos of a political system that is increasingly dominated by twenty-four-hour news, a fractured and fractious Congress, and a burgeoning number of special interest groups. Too much openness simply accelerated the inherent entropic tendencies of American politics.

Overload

If nothing else, Rumsfeld's attitude had the virtue of long consistency. The drive for greater secrecy was not precipitated by the demands of the war on terror. Concern about the executive's capacity to govern had preoccupied Rumsfeld and his allies for three decades, always constraining their enthusiasm for greater governmental openness.

Sometimes history was bent to avoid a direct acknowledgement of this fact. It was true, as Rumsfeld told the ASNE convention, that as a young Republican congressman he had been a co-sponsor of the Freedom of Information Act adopted by Congress in 1966. At the time he had even expressed sentiments about the virtues of open government that advocates of transparency would later deploy in a futile effort to embarrass him as Defense secretary. "Disclosure of government information is particularly important today," said Rumsfeld in 1966, "because government is becoming involved in more and more aspects of every citizen's personal and business life, and so access to information about how government is exercising its trust becomes increasingly important."[15]

Rumsfeld may well have believed this. However, the law that he co-sponsored – the 1966 FOIA – was only a shadow of the contemporary Freedom of Information Act. As Supreme Court Justice Potter Stewart said in a 1973 case interpreting the law, the 1966 FOIA provided no method of challenging a decision to withhold information that had been classified in the name of national security – no matter how "cynical, myopic, or even corrupt that decision might have been."[16] The 1966 law provided similarly broad protection for the FBI's investigative files.[17] The sort of openness that Rumsfeld had praised in 1966 was one that still allowed the President and his subordinates substantial control over the outflow of information.

Congress attempted to limit this control in the fall of 1974, after the resignation of Richard Nixon. It adopted amendments that allowed the courts to determine whether the authority to classify information in the name of national security had been properly exercised, and that required the FBI and other agencies to show that disclosure of investigative files would actually compromise its law enforcement activities. By then, Rumsfeld was Chief of Staff to President Gerald Ford. (Rumsfeld's deputy was Dick Cheney.) In November 1974, Ford vetoed Congress's amendments to the law, claiming that they would compromise national security and law enforcement.[18] Congress, angered by the Watergate scandal, voted to override Ford's veto. (Justice Antonin Scalia, then head of the Justice Department's Office of Legal Counsel, also supported a veto of the FOIA amendments, and encouraged intelligence officials to make their opposition known to President Ford.[19] The 1966 FOIA had been "a relatively toothless beast," Scalia said later, but the 1974 amendments were a "disaster."[20])

Today, the Nixon years are remembered as a time in which the American public realized the dangers inherent in an excessive concentration of executive authority. Nixon had put the capstone on an "imperial presidency," according to the historian Arthur Schlesinger, Jr.,[21] and the Watergate scandal provided a vivid reminder of the ways in which these broad powers could be misused. In the conventional view, subsequent investigations into abuses by the CIA and the FBI helped to drive the lesson home. This narrative – centered on the restraint of a too-powerful President – was widely, but not universally, accepted. For many in America's governing elite, the real story was actually about the *collapse* of executive authority in the United States and other advanced democracies.

This alternative narrative was articulated in a study commissioned by the Trilateral Commission in April 1974. The commission itself had been formed a year earlier and comprised 200 top policy makers – elected officials, businessmen, and academics – from the United States, Japan, and Western Europe. Its first major project was the Task Force on Governability of Democracies, set up (as the commission's director, Zbigniew Brzezinski, explained) to answer a question being posed "with increasing urgency" by leading statesmen in the West: "Is democracy in crisis?" Three leading scholars – Samuel Huntington, Michel Crozier, and Joji Watanuki – were enlisted for the study, completed in May 1975.[22]

Their report presented a gloomy view of the prospects for the trilateral democracies. Profound changes in the political and social order, the trio argued, had made "the governability of democracy...an urgent issue." Mass electorates had become more assertive in their demands on government, and less trustful of public authorities. Political parties had lost their capacity to channel public opinion, leading to a "disaggregation of interests" and proliferation of lobby groups. The influence of the old print media was being undercut by the new broadcast media, whose news coverage tended "to arouse unfavorable attitudes toward established institutions and to promote a decline in confidence in government." In the United States, Congress had also increased its role in the political system – but at the same time the "strong central leadership" that had focused the energy of Congress had been toppled, with its power broadly diffused throughout both chambers.

This broad "democratic surge," as Samuel Huntington called it, had led to a proliferation of demands on the executive branch of government. But here was the predicament: As the demands on government grew, its capacity to respond effectively to those demands had declined. In large part this was because of the leakage of power to Congress, to other levels of government, and directly to the public itself. Even within the executive branch, however, authority was eroding, with subordinates more willing "to ignore, to criticize, or to defeat the wishes of their organizational superiors." In general, warned Huntington,

> The publics in the Trilateral societies have expected much of their political leaders. . . . In many instances, however, political leaders have been left deficient in the institutional resources and authority necessary to achieve these goals. A pervasive suspicion of the motives and power of political leaders on the part of the public has given rise to the imposition of legal and institutional barriers which serve to prevent them from achieving the goals which the public expects them to accomplish.[23]

The "overload thesis," as it came to be known, gained widespread popularity among senior officials in many countries. It articulated their own frustration with the task of governing in societies in which power was increasingly fragmented, and entropic tendencies – the inclination of the whole system toward disorder – seemed increasingly strong. And the passage of time seemed only to aggravate the conditions that had been observed in the Trilateral Commission's 1975 report.

In the United States, the number of policy areas in which the federal government was involved continued to expand.[24] At the same time, the number of interest groups also grew substantially.[25] The Lobbying Disclosure Act of 1995 required organizations that spent more than $20,000 on lobbying in a six-month period to file a public report of basic information about their activity. In the first year, over 10,000 reports were filed.[26] The United States, said Jonathan Rauch in 1994, had reached a state of "hyper pluralism" – a world so thickly populated with special interests that vigorous government action had become impossible.[27]

The proliferation of interest groups was accompanied by "epochal" changes in the organization of national media.[28] The major broadcast networks, which thirty years ago undermined the power of national newspapers, found their own dominance in news undercut by the emergence of cable news networks. And the whole edifice of institutionalized news production has itself been challenged by the advent of the internet and the dramatic reduction in barriers to entry into the news business. Increasingly, citizens receive the "raw elements of news" in a "jumbled, chaotic" stream without synthesis or interpretation.[29] These technological changes produced a "never-ending news cycle" in which stories emerged and spread at "warp speed."[30] "The media is fracturing into more choices and more diversity," said Ari Fleisher, President Bush's first press secretary, in 2005:

> In the modern media world, marked by the Internet and three all-news, all-the-time cable networks that compete furiously with one another, the ability to digest news slowly when facts emerge and sometimes change is seriously hindered. Gone forever are the days when news would break, reporters and sources would discuss ongoing developments throughout the day, and most Americans would first hear the news in a carefully digested story hours later on the evening news. For reporters now, it's an immediate need to tell and a rush to air. The need for the public to "know" hasn't changed, but the urgency for reporters to "tell" has grown more intense.[31]

At the same time, the authority of major government institutions continued to wane. "By almost any measure," three scholars observed in a 2000 retrospective on the Trilateral Commission report, public alienation from governing institutions had "soared" over the following quarter-century. Public confidence in the executive and legislative branches of the federal government remained far below levels that had been recorded in the mid-1960s.[32] Congress itself undertook internal reforms in the 1970s that increased the power of committees and weakened the authority of senior legislators, producing "conditions of extreme fragmentation" that could be exploited by dissatisfied minorities. "The messiness and volatility of the political process that the reforms helped amplify," Julian Zelizer argues, "exacerbated the perception of Washington as a town that seemed incapable of action."[33]

Congress, in turn, ignored the Trilateral Commission's warning against the imposition of restrictions on the executive branch. The commission argued in 1975 that accountability had its limits: There was a need, it said, "to assure to the government the right and the ability to withhold information at the source."[34] Congress thought otherwise. The Freedom of Information Act, amended over President Ford's objection in 1974, now expanded access to national security and law enforcement information. The Presidential Records Act (1978) broke a long tradition and established that the documents of former Presidents were public property, eventually subject to public scrutiny.[35] The Privacy Act (1974) created an obligation for federal agencies to provide citizens with access to their personal information. The Ethics in Government Act (1978) required government officials to reveal details about their income and assets. The Government in the Sunshine Act (1976) compelled government boards and commissions to conduct their business in open meetings, while the Federal Advisory Committee Act (1972) imposed similar obligations on committees set up to solicit advice from individuals outside government.

The veil surrounding the executive branch was lifted through other laws as well. The Civil Service Reform Act (1978) provided new remedies for public servants who had been punished for "blowing the whistle" about misconduct within the federal government. (These remedies were bolstered in 1989 by the Whistleblower Protection Act, which was strengthened again in 1994.) The Inspector General Act (1978) led to the appointment of a cadre of almost sixty independent officers with a mandate to investigate and report publicly on mismanagement inside federal agencies.[36] The General Accounting Office Act (1980) expanded the power of the Comptroller General to obtain access to records held by uncooperative federal agencies.[37] Meanwhile, the Foreign Intelligence Surveillance Act (1978) compelled the federal government to disclose its case for counterintelligence search and surveillance operations to a new body, the Foreign Intelligence Surveillance Court.

These were the conditions that confronted Donald Rumsfeld in the 1990s, and that may have affirmed for him the dire warnings of the Trilateral Commission a quarter-century earlier. Rumsfeld captured the predicament of American government in an analogy: the Executive Branch as Lemuel Gulliver, the protagonist of Jonathan Swift's 1726 tale *Gulliver's Travels*. Gulliver, a ship's surgeon, joins an expedition to the East Indies that is shipwrecked on an unfamiliar coast. Believing himself to be the sole survivor, Gulliver struggles to shore, where he quickly falls asleep. "When I awakened," says Gulliver,

> ...it was just Day-light. I attempted to rise, but was not able to stir: For as I happen'd to lye on my Back, I found my Arms and Legs were strongly fastened on each Side to the Ground; and my Hair, which was long and thick, tied down in the same Manner. I likewise felt several slender Ligatures across my Body, from my Armpits to my Thighs. I could only look upwards; the Sun began

to grow hot, and the Light offended my Eyes. I heard a confused Noise about me, but in the Posture I lay, could see nothing except the Sky.[38]

Gulliver had been captured by the Lilliputians, a race of people "not six inches high" who had bound the stranger to earth with hundreds of thin ropes.

In 1995, Rumsfeld – then in the private sector, the head of a pharmaceutical company – visited Capitol Hill to provide advice on government reform to the new House Republican majority led by Newt Gingrich. "The federal government is, for all intents and purposes, an institution in Chapter 11," Rumsfeld told legislators. Over three decades, it had become a "complex and overwhelming behemoth" that had taken on too many functions ("I am convinced that probably one-half to two-thirds of the federal government's non-central departments are no longer needed in their current form"), and more to the point, lacked autonomy to perform any of these functions well:

> One of the problems in government . . . is legislative microman-agement of the Executive branch. As I recall from my days in the Executive branch, Congress imposes so many restrictions, requirements, and requests on the Executive branch that, while no one of them is debilitating, in the aggregate they are like the threads the Lilliputians used to prevent Gulliver from moving. . . . What Congress needs to do is tell the Executive branch generally the direction to go, where the sides of the road are, and what the speed limit is. Then Congress should stand back, over-see, and evaluate the administration on how well it does, and if necessary calibrate the directions or change the drivers. Too many hands on the steering wheel will put the truck in the ditch.[39]

Speaking to the National Defense University in 2002, Rumsfeld again invoked the image of Lemuel Gulliver:

> I don't know quite how it happened, but along the road between the time I left the government in 1977 and when I came back, last year, a good deal of distrust has developed between the Congress and the executive branch. . . . Something happened in the interven-ing period, where the executive branch has done something that causes distrust by the Congress, or the Congress has, for whatever reason, decided that they want to put on literally thousands of earmarks on the legislation that "You can't do this, you can't do

This image, first used in the nineteenth-century advertising of a British thread manufacturer, was reproduced in the Bush administration's 2003 budget to illustrate its frustration with legislative checks on executive authority.

that, you can't do this, you can't do that," where your flexibility is just – it's like Gulliver, with a whole bunch of Lilliputian threads over them. No one thread keeps Gulliver down, but in the aggregate, he can't get up. And that is where we are.[40]

Testifying to the House and Senate Armed Services Committees two weeks later, Rumsfeld reprised the complaint. "We find the department like Gulliver," Rumsfeld told legislators, calling for an end to "micromanagement" that had cast "thousands of Lilliputian threads over the Department."[41]

Gulliver is a familiar character in Western literature. However, he may also have had a special place in the minds of neoconservatives in the Bush administration. The political philosopher Leo Strauss was said to have invoked Gulliver frequently in his own critiques of the vulnerabilities of liberal democracies.[42] Strauss's intellectual heirs included Rumsfeld's deputy secretary, Paul Wolfowitz, and Richard Perle, the chair of a key advisory panel within the Defense Department.[43]

Soon Rumsfeld's colleague, Treasury Secretary Paul O'Neill, was invoking Gulliver as well,[44] while President Bush's budget director,

Mitchell Daniels, included the analogy in the administration's 2003 budget. ("It makes me wonder if the administration may not be requiring the members of the cabinet to read Jonathan Swift's masterpiece of satire," said Senator Robert Byrd.[45]) "At a time of national emergency," the 2003 budget said, it was critical that federal managers should have broad discretion "to get the job done." Yet many departments were "tied-up in a morass of Lilliputian do's and don'ts." The complaint was accompanied by an illustration that looked distinctly out of place in an American budget report produced in the twenty-first century: a lithograph of the Lilliputians ensnaring Gulliver in spooled cotton, first printed as an advertisement for a British thread manufacturer almost 200 years earlier.[46]

The zone of autonomy

The controversy over the National Energy Policy Development Group provided a good illustration of the forces that now attempted to constrain executive authority – and the Bush administration's determination to rebuff them. Chaired by Vice President Cheney, the NEPDG met throughout 2001 to draft the administration's proposed energy policy. The NEPDG purported to be a task force comprised of fourteen senior government officials, but critics argued that executives of private energy companies (including the now-disgraced Enron Corporation) had been closely consulted about the proposed policy while environmental groups were shut out entirely. Following a request by two senior Democratic congressmen, in May 2001 the General Accounting Office launched an investigation of the NEPDG's work. Two advocacy groups, the Sierra Club and Judicial Watch – joined later by nine other groups – sued the government for disclosure of NEPDG records under the Federal Advisory Committee Act.

The chairman of Judicial Watch, Larry Klayman, later called the Bush administration "the most secretive of our lifetime, even more secretive than the Nixon administration."[47] It was not clear that the NEPDG case did much to substantiate the claim. Thirty years earlier, the Federal Advisory Committee Act had not yet been adopted by Congress. The particular interpretation of FACA that allowed Judicial Watch to pursue the NEPDG case – known as the "de facto member doctrine" – was not affirmed by the District of Columbia Court of Appeals until 1993.[48] Judicial Watch itself was not established until 1994, and several of its supporters in the NEPDG litigation were post-Nixon creations as well. (These included the People for the American Way Foundation [established in 1980], OMB Watch [1983], the National Security Archive [1985], and the Center for American Progress [2003].) For its part, the General Accounting Office relied on investigatory powers given to it by Congress only twenty years earlier.[49]

For senior members of the Bush administration, the NEPDG case probably exemplified how the Lilliputians went about their work. The Vice President responded aggressively, refusing to cede any ground on either the GAO investigation or the FACA litigation. "In 34 years," Cheney told ABC's *This Week* in January 2002,

> I have repeatedly seen an erosion of the powers and the ability of the President of the United States to do his job.... We've seen it in cases like this before, where it's demanded that the President cough up and compromise on important principles.... We are weaker today as an institution because of the unwise compromises that have been made over the last 30 or 35 years.[50]

Cheney flatly refused to cooperate with the GAO's inquiry, arguing that it constituted an "unconstitutional interference" with the functioning of the Executive Branch.[51] The administration took the same position in the FACA case, asserting that the de facto member doctrine permitted an unconstitutional intrusion into the President's "zone of autonomy."[52] "I'm not going to let Congress erode the powers of the Executive Branch," President Bush told reporters. "I have an obligation to make sure that the Presidency remains robust."[53]

From its earliest weeks, protecting the "zone of autonomy" became one of the main aims of the Bush administration. According to John F. Stacks, a senior editor at *Time* magazine who had supervised its coverage of Watergate, the Bush administration became the most "closemouthed, closed-doored" in memory:

> President Bush has held fewer press conferences at this point in his presidency than any president since Richard Nixon during his truncated second term. He has had almost no private interviews with a major news organization other than the conservative Fox

Network and has made himself available only to a select group of conservative columnists. His cabinet officers are similarly inaccessible, and when they or their deputies do grant interviews, minders from the press office sit in to make sure there are no deviations from the official line.[54]

The administration also attempted to curtail many of the statutory incursions on presidential authority. In March 2001, White House counsel Alberto Gonzales issued the first of three orders delaying the release of records from the Reagan administration that had been scheduled for disclosure under the Presidential Records Act. In November 2001, the White House finally issued a new executive order that provided a more restrictive interpretation of its obligations under the law.[55] The order broadened the grounds on which an incumbent President could block the disclosure of documents and asserted that former Presidents had an independent authority to block disclosure, which could be exercised by a surrogate even after a former President's death. An incumbent President could also deny access to records even if a former President did not object to disclosure.[56]

The administration also sought to restrict access to documents through the Freedom of Information Act. In October 2001, Attorney General John Ashcroft issued a statement for federal agencies summarizing the administration's approach to the application of FOIA. Eight years earlier, the Clinton administration had promised that it would apply a "principle of openness" and fight FOIA cases only when agencies could show that disclosure of information was likely to cause harm. By contrast, Ashcroft encouraged agencies to "carefully consider" whether information could be withheld, and promised that the Justice Department would support agencies in litigation if their case had "a sound legal basis."[57]

The terrorist attacks of September 11 gave further impetus to efforts to narrow FOIA's impact. In March 2002, White House Chief of Staff Andrew Card, Jr., sent a second directive to federal agencies, urging them to give "full and careful consideration" to the restrictions contained in the FOIA when processing requests for information relating to homeland security or public safety.[58] The memo also gave license to the widespread "scrubbing" of information from agency websites, and in some cases the retrieval of documents that had already been distributed to libraries outside of government.[59] The law was also amended to include new restrictions on access. The Homeland Security Act adopted in November 2002 imposed a ban on access to information relating to "critical infrastructure" operated by the private sector,[60] while the 2003 defense authorization bill added a ban on access to the "operational files" of the National Security Agency, a federal agency responsible for surveillance of electronic communications.[61]

The Bush administration toughened policy on the handling of classified information as well. It overhauled the executive order on classification of federal documents, broadening the categories of information that could be classified on national security grounds and creating a presumption in favor of classification of information received from foreign governments.[62] The set of agencies with authority to impose national security classifications was expanded,[63] and the volume of information being classified increased substantially throughout the Bush administration. (Noting the trend, the official responsible for oversight of classification protested in 2004 that war was being used "as an excuse to disregard the basics of the security classification system."[64])

The administration also invoked its authority to classify information already in the public domain. This authority had been eliminated by the Clinton administration but was restored by Bush in 2003, at which time federal officials predicted that the change "should have little impact."[65] Within months, however, the Department of Defense classified an already-public report that was critical of the testing program for its national missile defense system.[66] In 2004 the Justice Department classified already-public documents relating to allegations by a former FBI translator that the bureau had missed critical terrorist warnings before the 2001 attacks.[67]

Meanwhile the administration made clear that it would adopt a more severe attitude toward the unauthorized disclosure of classified information. Secretary Rumsfeld repeatedly warned defense staff about the dangers caused by leaking information and the penalties for leakers.[68] In October 2001, President Bush ordered Cabinet members to restrict the circulation of classified information to a small number of senior Congressional leaders, complaining that members of Congress had acted irresponsibly by distributing sensitive documents. (The directive was rescinded after congressional protests, but the message remained clear.) In December 2001, Attorney General

Ashcroft established an interagency task force to review methods of preventing leaks of classified information. The task force's report concluded that federal agencies should "take aggressive steps" to identify and punish leakers.[69]

These changes in broad policy were accompanied by a series of decisions that confirmed the administration's determination to tighten its hold over information. Perhaps most provocative was the administration's refusal to release information about its handling of detainees taken into custody after the September 2001 attacks. In the weeks following the attacks, federal agencies took into custody hundreds of foreign citizens within the United States who were alleged to have links to the government's counterterrorism investigation. The exact number of detainees was unknown, because the Justice Department stopped providing a cumulative tally after November 2001.[70] The department subsequently refused FOIA requests for the detainees' names, the date of their arrest, and the place of their detention.[71] Many individuals detained for immigration violations were deported after hearings that were closed to the public and excluded from the public docket of forthcoming immigration cases.[72]

Abroad, the federal government established an "archipelago" of prisons for suspected jihadists that includes facilities in Afghanistan, the British dependency of Diego Garcia, Jordan, and Cuba, to which access was tightly controlled.[73] The total number and identity of individuals held at these facilities is not known.[74] The Department of Defense refused to identify the 600 foreign nationals known to be held at the Guantánamo Bay detention facility in Cuba, or to allow the detainees an opportunity to meet with legal counsel, or to concede that detainees had a right to challenge the legality of their detention in American courts.[75] This latter position was repudiated by the Supreme Court in June 2004.[76] Even after this ruling, however, newspaper reports suggested that federal agencies intended to deny habeas corpus rights to some detainees, who were to be "kept off the books" for intelligence reasons.[77]

At home, the Bush administration resisted congressional efforts to oversee its antiterror efforts. The joint congressional inquiry into the performance of the intelligence community before the 2001 terror attacks complained in its December 2002 report that its investigations had been compromised by the unwillingness of the intelligence community to provide documents.[78] Public disclosure of the report itself was held up for seven months as an administration working group scrubbed it by removing classified information.[79] The published version of the report excluded critical passages relating to pre-9/11 warnings of terror attacks and connections between "a foreign government" – widely believed to be Saudi Arabia – and the 9/11 attackers. Even after the Saudi government itself requested the publication of the excised portions of the report, the Bush administration refused.[80]

For a year, the administration also resisted congressional pressure to establish an independent commission with a broader mandate to investigate the government's response to terror threats and the 9/11 attacks.[81] President Bush's first choice to chair the commission, Henry Kissinger, was a Nixon administration veteran who shortly resigned from the position following controversy over his alleged conflicts of interest. He was replaced by Thomas Kean, former Republican governor of New Jersey, who later expressed frustration at the administration's refusal, on the grounds of executive privilege, to release documents that showed what the President had been told about terrorist threats before the attacks.[82] Bush also refused to allow his national security advisor, Condoleeza Rice, to give public testimony to the commission, again citing executive privilege.[83] In January 2004, the President resisted the commission's request for an extension of time to complete its final report.[84] The administration later refused to declassify and release a critical background report prepared for the commission, which showed that federal aviation officials had collected substantial evidence on the threat posed by suicide hijackers before the 9/11 attacks.[85]

As the Bush administration's attention shifted to war against Iraq, its concern for secrecy continued. Bob Woodward alleged that in 2002 the administration covertly diverted $700 million dollars that had been appropriated for counterterror efforts to finance its preparations for war in Iraq, an action that avoided congressional scrutiny of its pre-war planning.[86] At the same time, senior defense officials refused to provide Congress with estimates of the resources likely to be needed during post-war occupation, and punished military staff who offered their own views on the subject.[87] In April 2004, the Republican chair of the Senate Foreign Relations Committee, Senator Richard Lugar, complained about the defense department's unwillingness to allow officials to testify before the committee and its more general failure to communicate with Congress about "Iraq plans and cost estimates" since 2002.[88]

There were even stronger complaints about the administration's unwillingness to make a public showing of its case for war in Iraq.[89] It produced a National Intelligence Estimate on the threat posed by Iraq in September 2002 only after a request for an analysis was made by the Senate Intelligence Committee.[90] The estimate itself was classified. A CIA discussion paper that was publicly released in October 2002 was later criticized for omitting caveats contained in the classified Estimate that significantly weakened key claims about the threat posed by Iraq.[91] A July 2004 report by the Senate Intelligence Committee concluded that the discussion paper's omissions resulted in the misrepresentation of the more cautious assessments in the classified document. However, the administration blocked the committee from publishing its reasons for reaching that conclusion.[92] In all, the CIA insisted that about one-fifth of the Senate Committee report should be withheld for national security reasons. Some senators – including former majority leader Trent Lott – were so outraged by the agency's decision that they called for a new independent commission to make decisions on classification.[93]

The secretiveness that typified the handling of post-9/11 detainees also continued in post-war Iraq. At Abu Ghraib prison near Baghdad, military officials took steps to limit access by representatives of the International Committee of the Red Cross, even though the ICRC's reports are delivered in confidence to the United States government. Following a critical ICRC report in November 2003, military officials restricted the ICRC's ability to conduct "no-notice inspections" within parts of the prison.[94] The Taguba report later documented the practice of treating some Abu Ghraib prisoners as "ghost detainees":

> The various detention facilities operated by the 800th MP Brigade have routinely held persons brought to them by Other Government Agencies (OGAs) without accounting for them, knowing their identities, or even the reason for their detention. The Joint Interrogation and Debriefing Center (JIDC) at Abu Ghraib called these detainees "ghost detainees." On at least one occasion, the 320th MP Battalion at Abu Ghraib held a handful of "ghost detainees" (6–8) for OGAs that they moved around within the facility to hide them from a visiting International Committee of the Red Cross (ICRC) survey team.[95]

The practice, said Taguba, was "deceptive, contrary to Army Doctrine, and in violation of international law." But in at least one case, an Abu Ghraib detainee was hidden from ICRC officials on the direction of Secretary Rumsfeld himself.[96] News reports based on leaks from troubled military officials later described a common practice of holding ghost detainees at Army facilities in Afghanistan as well.[97]

Attempts to probe allegations of more widespread torture of detainees by defense and intelligence agencies were again compromised by secretiveness. Although the Army had for many years included its interrogation rules in publicly available field manuals,[98] new rules for more aggressive interrogation within the country's overseas detention centers, approved by Secretary Rumsfeld, were classified on his authority as secret documents.[99] The administration also resisted demands for disclosure of memoranda in which senior officials debated the extent to which its interrogation policies were constrained by domestic and international law. Its slowness in providing documents and witnesses undermined congressional inquiries into the torture controversy.[100]

Worse than Watergate?

The breadth of the Bush administration's attempt to restrict openness appalled many observers. The criticism was unsparing. The U.S. government, said the Reporters' Committee for Freedom of the Press, had "embarked on an unprecedented path of secrecy."[101] Comparisons to the generally acknowledged nadir of presidential accountability – the Nixon administration – were common. John Dean, Nixon's former counsel, argued in April 2004 that the Bush administration had created "the most secretive presidency of my lifetime. Their secrecy is far worse than during Watergate . . . Their secrecy is extreme – not merely unjustified but obsessive."[102] Arthur Schlesinger, Jr., endorsed Dean's view. The Freedom of Information Act was a "most beneficial law," Schlesinger said, "until Ashcroft got hold of it."[103]

This was hyperbole, which confused ambition with accomplishment. The Bush administration may have aspired to restore the degree of secrecy that had prevailed thirty years ago, but its capacity to achieve that goal was severely compromised because of the profound changes in the structure of American politics that had been wrought over those three decades. The Lilliputians (to continue the metaphor) had become more numerous, bolder, and more clever.

For example, the Bush administration did not attempt to revoke any of the ten major disclosure statutes that had been adopted by Congress between 1972 and 1980.[104] The administration attempted to change the interpretation of those laws, and sometimes to amend them – but these efforts, while serious, are different in degree than an effort at complete revocation. It would be difficult for the Bush administration to be "worse than Watergate" – in actual, rather than intended, secretiveness – while at the same time being subject to a battery of disclosure laws with which President Nixon never contended.

Broadly, there were two reasons why a complete rollback of this legislation was never attempted. The first was that public opinion would not tolerate a direct assault on post-Watergate controls. Trust in government institutions had corroded too far and openness had become too deeply entrenched in public opinion as one of the predicates of governmental legitimacy for a direct assault to succeed. The shift in public opinion may have been illustrated by the character of the reaction to the Bush administration's attempt (in the Patriot Act) to extend the role of the Federal Intelligence Surveillance Court. In 1978, creation of the FISC had been regarded as a liberal reform, providing a new check on the opaque process by which the federal government undertook electronic surveillance on its citizens.[105] By 2002, however, the secretiveness of the court made it the object of suspicion as well.[106] The taint of illegitimacy was now borne by the guardians as well as the guarded.

Public hostility toward secretiveness was now manifested in a new and immediate form: the internet poll. Should the Bush administration be forced to disclose the records of the National Energy Policy Development Group? Yes, said 58 percent of respondents to an Excite.com poll. Should National Security Advisor Condoleeza Rice be compelled to testify under oath before the 9/11 Commission? Yes, said 69 percent of respondents to an online poll by Milwaukee's WDJT TV. Should the President and Vice President be required to testify publicly before the commission? Yes, said 53 percent of respondents to a poll by New Haven's WTNH TV. Had Secretary Rumsfeld provided satisfactory answers about the Abu Ghraib abuses in his testimony to congressional committees? No, said a majority of respondents to MSNBC's online Question of the Day. These polls were ephemeral and methodologically suspect. In aggregate, however, they gave a new voice to a broad popular impatience with conventional arguments in favor of governmental openness. Even if the administration did not always bend to the pressure – as Cheney did not – the polls suggested that the administration paid a price for its secretiveness.

Popular resistance to radical reform of existing controls was stiffened by the larger number of advocacy groups who sounded the alarm when the executive branch attempted to restrict openness. *CNSS et al v. Department of Justice* (the legal challenge to the Bush administration's denial of access to information about detainees taken into custody within the United States after the 9/11 attacks) illustrated how the watchdogs had proliferated. Of the twenty-three advocacy groups that joined to pursue the case, all but five were established after Richard Nixon's election in 1968. In fact, most were established after Reagan's election in 1980. By contrast, only two groups filed amicus briefs in the 1971 Pentagon Papers case.[107]

Because they were not radically altered, many features of the post-Watergate apparatus continued to operate as it always had. For example, the Bush administration was stung by a series of reports from departmental Inspectors General, using powers given to them by a 1978 law, that offered severe criticisms of the administration's management of the war on terror. The reports documented weaknesses in airport security screening, patterns of abuse in the treatment of Justice Department detainees, and defects in contracting for Iraqi reconstruction. The Defense Department's Inspector General criticized its inattention to privacy rules contained in the 1974 Privacy Act. The Justice Department's Inspector General concluded that the department had not adequately investigated a whistleblower's allegation of security lapses in its translation office; details of the Inspector General's classified report were quickly leaked to the *New York Times*.[108]

The Freedom of Information Act also continued to cause irritation to the administration. Imposing a more restrictive interpretation of the law proved difficult, given the highly decentralized way in which the law is administered. A 2003 study concluded that many federal agencies made little or no change in their daily practice as a result of Attorney General Ashcroft's memorandum.[109] The Pentagon found that its ban on the distribution of images of coffins returning from Iraq was undone when Air Force officials accepted a FOIA request for photos taken by its own personnel.[110] While the White House resisted efforts to release key documents relating to the Cheney task force, the Department of Energy was ordered by a federal court to release records sought under FOIA by the National Resources Defense Council, which it said revealed the heavy hand of the energy industries.[111] Another nongovernmental group, the Center for Public Integrity, used FOIA to show that contracts for post-war reconstruction had gone to firms with close political ties to the Bush administration.[112] A third group, the Electronic Privacy Information Center, used FOIA to expose federal data-mining projects that it said threatened privacy rights.[113]

Even the Foreign Intelligence Surveillance Act, although weakened by Patriot Act amendments, provided a continuing check on executive authority. The law requires the Attorney General to provide an annual public report on the number of applications made to the Foreign Intelligence Surveillance Court that, although rudimentary, regularly gave advocacy groups and editorialists an insight into the federal government's surveillance activities.[114] In May 2002, the Court issued an opinion that rebuked the Justice Department for a longstanding practice of misrepresentations in its applications, giving encouragement to members of Congress who hoped to stiffen the law.[115] A few weeks later the Court refused an application based on new and less restrictive administrative procedures proposed by the Justice Department. Although its decision was overturned on appeal,[116] the refusal again fueled widespread editorializing against the erosion of civil liberties.[117]

Maelstroms of transparency

Not only was the administration vulnerable to disclosure through the routine working of the post-Nixon controls, but a new phenomenon was also at play. The Bush presidency was hit by a series of brief and intense controversies that often led to rapid and unprecedented levels of disclosure. These "transparency maelstroms" were fueled by at least three factors.

The first was the willingness of officials at all levels within the administration to ignore warnings against leaking and to reveal sensitive internal information anyway. The increased volume of leaks was itself the result of several considerations. One was the mounting evidence of policy failure and the desire of officials to express dissent over goals or to shift blame for results. Another was the breakdown of the basic norm of fidelity to the bureaucratic hierarchy along with stronger legal protection for dissenters. Finally – and from a technical point of view – leaking was also easier than ever before. When Daniel Ellsberg decided in 1969 to leak the Pentagon Papers, he spent six weeks covertly photocopying its 7,000 pages.[118] When Bush's first Treasury Secretary, Paul O'Neill, was dismissed in December 2002, he walked out of his office with a CD-ROM that contained 19,000 documents.[119]

The second factor was the increased ease with which internal documents could be broadcast to a mass audience. Again, a contrast with the Pentagon Papers case helps illustrate the radical change. By February 1971, Ellsberg had given up on efforts to have the Papers revealed by a friendly member of Congress, and decided that it would be "useful to make this history public – if it could be done fast." This required the cooperation of a major newspaper. Ellsberg approached the *New York Times*, which eventually published excerpts of the Papers *three months* later. The Nixon administration's subsequent effort to obtain a restraining order against the *Times* was also predicated on the assumption that this would be an effective method of blocking the mass distribution of the Papers.[120]

By comparison, what would Ellsberg have done in the internet age – and what could a contemporary President have done to stop him? Many of the most damaging of Paul O'Neill's documents were simply posted on a website by Ron Suskind, an author with whom O'Neill collaborated.[121] When photos of the coffins returning from Iraq were released under FOIA, they too were posted immediately on the internet.[122] The *New York Times*, like many other major media outlets, found itself reproducing material that was already widely accessible.

A third factor contributing to these transparency maelstroms was the transformation in the structure of the media itself. Increased competition meant that disclosures were likely to be treated more sensationally, while a faster news cycle led to stories that could explode much more quickly. Administration officials faced pressure to mount broad and immediate campaigns against damaging news stories – often making more extensive disclosures in an effort to defend their own interpretation of events.

Such maelstroms struck repeatedly throughout the Bush administration. Early efforts by the FBI to deny that it had evidence of impending terror attacks in 2001 were undone following the leak of a classified memorandum that described concerns about Arab students training at U.S. flight schools. Special Agent Colleen Rowley became one of *Time* magazine's "Persons of the Year" when she revealed internal disputes about the handling of evidence in the FBI's Minneapolis field office before 9/11. (Rowley relied on protections in the 1989 Whistleblower Protection Act.) By June 2002, *Time* reported that federal officials were "banging down our doors, seeking sanctuary" and hoping to avoid blame for failing to anticipate the attacks.[123]

More damage was done to the administration in March 2004, when former counterterrorism advisor Richard Clarke published a book alleging that its agencies had failed to act on warnings of an imminent terror attack.[124] The book, and Clarke's appearance on *60 Minutes*, provoked a "ferocious" counterassault by the White House.[125] Within hours of the broadcast, the White House booked more than twenty interviews with Condoleeza Rice and other officials on network morning shows and cable news channels. This had the perverse effect of undercutting the White House's refusal of the 9/11 Commission's request that Rice give public testimony under oath on pre-attack planning. How, after all, could the administration insist that the President's relationship with his national security advisor was "unique and confidential and private,"[126] if the mass media was saturated with Rice's defense of the administration's performance? Within days, the White House abandoned its claim of executive privilege, warning that Rice's testimony would not set any precedent for the future[127] – which of course it did.

A similar dynamic led to the release of a contentious copy of the President's Daily Brief, documents prepared by the CIA and regarded as one of the government's "most closely guarded secrets"[128] ("the family jewels," as Vice President Cheney called them[129]). In May 2002, CBS reported that the PDB for August 6, 2001, had given the President a warning of an imminent threat of a massive terrorist attack in the United States. The White House refused to release the document, but questions about what the President had known in the days before 9/11 festered. In October 2003, the 9/11 Commission threatened to issue a subpoena for the document. Seeking to deflect growing public sentiment that it was hiding incriminating evidence, the White House allowed a few commissioners to inspect the PDB in November 2003. This was heralded as a "watershed moment" in the history of presidential–congressional relations,[130] but still it was not enough. A succession of leaks suggested that the PDB had provided the President with an unambiguous warning,[131] and in April 2004 Condoleeza Rice – testifying publicly before the commission – conceded that the title of the briefing had been, "Bin Laden Determined to Strike in the United States." Later that day the White House relented and agreed to release the PDB, which was quickly posted on the internet. For the second time in two weeks, the White House warned that its action should not be taken as a precedent.[132]

The 9/11 Commission's report, released in July 2004, quickly became a national bestseller. The report "shattered the ceiling on access" to internal government information, providing a detailed and damning account of the political and bureaucratic missteps that preceded the 9/11 attacks.[133] The commission provided details of an aborted CIA plan to capture or kill Osama bin Laden, and used classified evidence from the interrogation of Khalid Sheikh Mohammed – an al Qaeda leader captured in Pakistan a year earlier – to describe how the 2001 attacks had been planned. Alleged connections between the Iraqi government and bin Laden's terror network were disputed, while new evidence was proffered to show that Iran had aided the hijackers. Another of the "family jewels" – a 1998 PDB on an al Qaeda plot to hijack U.S. airliners – was released. And the commission put more emphasis on the significance of the August 6 PDB: CIA analysts, it said, had tried to make clear that in August 2001 the threat from al Qaeda was "both current and serious."[134]

Another maelstrom led to remarkable disclosures about the Bush administration's planning for war in Iraq. By July 2003, the failure of American forces to find substantial evidence of weapons of mass destruction in Iraq led to widespread questioning of the soundness of the Bush administration's case for war. Debate was stirred further when a former diplomat, Joseph Wilson, revealed in the *New York Times* that he had been asked before the war to investigate a claim that Iraq had sought nuclear material in Africa, and told the CIA that the claims were unfounded. President Bush included the claim in his State of the Union address anyway. The administration, said Wilson, had "twisted" intelligence to bolster its case for war.[135]

Wilson's claim drove a wedge between the White House and the CIA. In its effort to show that the President had not willfully distorted evidence, White House officials relied on the fact that the CIA had included the claim in its classified 2002 National Intelligence Estimate – in their view, "the gold standard of our intelligence about Iraq."[136] CIA officials argued that they had made efforts to tell White House staff that the intelligence supporting the Estimate had become suspect. On July 17, 2003, a Democratic proposal to establish a commission to probe the conflicting claims was defeated in the Senate. The next day, the White House attempted to bolster its position by declassifying the key findings of the 2002 Estimate. The disclosure actually fueled more controversy, by revealing other inconsistencies with the administration's public statements in the run-up to war.[137]

The next months saw a further unraveling of the secrecy surrounding the administration's pre-war planning. In January 2004, internal documents posted on the web by Paul O'Neill's collaborator, Ron Suskind, suggested that the administration had begun planning for a "post-Saddam Iraq" within days of Bush's inauguration.[138] In March, Richard Clarke's book *Against All Enemies* reported on a private conversation with the President the day after the 2001 attacks in which Bush pressed for a report on the possible involvement of the Iraqi government. In April, Bob Woodward's book *Plan of Attack* (widely believed to have been written with the close cooperation of Secretary of State Colin Powell[139]) revealed more compromising details about conflict within the administration about the build-up to invasion. In June, a veteran CIA official wrote an anonymous book, *Imperial Hubris*, that was harshly critical of the administration's execution of the war on terror.[140] In August, General Tommy Franks, commander of U.S. forces in Iraq until his retirement in July 2003, published his own memoir describing tensions within the administration over war planning. Franks was a friend of the administration who endorsed the reelection effort of President Bush. This did not cause him to be any more reticent in his assessment of the country's civilian and military leadership: Defense Undersecretary Douglas Feith, Franks wrote, was the "dumbest fucking guy on the planet."[141]

The Abu Ghraib abuses stirred yet another maelstrom. In this case, technology, internal dissent, and media competition combined powerfully. In an earlier age, censorship of soldiers' correspondence might have slowed the diffusion of knowledge about the abuses: Today, however, soldiers have digital cameras and ready access to high-speed internet, even in the field. Soldiers and their families had also become less willing to rely on military justice, instead giving documents or interviews to the media about the complicity of higher levels of command. Tensions within components of the defense and intelligence community – military police against military intelligence, CIA against the military, career officers against politically appointed overseers – also encouraged each to resort to disclosure as a technique for shuffling blame. The effect of these disclosures was amplified in the internet, cable, and broadcast media.

Quickly the Abu Ghraib controversy transformed into a larger debate about the administration's policy on the torture of detainees. Secretary Rumsfeld promised that the administration was adhering to international accords banning the use of torture,[142] but at the same time classified the documents that would allow a judgment about whether the claim was defensible. Within the military, however, there was substantial disagreement about the legality of interrogation methods approved by Rumsfeld. In spring 2003, a group of military lawyers concerned by an internal March 2003 report that upheld the new techniques approached a human rights lawyer in New York for confidential advice on their predicament.[143]

Abu Ghraib brought this internal dispute into the public domain. On the morning of Monday, June 7, 2004, the *Wall Street Journal* reported that it had received a leaked copy of the troubling (and still classified) March 2003 report.[144] On Tuesday, the *New York Times* and *Washington Post* reported that each had received internal Justice Department memos written in 2002 that provided a legal justification for the torture of detainees.[145] On Wednesday, the *Los Angeles Times* reported on leaks from Defense Department staff who said that

Rumsfeld's legal counsel had authorized interrogators to "take the gloves off" in late 2001.[146]

Appearing before the Senate Judiciary Committee that Wednesday, Attorney General Ashcroft refused to release the series of memos on interrogation rules, arguing that the advice had been given in confidence to the President. However, Ashcroft's position was quickly undercut. The nongovernmental Center for Constitutional Rights had already posted its own leaked copy of the March 2003 report on the web, and the *Washington Post* posted its copy of the most damaging of the Justice Department's documents a few days later. As public support for the administration softened, the White House relented, releasing hundreds of pages of Justice and Defense Department documents on its interrogation policy – including Secretary Rumsfeld's previously classified directions on questioning of detainees. It was an "extraordinary" step, said administration officials, designed to fight leaks that had combined into a "constant drip" of damaging disclosures.[147]

Nevertheless, the "constant drip" continued. In August, *Rolling Stone* magazine reported that it had received 6,000 pages of classified Army files detailing abuses within Abu Ghraib prison; many of these files were subsequently posted on the internet by the Center for Public Integrity.[148] Responding to a FOIA lawsuit brought by the ACLU, a federal court ordered the Defense Department to release thousands of pages of documents that showed patterns of abuse in military facilities in Afghanistan and Pakistan as well; again, the ACLU posted the documents on its website.[149] The report of an independent review panel led by former defense secretary James Schlesinger confirmed "widespread abuses" sometimes leading to the death of detainees, for which it said there was "both institutional and personal responsibility at higher levels."[150] In a book published three weeks later, Seymour Hersh drew on anonymous government sources to claim that top officials in the White House and Defense Department had been warned repeatedly about abuses as early as 2002.[151] By Election Day of 2004, American voters could not reasonably claim to be in the dark about the breadth or severity of the abuses committed by American forces, or about the link between the behavior of soldiers in the field and the administration's overarching determination to use "more aggressive methods" in the war on terrorism.[152] The material question was the extent to which they cared.

Not without a fight

The Bush administration and its sharpest critics had one thing in common: a misapprehension about the reversibility of history. The Bush administration believed that it could roll the clock back to the pre-Watergate years, and so launched an assault on the many rules it believed had undercut the power of the presidency and, more broadly, the governability of the American system. The administration's critics accepted the premise that the clock could be rolled back – not only that, but also that it *had* been rolled back.

Of course, neither side was right. Shifts in the political, cultural, and technological context of American politics over the last three decades have been too profound to allow an easy reversal of history. These changes in context made a direct assault on the regime of post-Watergate controls impossible. Nevertheless, the Bush administration did its best to hedge and qualify these controls. At the same time, however, the more complex and turbulent environment surrounding the Presidency often generated maelstroms that precipitated brief but extraordinary moments of transparency. The result was paradoxical: By the end of 2004 we had come to know a great deal about the internal workings of an administration that was, at the same time, widely damned for its secretiveness.

Freeing Gulliver – a domestic project of regime change – had proved much more difficult than Donald Rumsfeld and his colleagues expected.

Furthermore, there were some observers who believed that freeing Gulliver was simply impossible, at least so far as keeping secrets was concerned. We might call these the technological fatalists – or utopians, depending on your predisposition about a world of uncompromised openness. They saw transparency maelstroms as the early signs of more profound climate change. In 2003 the futurist William Gibson warned:

> We are approaching a theoretical state of absolute informational transparency. . . . It is becoming unprecedentedly difficult for anyone, anyone at all, to keep a secret. In the age of the leak and the blog, of evidence extraction and link discovery, truths will either out or be outed, later if not sooner. This is something I would bring to the attention of every diplomat, politician and corporate leader: the future, eventually, will find you out. The future,

wielding unimaginable tools of transparency, will have its way with you. In the end, you will be seen to have done that which you did.[153]

By the summer of 2004, it might have been possible to imagine that Gibson was right. There was so much compromising material from the Bush administration posted on the web that an enterprising student at a New York law school set up a peer-to-peer computer network ordinarily used for illicitly sharing music to distribute it. He called it "downloading for democracy."[154]

But if critics who saw a reprise of Watergate were misguided, so too were the technological fatalists. Periodic maelstroms may have produced important disclosures, but their effect was not always timely or comprehensive. Often – as in the case of the controversies over the quality of U.S. intelligence on Iraq – the storm came too late to prevent harm. Allegations of abuse in prisons run by the U.S. military could be found in the American press throughout 2003, but it was not until April 2004 that a combination of circumstances finally put pressure on the Bush administration to disclose much more about its policies. And even then, the effect of the maelstrom was incomplete: While the *Army's* handling of detainees was closely examined, the *CIA's* treatment of detainees suffered from "a complete absence of scrutiny"[155] despite credible evidence of serious abuses.

Furthermore, there were many areas in which the Bush administration did succeed in rolling back openness. We do not have to believe that Bush administration policies were "unprecedented" or "worse than Watergate" in order to reach the conclusion that they were, nevertheless, deeply troubling. The administration's secretiveness undermined the political and civil rights of Americans, as well as the human rights of many others affected by the exercise of American power. National security was compromised by the secrecy that surrounded war planning and efforts to improve homeland security.

Nor was it reasonable to believe that the policymakers in the Bush administration would conclude from their experience that efforts to reduce transparency had been wholly misguided. The administration may have underestimated how difficult it would be to restore presidential prerogatives; Donald Rumsfeld's moment of apparent bewilderment before the House and Senate Armed Services Committees in May 2004 was probably genuine. Nevertheless, officials who entered into power in 2001 with a belief that the authority of the executive had been badly compromised might have viewed the following four years as a vivid demonstration that the problem was even worse than expected; even in a moment of national crisis, Gulliver was kept down by Lilliputians. The prescription in this case was clear: not a retreat, but an intensified and more clever campaign to reclaim the zone of autonomy.

4

MESSAGE DISCIPLINE

Cultural change in Whitehall is exactly like turning round the classic ocean liner. Opening up Whitehall and introducing freedom of information is a titanic task.
– Charles Falconer, UK Secretary of State for Constitutional Affairs, 2004.

In the United Kingdom, debate about the way in which the Labour government of Prime Minister Tony Blair had managed intelligence about the threat posed by Iraq quickly took a tragic turn. In May 2003, the British Broadcasting Corporation featured an interview with journalist Andrew Gilligan in which he alleged, based on information from an unnamed source, that the government's pre-war intelligence brief had been "sexed up" with false information. The Blair government reacted furiously against the allegation. When the country's top WMD scientist, David Kelly, revealed to his superiors that he might be Gilligan's source but that Gilligan had misconstrued his statements, senior Blair advisors effectively leaked Kelly's name to the media.[1] After a week at the center of an intense controversy, Kelly committed suicide. Prime Minister Blair appointed a special investigation – the Hutton Inquiry – to examine the events leading to Kelly's death.

In a country notorious for official secrecy, the Hutton Inquiry was remarkable. Internal government documents – memoranda, e-mail, diaries – written with extraordinary candor only weeks before were not only handed to the inquiry, they were posted on the internet for universal inspection.[2] Lord Hutton's report concluded that the government had not treated Kelly unfairly, and that the intelligence brief had not been "sexed up" – if the phrase implied the deliberate inclusion of false intelligence.[3] In a looser sense, however, the charge clearly held. Media staff in the Prime Minister's office had been deeply involved in the drafting of the dossier, pushing intelligence staff to make a case against Iraq that would produce compelling media coverage. Blair's senior press officer had even chaired a meeting of the Joint Intelligence Committee charged with preparing the brief.[4] The usually nuanced language of intelligence analysis, said commentator Peter Riddell, had clashed with "the megaphone communications of 'spin doctors' and the twenty-four-hour news cycle."[5]

That Blair's media advisors had played such a critical role was, for most observers, no surprise at all. Even before the Iraq crisis the Blair government was criticized for a culture of "top-down centralism" and a preoccupation with imposing "message discipline" in government.[6] The number of political appointees with a "license to spin" grew substantially after Labour's election in 1997.[7] Career civil servants working in public relations were pressured to present the government's program more forcefully, leading to widespread complaints about their politicization.[8] Overall authority for communications functions was concentrated within the Prime Minister's Office even more than it had been under preceding Conservative governments, with the task of news management tightly controlled by Blair's press secretary, Alastair Campbell.[9] Campbell, one commentator wrote, "realized that contemporary journalism, brutally competitive and relying on the day-by-day manufacture of sensational, attention-grabbing headlines . . . had come to constitute a permanent obstacle to the smooth practice of government."[10]

However, the Labour government's program was not without its paradoxes. It had been elected in 1997 on a promise to undertake broad constitutional reforms intended to diffuse the power of the central government. Some reforms (such as new national assemblies for Scotland and Wales) had been completed; some (such as reform of the electoral system) had been abandoned; some (such as reform of the House of Lords) were mired in a no-man's-land. One that had survived, scheduled to go into force eight years after Labour's 1997 election, was the Freedom of Information Act.

The Blair government had once made bold promises about the new law. In 1997, Blair himself said that it would break down the "traditional culture of secrecy" within the UK government and produce a "fundamental and vital change in the relationship between government and governed"[11]; in 1999, Home Secretary Jack Straw lauded the law as a landmark in constitutional history that would "transform the default setting" of secrecy in government.[12] The government also anticipated that after the date of implementation – January 2005 – departments would administer the law in a highly decentralized way: Requests for information would be received and processed "at a local level, by the relevant policy official."[13]

The tension between these bold promises on openness and the government's own tendency to centralize control over the outflow of information seemed to go unrecognized. The government had promised a much freer flow of information, with decisions on access being made at low levels of the bureaucracy. However, experience from other countries made clear that the new law would be used extensively by journalists, legislators, and advocacy groups seeking information for the purpose of scrutinizing or embarrassing the government or shaping its policy agenda. How would a top-heavy public relations system respond as the Freedom of Information Act began to corrode its foundations?

The center cannot hold

The United Kingdom was not the first country to wrestle with this question. In 1997, the Irish government had adopted its own Freedom of Information Act. At first blush, there were similarities between the history of the two laws. As in the UK, the Irish legislation was introduced by a new center–left government – the "Rainbow Coalition" of the Fine Gael, Labour, and Democratic Left parties – as part of a program of constitutional modernization. The coalition's commitment to freedom of information was meant to signal a break from the Fianna Fáil government, which had invoked the doctrine of cabinet confidentiality to withhold information from a judicial inquiry into allegations of official corruption, and eventually collapsed following revelations that the prime minister had withheld information from the parliament in a controversy over the extradition of a pedophile priest.[14] The new law promised an end to the "antiquated procedures of secrecy" in the Irish government.[15]

Irish journalists became early and enthusiastic users of the new law, filing over 7,000 requests – roughly one-fifth of the total sent to central government – in its first five years.[16] The *Irish Times* showed that the European Investment Bank had expressed concern to Finance Minister Charlie McCreevey about his attempt to appoint to the Bank's board a judge who had been forced to resign from the bench following allegations of judicial misconduct. Later the *Times* revealed that civil servants had called the case for a new national stadium (soon nicknamed the 'Bertie Bowl') proposed by Prime Minister Bertie Ahern "flimsy." (The project was cancelled.) The *Irish Sun* published documents that suggested McCreevey had misled voters about the state of public finances before the 2002 election, prompting calls for his resignation. Other documents revealed conflict between the finance and health ministers over the control of health service costs, and concessions by the education minister in negotiations with the Catholic Church over compensation of abuse victims.

Within the government, frustration over the law began to mount. In 1999, an internal committee proposed new restrictions on "large and disruptive" requests for information.[17] In 2002 the country's Information Commissioner, Kevin Murphy – an independent officer responsible for investigating complaints about denial of information – acknowledged that many public servants were exasperated by news stories that used government documents "in a selective, unfair or sensationalist manner."[18] Murphy's successor, Emily O'Reilly, a former journalist, speculated that ministers "felt that FOI had made governing a democracy even less easy."[19] Justice Minister Michael McDowell confirmed the speculation, telling a radio audience that the law prevented frank conversation inside government:

> One of the consequences of the Freedom of Information Act which isn't generally appreciated is the huge negative effect it has had on the process of government itself. Unless you are sitting at a minister's desk ... you would not be aware of the extent to which it has corroded the process of government.[20]

Some government officials began to develop techniques for limiting the damage done by the release of information under the law. Journalists complained that government departments encouraged other reporters to duplicate their requests for documents – a step that heightened the department's ability to ensure a "more sympathetic spin" on the story.[21] The Justice Minister himself acknowledged that he had "pre-released" information requested by opposition politicians to friendly journalists, telling the Parliament that he would not allow "my opponents to spin against me without having at least the opportunity to put my side of the story into the public domain."[22] One government department began posting details about new requests, including journalists' identities, on its website, a practice the department defended as an advance in transparency but journalists condemned as a tactic to reduce the "scoop value" of an information request.[23]

In 2002, the coalition government went even further. Acting on the Prime Minister's instructions, a group of senior civil servants drafted new restrictions that were incorporated into a bill to amend the FOI Act. The bill was introduced in March 2003, only weeks before a provision of the law allowing access to five-year-old Cabinet records was scheduled to go into effect. The amended law extended the delay in releasing Cabinet records to ten years, and broadened the Cabinet confidentiality rule to include advisory committees that did not include a Cabinet minister at all. Ministers were allowed to block requests for information relating to other deliberative processes within the public service, and national security restrictions were toughened as well.[24]

The amended law also introduced new fees for information requests: 15 euros for an application, 75 euros to have a department reconsider its decision on denial of information, and 150 euros for an appeal to the Information Commissioner. The fees had a predictably sharp impact on the demand for information. A year later, the Commissioner reported that requests for information had declined by over 50 percent. Requests by journalists dropped more precipitously – over 80 percent within the space of a year.[25] The changes, an opposition critic charged, "rendered the whole concept of Freedom of Information almost useless."[26]

Amberlighting

The United Kingdom and Ireland were latecomers to the concept of freedom of information. Canada, by contrast, was not. Throughout the 1970s, a combination of circumstances – frustration over the declining power of Parliament,[27] deteriorating economic performance, constitutional instability, fiscal indiscipline, and abuses of power by the national police force – contributed to disillusionment with central government in Canada. One of the consequences was mounting pressure for adoption of a version of the United States' Freedom of Information Act. "What we are talking about is power," said Joe Clark, leader of the Conservative opposition that pushed for the law:

> We are talking about the reality that real power is limited to those who have facts. In a democracy that power and that information should be shared broadly. In Canada today they are not, and to that degree we are no longer a democracy in any sensible sense of that word. There is excessive power concentrated in the hands of those who hide public information from the people and Parliament of Canada.[28]

Canada's Access to Information Act (AIA) was adopted in 1982.[29] The Liberal government led by Prime Minister Pierre Trudeau promised that the law would promote "effective participation of citizens and organizations in the taking of public decisions."[30]

Ironically it was the Conservative Party – elected in a landslide in Canada's 1984 election – that bore the early brunt of the new law. Its enthusiasm for openness soon waned. It was later revealed that senior officials quickly took steps to hide background papers prepared for Cabinet that drafters of the AIA had intended should be subject to the law.[31] Officials responsible for oversight of the national blood system secretly shredded records that showed how they had responded to contamination of blood supplies by the AIDS virus in the 1980s, in an effort to thwart requests for the documents.[32] Cabinet officials also resisted requests for the results of its public opinion polls on constitutional reform, arguing that disclosure of polling data would undermine "the very existence of the country."[33] John Crosbie, who as Justice Minister was responsible for the Act in its first years, dismissed it as a tool for "mischief-makers" whose objective "in the vast majority of instances" was to "embarrass political leaders and titillate the public."[34]

The Liberal government elected in 1993 confronted a dilemma. On the one hand the principle of openness had become broadly accepted, and had to be acknowledged. ("Open government will be the watchword of the Liberal program," said the 1993 Liberal platform. "The people are irritated with governments . . . that try to conduct key parts of the public business behind closed doors."[35]) On the other hand, Liberal policymakers shared Crosbie's impatience with the AIA. The country seemed under serious threat – from secessionist pressures from Quebec, interregional conflict, and tensions engendered by new trade policies and fiscal controls. The Liberal response to these threats was to continue concentrating authority at the center of government, developing an increasingly sophisticated capacity to gauge public opinion and craft communications programs that advanced its agenda.[36]

The AIA posed a growing challenge to the government's capacity to keep a firm hand on the tiller. "Requests are more probing than they used to be," an AIA officer observed in 2002. "There are many more of them and their requests frequently involve far more, and more sensitive, records. The result is that [the Access to Information Act] is much more complex . . . more challenging for us and more threatening for government-side politicians."[37] Senior officials confronted a work environment "analogous to the perfect storm," a Liberal advisor said in 2003. "They might as well be working in a glass house, given access-to-information legislation, several oversight bodies policing their work, and more aggressive media."[38]

The Liberal government attempted to resolve its dilemma by pursuing a policy that honored the disclosure law in principle while limiting its disruptive potential in practice. One tactic relied on litigation. Throughout the 1990s, the government attempted to block the investigation of alleged abuses of the disclosure law and argued for more expansive interpretation of key sections of the law, such as the provision protecting Cabinet decision making. In a long series of legal challenges, it attempted to argue that the disclosure law did not provide any right to records held within the offices of Cabinet ministers, or the Prime Minister's own office.[39]

A second tactic consisted of repeated acts of omission. The AIA requires that policy makers add newly created government organizations to a list within the law in order for them to be subject to disclosure requirements. In its drive to slim central government, the Liberal government spun off many tasks to new quasi-governmental organizations that were not listed within the AIA. (The omission was not inadvertent: Other federal statutes often continued to apply.) The possibility of a reprise of the controversy over destruction of blood system records was eliminated when federal responsibilities were shifted to a quasi-governmental organization that was no longer subject to the law. A host of other functions – air traffic control, man-agement of major airports and the national pension plan, disposal of nuclear waste from electricity generators, major research granting programs – were excluded from the AIA in a similar way.[40]

Changes in administrative policy also led to a weakening of the disclosure law. Cuts in bureaucratic resources for processing infor-mation requests led to widespread problems of delay; the consequen-tial spike in the number of complaints about delay overwhelmed the Information Commissioner of Canada, the independent offi-cer responsible for investigating cases of noncompliance. Declaring the problem one of "crisis proportions," the Commissioner served subpoenas on senior officials to account for their management of information requests – an action that prompted improvements but also corroded relations with the bureaucracy even further.[41]

All of these responses to the disclosure law had the advantage of being easily observed. At the same time, however, the government developed elaborate procedures for handling potentially contentious requests for information. The internal rules for dealing with difficult requests were largely unknown to Canadians until 2003, when jour-nalist Ann Rees obtained documents through the AIA that showed how one major ministry, the Department of Citizenship and Immi-gration, had recently refined its procedures. Subsequent AIA requests revealed comparable routines in several other ministries.[42]

The procedure for handling politically sensitive requests within the Immigration Department – and many other ministries – is known as the "amberlight process." (Some other departments used different color schemes: In the Privy Council Office (PCO) – the secretariat to the Canadian Cabinet – sensitive cases are called "red files.") The name of the amberlight process signaled its intent; the aim of the procedure (one senior communications officer explained in 2002) is to "achieve the objective of proactive issues management" on sensitive AIA requests.

As in other ministries, the Immigration Department's amberlight process begins the moment an AIA request is received by the depart-ment. A "risk assessment officer" reviews incoming requests to identify those that are potentially sensitive. In practice, there is a presumption of sensitivity for requests submitted by journalists or representatives of political parties, including the offices of opposition legislators. The amberlight process requires that notice about incoming media or party requests should be sent to the Minister's Office and the ministry's media staff within one day.

In addition, the AIA offices of several departments circulate a weekly inventory of new requests that have been flagged for potential sensitivity. In the Justice Department, for example, the weekly inventory is sent to the Minister's Office, the Deputy Minister's Office, the Parliamentary Affairs Unit, and the Communications Branch. The inventory serves as the basis for a weekly review meeting, as an official from the Public Works ministry told a public inquiry in 2004:

> I took part in a weekly meeting – normally, there was a person from the minister's office, a person from the office of the deputy minister, a person from communications, a person from the office of the corporate secretary, and a person from access. The goal of the meeting was to review the requests in progress.[43]

If participants in the meeting decide that a request is particularly risky – that there is "potential for the issue/incident to be used in a public setting to attack the Minister or the Department" – then it may be tagged for special attention, or "amberlighted." In some departments, the proportion of requests that are amberlighted may be very high: According to internal memoranda, the Department of Foreign Affairs and International Trade amberlighted between 50 and 70 percent of its AIA requests in 2002.

The office that holds the documents sought by a request – known within the bureaucracy as the office of primary interest (OPI) – is immediately advised when a request has been amberlighted. AIA staff work with the OPI to "identify and assess issues for sensitivity and media product development," while communications staff develop "media lines" – a memorandum that outlines key messages that should be emphasized by departmental spokespersons in response to questions raised after the disclosure of information. "House cards" are also prepared that provide the Minister with responses to questions that may be raised in Parliament.

The complete "disclosure package" – including the documents to be released to the requester and the "communications products" – is sent to the Minister's Office for review. The role of the Minister's Office at this final stage is a sensitive matter for AIA officers. The formal position is that the purpose of this review is simply to give the

Minister's Office a warning about the impending release. In practice, however, the Minister's Office may raise questions about disclosure decisions as well as the communications strategy. After approval by the Minister's Office, the disclosure package is returned to the AIA office, and documents are sent to the requester. At the same time, an e-mail notice that contains the communications products for the request is sent to senior managers within the department.

These amberlight procedures rely significantly on new information technologies. Within ministries, software initially acquired to aid in the management of AIA caseloads has been adapted to facilitate the handling of politically sensitive requests. The software allows requests to be categorized as coming from journalists, political parties, or legislators.[44] The capacity to classify requests in this way is important because, under Canadian law, AIA offices are generally barred from disclosing the identity of a requester to other parts of the ministry. However, there are no prohibitions on the disclosure of the requester's occupation.[45] The software also allows requests to be categorized by their sensitivity or amberlight status.[46] These features make the process of managing the inventory of sensitive requests much simpler.

In 1990, the Conservative government added another, government-wide database of incoming information requests, known as the Coordination of Access to Information Request System (CAIRS). Government policy requires all ministries to enter information about new requests – including details on whether the request was made by a journalist or legislator – into CAIRS within one day of receipt.[47] At the time of its adoption, CAIRS was criticized as a tool for "computer surveillance" of the entire federal AIA system.[48] Government officials argued that the database would allow it "to monitor the progress of Access to Information (ATI) requests made, facilitate the coordination of responding to requests with common themes, and facilitate communication and consultation with central agencies and institutions."[49]

The monitoring capacity of the CAIRS database is used most heavily by central agencies of the Canadian government, and is a key component of a centrally run process for overseeing potentially sensitive requests. A PCO official conceded in 2003 that it actively manages the government's response to sensitive requests received throughout government. ("It is our role," the official said, "to make sure that ... the department releasing the information is prepared to essentially handle any fallout."[50]) A former Liberal Party official said that the task of overseeing requests within the PCO was handled by a "communications coordination group" that included representatives from the Prime Minister's Office, other senior ministerial aides, and top communications officers. The group was "[an] egregious example of bureaucratic politicization," said the official. "While the CCG's mandate is supposedly to 'coordinate' the government message, in practice much of the committee's time each week is taken up discussing ways to delay or thwart access-to-information requests."[51] The PCO's power to oversee ministries' handling of AIA requests is clear. "When Privy Council Office says they want to see a release package," an Immigration communications officer explained in an internal note in 2001, "I am not at liberty to do anything but what they ask."[52]

These surveillance and review procedures have significant effects. The first, as empirical analyses have now shown, is substantial delay in the processing of sensitive information requests. A review of AIA practices within Canada's Department of Human Resources Development showed that sensitive requests received from journalists or political parties took an extra month for processing, even when other factors (such as the breadth of the request or type of information sought) were taken into account. Many of these requests were for documents relating to allegations of mismanagement in a major grants program, which were caught – in the Information Commissioner's words – by the department's "reflexive need to control the story."[53] A broader study of AIA practices in several ministries found comparable effects: In the Immigration Department, for example, media requests required an extra one-and-a-half months, even when other factors were taken into account. Even the Justice Department, with oversight responsibility for the law, treated journalists' or legislators' requests unequally.[54]

In moments of controversy, delay often provides a significant advantage to the government. The amberlight process also gave other benefits: an ability to prepare a brief that minimizes the harm done by disclosure of documents. Journalists are caught by their professional norms, which oblige them to seek comment from the department – and the department is ready, with a spokesperson already selected and "media lines" drafted.

There is also evidence that Canadian departments may sometimes go further than simply drafting "media lines," as Canadians learned during a 2004 inquiry into political corruption in another grants program. Four years earlier, a journalist for the Toronto *Globe and Mail*, Daniel Leblanc, acting on rumors of mismanagement, had filed an information request with the federal Department of Public Works, which ran the program. An official testified in 2004 that the department had anticipated the possibility of such requests: Acting on instructions from the Prime Minister's office, it kept "minimum information" on the program's spending.[55] Another official admitted that Leblanc's request had been caught by the department's amberlight procedures, and that Leblanc's identity was disclosed within the ministry.[56] Leblanc's request prodded the department to develop guidelines designed to create the impression that the program contained appropriate controls against political interference on spending. The guidelines had no real effect on the operation of the program: They were drafted, the official conceded, "for cosmetic purposes."[57]

This was not the first time that a federal government department had actually created documents following an information request. In an earlier case, another federal department commissioned a special audit of a government-funded group after a journalist filed a request regarding possible links between the group and Tamil terrorists. The department took almost two years to respond to the request; in the end, it was able to counter damaging inferences from older documents by relying on the positive results of the specially commissioned audit.[58]

Lying in unison

Canada was one of three countries that adopted access-to-information laws in 1982. The others were Australia and New Zealand. The three had much in common. All were affluent, anglophone, stable, parliamentary democracies. As such, they were susceptible to the importation of an American innovation and able to absorb the costs and disruptions that would follow from its adoption. For many years the three countries were classed together as examples for other countries considering the adoption of a disclosure law.[59] By the century's end, however, the access regimes seemed to share a common infirmity, as officials attempted to tighten control over the release of politically sensitive information.

An appraisal of the health of New Zealand's Official Information Act – often regarded as the most progressive of the three – was compromised by the lack of good data on the use of the law or its internal administration.[60] However there was evidence of a shift in dynamics in the operation of the law. In 2003, New Zealand's ombudsman, Sir Brian Ellwood, told legislators that his decade of service as a referee on disputes over access to information "had not been an easy time." There had been rapid growth in the number of information requests, Ellwood reported, and requests themselves were "increasingly targeted and sophisticated."[61] A similar conclusion was reached by British officials who conducted a study tour of New Zealand and Australia in 2003:

> The picture as described to us is clear: in the early days, requests were typically made by individuals or local groups wanting information of interest to them, or relating to specific causes in which they were interested. But, twenty years on, such information was now nearly always made available through proactive disclosure or through informal disclosure. Most of the formal FOI requests in 2003 came from journalists or by the research departments of opposition parties. . . . Such requests were perceived by officials as being nearly always politically motivated.[62]

A senior Cabinet official had earlier acknowledged that the government sought to "manage the process" of disclosing information, for example by releasing information sought by a journalist simultaneously to the entire press gallery.[63] In 2003, Cabinet Office staff told the British visitors that they were increasingly concerned about their capacity to coordinate the government's responses to "politically inspired" information requests. "We encountered here," the British officials reported, "a real sense of the institutions of Government beginning to creak."[64] A veteran user of the New Zealand law confirms this impression, blaming the problem on the growing number of "professional 'communications' or PR people whose job it is to manage and restrict the information that reaches the public":

> There is plenty of scope for deliberate bending of Official Information Act requirements for tactical political reasons. Sometimes it is blatant. I recently waited seven months through an Ombudsman's

investigation to get some information from the Ministry of Economic Development. Yet two weeks before the Minister, Paul Swain, released the information to me, he had his staff drop a bundle of the key papers I had requested to every parliamentary journalist. Why? This is a trick used by [ministerial] staff to stop the requester, who has done the work of obtaining the information, from being able to write an exclusive story. After waiting seven months and then being scooped by the Press Gallery, there was no point in using the information I finally received.[65]

The strains on New Zealand's disclosure law were illustrated by the "lying in unison" controversy. The dispute arose in December 2002 when the *New Zealand Herald* contacted the media advisor of the New Zealand Labor Department, Ian Smith, to confirm rumors that one of the department's components, the Immigration Service, had detained a suspected terrorist. Smith said he was unaware of any such detention. When Smith's minister publicly acknowledged the detention, The *Herald* wrote an editorial that charged Smith with duplicity. "I was let down badly," Smith wrote in an internal media log that day, in words he later said were meant sarcastically. "Everyone had agreed to lie in unison, but all the others caved in."[66]

The next week, the Immigration Service received a request under the Official Information Act from the office of Bill English, leader of the opposition National Party. The request was intended to determine how much Smith had known about the detention when he spoke to the *Herald*. The Immigration Service did not provide the media log that contained Smith's comment. English's office complained to the ombudsman, suggesting that the Service had not provided all of the documents covered by its request, and asking specifically about media logs. The ombudsman, relying on the assurances of the Immigration Service, concluded that it had provided all of the relevant information.

Soon after, however, the *Herald* published a leaked copy of Smith's comments in the media log, stirring further controversy over the detention. Presented with evidence of misbehavior, the ombudsman reopened his investigation. In 2004, he concluded that Smith had consciously obstructed the original request and the ombudsman's initial investigation by withholding documents, and that the official responsible for handling the request had been aware of Smith's efforts at obstruction.[67] Smith was fired soon afterward. The case had stretched on for more than a year, providing a vivid demonstration of the extent to which the Official Information Act, and the officials responsible for administering it, had become entangled in partisan politics.

In Australia, concern about government preoccupation with the management of communications has been more pronounced – comparable, indeed, to complaints made against the Blair government. Two incidents during the 2001 federal election – one surrounding the Howard government's misrepresentation of its handling of asylum seekers on the ship *Tampa*,[68] the other stemming from its misrepresentation of the handling of asylum seekers on another ship, soon to become notorious as the "children overboard" case[69] – encouraged complaints about the government's obsession with spin. Patrick Weller charted the ways in which the structure of central government had been transformed: through the politicization of the highest civil service, the cowing of lower levels of the service, the growth in the number of political advisors (some acting as "junkyard attack dogs"), and the centralization of authority over communications.[70]

This transformation in the structure of Australia's central and state governments has affected the operation of the nation's disclosure laws. Procedures for managing politically dangerous requests are now "well entrenched" in Australian government, according to Rick Snell, who calls this the "dry rot" within the country's disclosure systems. The techniques of control parallel those in Canada. Ministers in all Australian governments, says Martin Chulov,

> . . . are quickly told by their mandarins when requests from journalists, or members of the public, come in that are likely to give them headaches. In many cases, what seems to happen from then on is not an independent, detached assessment of the request on merit, but rather a rationalisation process, with the political pros and cons of releasing the information delicately weighed up.[71]

Senior policymakers, journalists complain, routinely attempt to obstruct or delay responses to sensitive requests. And if obstruction fails, ministries will use "a series of tactics . . . to swamp or divert attention away from the newsworthiness" of released information.[72] In 2002 a state ombudsman noted instances in which opposition legislators who had asked for information read about the results of their requests – with their names included – in the media, before they had themselves received a response.[73] "Examples of FOI requests being released and placed strategically to counter their negative impact are no longer rare," a *Sydney Morning Herald* editorialist wrote in 2002:

> All requests for documents from Opposition or journalists under FOI legislation are now vetted for the potential political impact of their release. . . . As they are thoroughly screened for their potential newsworthiness, the government is then well-placed to respond immediately when the issue is made public or . . . to release the information with a particular spin attached.[74]

Evidence of similar practices has also emerged within Canada's provincial access systems. The province of Ontario adopted a Freedom of Information Act in 1988; within a few years, there were indications that ministries had begun to treat requests for information on "contentious issues" gingerly. By 2001, the province's Information Commissioner suggested that the government had developed formalized procedures managed by the Cabinet for dealing with sensitive requests filed by journalists, opposition legislators, or advocacy groups, which seemed to raise a "systemic problem" of noncompliance with the law. "Our understanding of the process is sketchy," the Commissioner said, "and ministry [staff] are extremely reluctant to provide us with details."[75] Two years later, an investigation by journalist Ann Rees confirmed the existence of a special process for handling sensitive requests, involving routine disclosure of the identity of requesters and consultations with communications specialists in the Cabinet Office.[76] The provincial government had also hiked fees for processing information requests in ways that caused a dramatic decline in the number of requests for sensitive information.[77]

The province of British Columbia adopted a Freedom of Information Act in 1993 and also developed sophisticated methods for monitoring sensitive information requests. Officials designed a government-wide computerized tracking system that allows communications specialists in the office of the province's premier to monitor the flow of information requests into government departments. More sophisticated than the software used by Canada's federal government, the system allowed officials to categorize incoming requests by six levels of sensitivity.[78] Requests from legislators, journalists, and advocacy groups were typically classified as highly sensitive, and the identities of requesters were routinely disclosed to communications aides, in violation of provincial privacy law.[79] The practice of tracking sensitive requests had begun in 1993,[80] but the public remained unaware of the technology and routines used for surveillance until a legislative inquiry in 2004.

Centripetence and centrifugence

At one level, the tactics employed by governments newly encumbered by disclosure laws were simply explained. Each law compelled officials to give up power, and officials – as rational, self-interested actors – did not wish to do this. As a consequence, they developed a range of strategies consisting of changes in administrative routine and also the law itself intended to dull its effect.

At a certain level, official resistance is a universal and timeless phenomenon. In the first years of the American Freedom of Information Act, advocacy groups had also protested about noncompliance: In 1972, a young lawyer in Ralph Nader's Center for the Study of Responsive Law complained that the Act had "foundered on the rocks of bureaucratic self-interest and secrecy."[81] (The lawyer, Peter Schuck, is now a distinguished professor of law at Yale University.) And as we saw in Chapter 3, complaints about official resistance persisted in the United States three decades later.

There are, however, potential dangers in over-simplifying the problem of official resistance. In important respects, it is not a universally consistent phenomenon: On the contrary, different governmental systems have reacted to the introduction of disclosure laws in different ways. Such variation should not be surprising. The legal scholar Otto Kahn-Freund observed in 1974 how "legal transplants" – the attempt to transfer laws from one country to another – could be compromised by political and constitutional differences between countries.[82] (Kahn-Freund remembered Montesquieu's famous warning that it would be "pure chance" if the laws of one nation could meet the needs of another.) Gunther Teubner later suggested that Kahn-Freund's metaphor was inapt. Transplants are accepted or rejected, Teubner argued; imported concepts (such as freedom of information) are better regarded as "legal irritants" that may trigger "a whole series of new and unexpected events" that lead to a quite distinct end result.[83]

Many of the countries that adopted disclosure laws after the United States had the advantage of also being wealthy democracies, but beyond this there were substantial differences in political conditions. Many of these countries have parliamentary systems of government and more disciplined political parties – two factors that may give political conflict a simpler and more intensely adversarial structure. These countries often have a smaller bureaucracy and a unified civil service (as opposed to the United States' more fragmented service), features that make it easier to develop consistent internal systems to control the disclosure process. At the same time these countries lack equally powerful legislative branches or vigorous nongovernmental sectors who are able to monitor and check attempts to restrict access.

The result of this may be that bureaucratic resistance differs in both quality and intensity in the countries outside the United States that first emulated its Freedom of Information Act. Administrative routines designed by departments to blunt disclosure rules appear to be more highly formalized; senior communications and political staff appear to play a larger role in vetting proposed responses to information requests; and the capacity to coordinate the response to sensitive requests across several government departments appears greater. In short, disclosure systems appear more highly centralized and politically attuned. (The phenomenon may not be limited to the anglophone parliamentary systems. In 2002 the Japanese Defense Agency acknowledged it kept a list of individuals who made requests for information under the country's disclosure law, adopted in 1997; the list also contained details about occupations and political beliefs. A subsequent investigation by the Public Management Ministry showed that over thirty agencies – including the management ministry itself – had circulated details about information seekers, in violation of privacy rules.[84])

Within the anglophone parliamentary democracies, the problem of official resistance has also intensified over time. The sense that disclosure systems have been transformed is palpable in all of these jurisdictions. The reasons for this may be straightforward. Journalists and legislators have acquired more experience and learned more about the intricacies of the bureaucratic system, which enables them to make sharper and more dangerous requests. (It may also be true, as some observers suggest, that bureaucracies have learned to deal with simpler requests informally, leaving only hard cases within the formal disclosure process.[85]) At the same time, politicians and bureaucrats have had the time to refine and formalize their own procedures for dealing with hard cases. New technologies have created opportunities for surveillance that were not available two decades ago.

In addition, the context in which governments operate has changed. Donald Rumsfeld is not the only policymaker who believes that the problem of overload – the problem of too many voices making too many demands on government – has worsened over the past three decades. It is a perception that is widely shared by bureaucrats and elected leaders of all ideological leanings in most advanced democracies. The frustration was articulated in a 1995 report produced by officials from OECD countries. "Governance capacities are being challenged," the study said:

> Citizen demand is more diversified and sophisticated, and, at the same time, the ability of governments to deal with stubborn societal problems is being questioned. The policy environment is marked by great turbulence, uncertainty and an accelerating pace of change. Meanwhile large public debt and fiscal imbalances limit governments' room for manoeuvre. Traditional governance structures and managerial responses are increasingly ineffectual in this context.[86]

A similar anxiety was manifest at a conclave of OECD ministers held in Paris the following year. Governments, the ministers agreed, were facing "intense pressure from citizens, transmitted or provoked by the media, and demanding rapid responses." Mechanisms for prompting responsiveness – "policies of consultation with the public, freedom of information, and transparency" – could be abused, blocking constructive governmental action. It was important, the ministers concluded, to resist "excessive pressure" from the media and pressure groups: Governments needed "to pursue more active communication policies, to keep control of their agendas and not just react passively to the pressure of events."[87]

The official preoccupation with agenda control is evident in the United Kingdom, as several recent inquiries have shown. In 2003, an independent investigation into the controversial work of politically appointed advisors in the Blair government suggested that their expanding role was a response to "a dramatic change in media pressure" on government, caused by a proliferation of media outlets, an erosion of media deference, and the advent of a twenty-four-hour news cycle.[88] When the Blair government was criticized by a second inquiry in 2004 for the informality of its decision making before the Iraq war – marked by a lack of briefing papers and ad hoc, unminuted meetings – ministers retorted that this, too, was the result of changed circumstances. A "24/7 news agenda" and the need to react quickly to events was said to have rendered more formal – and better documented – decision-making processes obsolete.[89] The Phillis inquiry, established in 2003 following allegations of misconduct within the Blair government's communications service, echoed these concerns. While condemning the practice of "misleading spin" of government policies, the Phillis report acknowledged that government confronted a broad decline in public trust and "extraordinary pressure" from the rapid growth in media outlets and intensification of media competition.[90]

In his recent book *The Shield of Achilles*, Phillip Bobbitt presents a diagnosis of the predicament of the contemporary state that shares this concern with media influence. The state, says Bobbitt, confronts a crisis of legitimacy that is largely media-driven:

> The press and electronic media, far more than the drab press releases of any government, are the engines of mass propaganda today, and it should be borne in mind that the press, when it is not controlled by the State, is driven by the need to deliver consumers to advertisers, and whether State-owned or not, is animated by the conditions of competition among all news media. Whatever the individual aspirations of its reporters and editors, the ideology of media journalism is the ideology of consumerism, presentism, competition, hyperbole (characteristics evoked in its readers and watchers) as well as skepticism, envy, and contempt (the reactions it rains on government officials). No State that bases its legitimacy on claims of continuity with tradition, that requires citizen self-sacrifice, that depends on a consensus of respect, can prosper for very long in such an environment. It must either change so as to become less vulnerable to such assaults, or resort to repression. Some nation-states do the latter; the liberal democracies, whose claims to ensure civil liberties are as much a part of their reason for being as any other functions, cannot do this. At best they

can manipulate information and resort to deception, thus poisoning the history on which they themselves must ultimately depend. This is the province of the "spin doctor" whose role in government has become correspondingly more important.[91]

To place the whole responsibility for the state's crisis of legitimacy on the shoulders of the media, however, would be mistaken. Bobbitt concedes the relevance of the other factors – such as the contemporary state's declining ability to fulfill the basic responsibilities of assuring national security (given the advent of new threats) or public welfare (given the state's inability to sustain social insurance programs).

Perhaps more important are fundamental changes in governance structures in the wealthy anglophone democracies over the last thirty years. Many of these countries have witnessed a weakening of a set of institutions that once bounded and tempered political conflict. In most countries, legislatures declined in influence, media elites were undercut, and the social ties that bound together old governing establishments frayed.[92] At the same time, mass enfranchisement was extended, either in the strict legal sense that more people were entitled to participate in political life,[93] or in the practical sense that people were more forceful in using their political rights to demand a larger share of society's resources. Good arguments can be made about the desirability of renovating old governance structures, but the effect has been to create a situation in which political executives are compelled to negotiate for power directly with a mass public that is distrustful of central authority.[94]

The new terrain is one that, from the point of view of political executives, is characterized by turbulence and fraught with uncertainties. It also creates an important new paradox. On the one hand, it compels governments to move into a state of "permanent campaign," in which executives are constantly engaged in an effort to maintain the support of the mass electorate. (The phrase, coined by Sidney Blumenthal, is American in origin, but has crossed the Atlantic: The 2003 inquiry into the role of special advisors concluded that their proliferation was attributable to the fact that British governments lived in the same condition.[95]) This reality has a powerful *centripetal* influence within government. Power over policies that are critical to key portions of the electorate – such as health or education – must be concentrated at the center; the power to make key political judgments and craft key messages must be concentrated as well. Recent and widespread complaints about the "presidentialization" of parliamentary systems may be a result of this centripetal pressure.[96]

At the same time, executives face powerful *centrifugal* pressures. Precisely because they must maintain broad popular support, governments are unusually susceptible to populist demands for reforms that check or disperse the power of the executive. This may include calls for devolution of responsibilities, reform of legislative and electoral systems, introduction of referendum procedures – and more powerful disclosure laws. These reforms, if taken seriously, weaken the capacity of executives to wage a permanent campaign. The challenge, therefore, is to find ways of acknowledging populist sentiment without actually undercutting the necessary concentration of political authority. This accounts for the start-and-stop character of governments' handling of disclosure policies, and in particular for strategies that honor the principle of disclosure while seeking, as a matter of practice, to minimize its disruptive potential. Governments maintain a law on the statute books but develop less obvious techniques – exclusion of certain institutions, increases to fees, internal procedures for sensitive requests – for restricting its actual impact.

The conventional narrative about official resistance to disclosure laws typically attributes simple motives – self-interest, embarrassment – for such behavior, and in some cases this is enough of an explanation. However, executives are increasingly driven to act as they do for other reasons, rooted in deep and perhaps irreversible changes in social and political conditions. Furthermore, their behavior is rationalized (at least internally) by a roughly articulated story about the challenges confronting contemporary governments, which is reinforced in those forums (such as the OECD) where ministers and officials can privately commiserate with one another. Executives, in other words, have developed their own ideology of resistance, articulated through continuing efforts at covert subversion of disclosure laws.

Anxiety in Whitehall

The Phillis inquiry's recommendations unwittingly gave evidence of the paradox confronting the Blair government. On the one hand, the inquiry urged departments to develop strong communications offices that were closely involved in daily administration, as well as a firmer central role in overseeing communications functions, in an effort to assure clearer and better coordinated communications to the public.[97] On the other, it urged a strengthening of the new Freedom of Information Act, to boost transparency and "active citizenship." The report dismissed concerns that the new law might aggravate the government's preoccupation with spin:

> There are some in government who fear that an effective FOI regime would worsen relations with the media by providing the national press with more ammunition with which to attack it. We do not think this argument can be sustained. Full disclosure allows context. It is a disincentive to spin (by both sides) as the public itself will have access to the material and will be able to form its own view of the accuracy of reporting.[98]

There is, unfortunately, little evidence from overseas to sustain this benign view of the likely impact of the new disclosure law. At the same time there is mounting evidence that officials in Whitehall might follow the path already trod by other parliamentary governments.

Although the Labour party had advocated for the adoption of a Freedom of Information Act throughout its long years in opposition, the Blair government's enthusiasm waned quickly after the 1997 election. Advocates of a disclosure law noted that a promise on adoption was conspicuously absent from the government's first major statement of priorities.[99] Although a junior minister later produced a promising discussion paper on the outlines of a disclosure law, Blair's powerful Home Secretary, Jack Straw, soon led an effort to weaken the government's commitments.[100] After its eventual adoption in December 2000, Blair himself pressed successfully for a four-year delay in implementation.[101]

As the government temporized, internal concern about the pressure for openness began to mount. With the new Freedom of Information Act in abeyance until 2005, government departments remained subject to a weaker administrative code promising limited access to documents that had been adopted by the Conservative government in 1994.[102] Between 1997 and 2002, journalists and legislators became increasingly aggressive in using the code; the number of information requests from these sources increased eightfold, eventually accounting for 40 percent of all requests.[103] The Cabinet Office was reported to be particularly unhappy about journalists' increasing skill in making "round-robin" requests, in which several departments received comparable requests for information about internal policy debates.[104]

In an internal memorandum written in January 2003, a senior official responsible for implementation of the Freedom of Information Act reported that at the center of government there was "an increasing level of anxiety" about departmental decisions on requests under the administrative code, which were felt to compromise the government's ability to assure the secrecy of the policy-making process.[105] Throughout 2003 and 2004, officials worked to develop "measures to ensure consistency" in dealing with difficult requests under the new law.[106] In May 2004, Blair acknowledged that he had established a special ministerial committee to oversee its implementation.[107] In July 2004, the *Mirror* newspaper reported that the Blair Cabinet had agreed to create a central "clearing house" for information requests, as part of "emergency discussions" on the potential impact of the law.[108]

As the deadline for implementation of the law approached, the Blair government considered other familiar tactics for dampening the impact of the new law. In May 2004 the *Guardian* reported that key government departments were lobbying for steep increases in the fees that could be charged to persons making requests for information.[109] An internal government working paper justified the increase as a way of avoiding costs that "could have a serious impact on the ability of departments to function."[110] The government reversed course following public protests.[111] In December 2004 – only one week before the Act was scheduled to go into effect – the minister responsible for the law, Charles Falconer, announced that the Cabinet had approved a new policy under which information requested by journalists would be released simultaneously on government websites – a more subtle form of practices adopted by Irish policymakers a few years earlier. Journalists protested that the effect of the policy would be to discourage editors and journalists from pursuing costly and time-consuming requests. Falconer responded by playing on the logic of the law itself: "Surely media organisations, for so long campaigners for open government and for freedom of information, cannot be suggesting that their own commercial interests are of greater importance to them than the public's right to know?"[112]

The Blair government's fears about the law were soon justified. On the second day of implementation, the Conservative opposition announced that it had used the Act to file a barrage of 120 "embarrassing questions" with government departments.[113] (Many backbench Labour Members of Parliament responded by filing requests for information about the performance of the Opposition leader, Michael Howard, during his years as a minister in Conservative governments in the 1990s.) The new FOI Clearing House struggled to keep up with the inflow of politically dangerous requests. In February 2005 it finally issued directions to other government departments: The center was to be consulted on "sensitive cases with a potentially high public profile"; and the Cabinet Office would become involved on cases "in which the Prime Minister takes personal interest."[114] It was remarkable that the Blair government – with *four years* to plan for the new law – was still inventing these routines at the last moment. But the direction was now clear: The British government, like other parliamentary governments before it, was headed down the path of centralization.

5

SOFT STATES

The countries that first adopted national disclosure laws – for convenience, let us focus on the fourteen that adopted laws up to 1990 – had much in common. They were among the richest countries in the world. Almost all were politically stable democracies with a long tradition of respecting citizen rights and the rule of law, a lively popular press, and healthy and independent nongovernmental organizations. Many had a political culture that included a skepticism about state authority – whether in the strong form (as in the United States), or in the moderate form peculiar to the older Commonwealth countries and the states of Northern Europe. (In 2000, one European Union official dismissed the call for tougher disclosure rules as a pathology of "protestant Puritanism."[1]) All of these considerations eased the adoption of a disclosure law and made it more likely that the law would work in practice.

Indeed, it was common to think that some mix of these considerations was probably *necessary* as a prerequisite for the adoption of a disclosure law. One scholar suggested two conditions that were essential for a law to be adopted. One was a "fundamental commitment" to the institutions of liberal democracy, manifested in a long history of democratic rule. Such states, it was thought, would be more responsive to the case for protecting citizens' rights against state authority and robust enough to tolerate the uncertainties that could be generated by a new disclosure law. A second prerequisite was a period of significant growth in the public sector, or at least a perception of growth, leading to concerns about the erosion of accountability.[2] This seemed to capture the realities of the 1970s and 1980s: disgruntled

Table 1 Perceptions of governance in nations adopting disclosure laws

The five "perceptions of governance" measures used in this table were developed by Kaufmann, Kraay, and Mastruzzi in research for the World Bank. A higher number reflects a more positive perception; each measure is calculated so that its "world average" is 0. Figures are averages for countries adopting in each period.[3] Data on per capita gross national income is US$ for 2000, provided by World Bank.

	1990 and earlier	1991–2000	After 2000
Per capita GNI	$21,082	$10,516	$3,626
Political Stability	0.81	0.45	−0.13
Rule of Law	1.36	0.57	−0.08
Control of Corruption	1.31	0.44	−0.13
Government Effectiveness	1.26	0.52	−0.01
Voice and Accountability	1.27	0.68	0.10

electorates in affluent welfare states, distrustful of their leaders and pressing for openness.

By the mid-1990s it was clear that this account was inadequate. The pace at which disclosure laws were being adopted was quickening: While it had taken more than a quarter-century for the first fourteen laws to be adopted, twenty-eight more were adopted in the nineties alone. The profile of this second wave of adopters was decidedly mixed. Some, such as the Netherlands or the United Kingdom – affluent, mature democracies – fit the pattern. But many did not, such as the countries of Central and Eastern Europe – new democracies determined to repudiate the secrecy of the Soviet era, and perhaps to emulate the policies of the remaining superpower.[4] On the whole, countries that adopted disclosure in the nineties were much less wealthy than the first adopters, less politically stable, less able to enforce the rule of law, and more prone to corruption. Political rights, including the right to free expression, were not as deeply entrenched (see Table 1).

There were equally sharp disparities between this group and the nations that adopted disclosure laws in the first years of the twenty-first century. These countries had, on average, only one-sixth of the per capita income of the first wave of adopters; and by all of the measures of governance – including stability, rule of law, control of corruption, respect for civil liberties, and political rights – were in poorer condition than either of the preceding two groups of adopters. The conventional wisdom about the necessary conditions for adoption of a disclosure law had been turned on its head: The typical case was now far from being a mature democracy, populated by an enfranchised citizenry disturbed by sprawling bureaucracy. On the contrary, some new adopters were countries once described by Gunnar Myrdal as "soft states" – struggling with poverty, political disenfranchisement, and widespread corruption.[5]

One could imagine several explanations for this shift in the profile of adopting states over time. One simple explanation might be that all the affluent democracies have now adopted laws – meaning that any new adopters must, by definition, be poorer and rank lower on governance measures. The fact of pervasive adoption in the First World also helps to establish a disclosure law as a marker of democratic and economic advancement – thus encouraging other countries to adopt similar laws, if only to emulate the better-off states.

Many intergovernmental organizations have also prodded poorer and more fragile states to adopt disclosure laws. In 2002 the Council of Europe – a body distinct from the European Union, without comparable authority – recommended the adoption of disclosure legislation to its forty-six members, including over twenty countries in Central and Eastern Europe.[6] In the same year, Commonwealth justice ministers approved a model freedom of information law for that organization's fifty-three member countries[7]; in 2004, the thirty-five members of the Organization of American States adopted a resolution endorsing legislation to recognize a right to information.[8]

Countries have also been pressured by an increasingly sophisticated transnational network of nongovernmental organizations interested in transparency issues. ARTICLE 19, the London-based free expression group, has played a critical role in promoting the adoption of disclosure laws and in critiquing proposed laws.[9] (In 2004, ARTICLE 19 also orchestrated a joint declaration by the free expression monitors of the United Nations, the Organization of American States, and the Organization for Security and Cooperation in Europe that the right to access information held by public authorities "is a fundamental human right."[10]) So, too, has the Delhi-based Commonwealth Human Rights Initiative,[11] as well as the International Helsinki Federation for Human Rights (particularly in Eastern Europe and the Caucasus)[12] and the Atlanta-based Carter Center (in Latin America and the Caribbean).[13] The Open Society Institute, a philanthropy established in 1993 by investor George Soros, also provides substantial support to groups advocating for the adoption of disclosure laws. An arm of the OSI, the Open Society Justice Initiative, now has the adoption of disclosure laws as one of its main priorities.[14]

One of the most influential of these nongovernmental organizations has been Transparency International, established in 1993 by Peter Eigen, once a World Bank official frustrated by the Bank's failure to address the problem of corruption in borrowing countries.[15] TI publishes a Corruption Perceptions Index that annually ranks countries based on the international business community's view about the pervasiveness of corruption within each. Arguing that there is "an obvious link between access to information and low levels of corruption," TI has also recommended the adoption of a disclosure law as one of the central elements of a national anticorruption strategy. In 1998 it observed that almost all of the "clean countries" in its index had a Freedom of Information Act.[16]

The identification of disclosure law as a tool for dealing with the problem of corruption has become a principal reason for the widespread adoption of such laws among "soft states," many of whom are attentive to their ranking in TI's Corruption Perceptions Index because of its potential impact on foreign investment. Other intergovernmental organizations such as the OECD and the United Nations Development Programme have endorsed TI's view; the UNDP has called freedom of information acts "an important precondition" for reduction of corruption.[17] The Bretton Woods institutions – the World Bank and the International Monetary Fund – have encouraged adoption of national disclosure laws on similar grounds. Governments have also realized that disclosure laws might serve their own ends, by helping them to improve control over a vast and unresponsive bureaucracy. This was the case in China, where in 2003 senior party officials endorsed transparency as an important tool "for the control and supervision of administrative powers, so as to prevent and control corruption."[18] "External supervision" by citizens would be enlisted to serve the interests of the Party.

In other words, "soft states" were adopting disclosure laws precisely *because* of their softness, not in spite of it. Here was another case of "legal transplantation" (to continue with Otto Kahn-Freund's phrase) to new bodies politic – and this time the differences in con-text were perhaps even more substantial than those between one rich democracy (such as the United States) and another (such as the United Kingdom). The contrast between the early and late adopters was so stark that it raised a reasonable question of whether the trans-plant could thrive at all.

In some instances, an obvious issue was whether the new adopter-governments felt any "ownership" (to use a favored phrase of the International Monetary Fund) of their new disclosure law. There was always the possibility that legislation had been adopted purely for the sake of appearances. Pakistan may have illustrated the poten-tial for backsliding. Routinely ranked by TI as one of the most cor-rupt countries in the world, Pakistan eventually agreed to adopt a Freedom of Information Ordinance in September 2002, as part of an anticorruption program promised in return for US$1.4 billion in aid from the IMF.[19] Two years later, Pakistan's Human Rights Commission complained that the government led by General Pervez Musharraf had done little to encourage bureaucratic compliance with the ordinance. "Nothing has turned around," lamented the head of a Pakistani lawyers' association. "Such legislation serves best in a civilized society. Our case is different. Either we make laws to violate or not to implement them at all; and this is our national tragedy."[20]

Governmental capacity

Disclosure laws will also test the administrative capacities of devel-oping countries. One mundane but nonetheless critical issue is the ability of governments to document their work and organize their records so that they can be retrieved later. The right to information is meaningless if files do not exist or cannot be found.[21] Even in affluent countries, good record keeping is a challenge. Preparing a documen-tary record of official activities, sorting and filing documents – all of this takes time and staff. As the public services of the advanced democracies have been cut back over the last decade, record keep-ing – often regarded as one of the ancillary functions of government – has deteriorated in many of these countries. In 1997 the Australian Law Reform Commission concluded that prolonged efficiency drives in the Australian government had led to widespread problems of "mediocre and fragmented recordkeeping"[22]; the complaint was echoed in several other rich states.

The problems are substantially worse in developing countries. Anne Thurston, founder of the International Records Management Trust, says that the record-keeping systems of many developing countries are "in decline, and in some cases total collapse" for lack of proper policies, trained staff, or adequate facilities.[23] An early Trust study of government personnel records in Uganda reported dire conditions: "No temperature, humidity or pest control exist, so paper is rotting, metal is rusting and there are layers of insects on or in files (termites have damaged shelving and wasps have nested among files)."[24] In Tanzania, the Trust found that the ability to monitor financial and personnel systems was compromised because "the system is overwhelmed by huge volumes of unmanaged paper. For example, it is very difficult to audit the payroll because the relevant documents are scattered in different files in a variety of locations. . . . [Personnel] files are frequently incomplete, missing or misplaced."[25] Another study found that the Ecuadorian court system's archives had accumulated 2.5 million files – 500,000 on shelves, and the other 2 million on the archive's floors. File retrieval depended on the "knowledge and memory of the Director."[26]

In Kenya – which will have a constitutional right to information if a Bill of Rights drafted in 2004 is put into force – missing government files were found to be a major problem. A government archivist believed that a major reason for the loss of files was corruption; officials were simply destroying incriminating documents.[27] This highlights one of the perversities of disclosure law as an anticorruption tool: It operates on the premise that the administrative system is, in large part, not corrupt. One of the remarkable features of disclosure systems in advanced democracies is the frequency with which they result in the release of documents that citizens did not know existed in the first place. That these documents are released, and not destroyed, is a testament to the professionalism of the civil service. Even in the cleanest civil services, however, cases of document destruction are occasionally uncovered. The problem is likely to be more severe in weakly professionalized civil services, particularly when missing documents can be blamed on notoriously poor record-keeping systems.

A decent system of record keeping and a reasonably professional civil service are likely to be two prerequisites for an effective

Documents stored in the archive of the municipality of Independencia, Peru, August 2004. Photograph by Helen Darbishire.

disclosure law. A third will be adequate resources for administering the law. Proponents of disclosure laws have sometimes been reluctant to discuss the potential burden of administering new laws, but they can be substantial if the law is to be applied properly. Staff need to be trained so that they know how to receive and respond to requests. In departments likely to receive a large number of requests, special offices may need to be established. The processing of requests will require some officials to retrieve records and review them to separate those that are sensitive from those that are not. Lawyers may be needed to give advice on the interpretation of exemptions in the law. Copies of documents containing sensitive material will have to be made, and the sensitive portions blacked out.

In short, a functioning disclosure law will spawn its own administrative routines and bureaucracy, and this will impose significant costs on government. In 2004, the Australian government estimated that the annual cost of administering its Freedom of Information Act was about $14 million, or about US$330 for each request.[28] In 2000, the Canadian government estimated that the annual cost of administering its Access to Information Act was US$19.4 million, or about US$1,340 for each information request received that year.[29] The difference in the two estimates is likely a result of the relative complexity of requests being handled in the Canadian system[30]; the Canadian estimate also included the budget of the independent Information Commissioner, who investigates complaints about the handling of AIA requests.

In 2003, the cost of administering the U.S. Freedom of Information Act was estimated to be $323 million, or about $100 per request.[31] This is significantly lower than either the Australian or Canadian estimates. Again, part of the difference is attributable to a variation in the kind of requests received by the three governments. Eighty percent of the 3.2 million FOIA requests received by the U.S. government in 2003 consisted of requests made by clients of the Veterans Health Administration or the Social Security Administration for personal information files; these requests are simple and highly standardized, and can be processed quickly and at low cost.[32] The average processing cost for requests received elsewhere in the U.S. government in 2003 was $405. The U.S. estimate also excluded some costs – such as the time taken by bureaucrats outside FOI offices to gather files – that were counted in the Canadian estimate. Nor is there an information commissioner in the U.S. system, as there is in Canada. In the United States, much of the enforcement cost – consisting largely of the cost of FOI litigation – is shifted to the federal court system and individuals who litigate FOIA cases.

These estimates are rough, but they suggest that the cost of processing an information request in these three countries is likely several hundred dollars, unless the process is highly routinized. In principle, it is possible to levy charges on citizens to recoup much of this cost. Indeed, a model right to information law drafted by ARTICLE 19 and the Commonwealth Human Rights Initiative in 2001 would allow fees up to "the actual cost of searching for, preparing and communicating" information, with waivers for personal information and public interest requests.[33] In practice, however, the Australian, Canadian, and U.S. governments rarely charge actual costs; revenue from fees is equal to roughly 1 or 2 percent of each government's expenses. There is evidence that a fee policy based on full cost recovery would cause the demand for information to collapse entirely.[34]

A working disclosure system cannot sustain itself financially; it requires almost complete subsidy from government coffers. There are sound arguments for such a subsidy in affluent nations. For example, governments in these countries spend a vastly larger amount on advertising and other promotional activities aimed at conveying information in ways that favor official priorities. In these countries, however, the subsidy for disclosure is explicitly recognized in government budgets: To put it another way, an allowance is made for the burden that will be put on departments by new disclosure laws. It is not clear that countries now adopting disclosure laws have done this; on the contrary, the assumption appears to be that the cost of implementation will be absorbed within existing budgets.

The disparity between the approach to implementation in richer and poorer countries was clear in 2004. The British government was in its fourth year of planning for the roll-out of its new Freedom of Information Act; adopted in December 2000, the law was scheduled to go into effect in January 2005. There had been heavy investment by government agencies in training, promotional material, and computer systems to handle anticipated requests. Parliamentary committees had scrutinized the implementation effort, as had the National Audit Office. In 2004 alone, the new Office of the Information Commissioner was given US$7 million to prepare for the law; the office within the central government's Department of Constitutional Affairs that had responsibility for providing guidance and overseeing implementation had, in that year, a budget of US$15 million.[35] Consultants had been hired; advisory boards had been appointed; "project risks" associated with the roll-out had been carefully monitored. Constitutional Affairs' public relations office announced that it would distribute complimentary coasters and pens bearing a new FOI logo[36] (thus raising, for FOI requesters, the perverse possibility that their denial letter would be signed with a pen celebrating the government's openness).

Jamaica, a poorer relation of the United Kingdom, put its Access to Information Act into force in January 2004, after only fifteen months of preparation.[37] This was, admittedly, a smaller effort than in the United Kingdom, but scale alone could not account for the disproportion in resources available for implementation in Jamaica. The budget for central guidance of the British FOI implementation effort exceeded the budget of the Jamaican Access to Information Unit (with its staff of four), the government's Archives and Records Department, the other parts of the Prime Minister's Office, and the Jamaican Houses of Parliament – combined.[38]

In September 2004 the Open Society Justice Initiative issued a report on the results of a test in which requests for information were submitted to government agencies in three countries that had recently adopted disclosure laws – Bulgaria, Peru, and South Africa.[39] The findings were discouraging. Officials frequently refused to accept requests for information, particularly if they were submitted by members of "vulnerable and excluded groups," while over 40 percent of requests that were accepted by officials were simply ignored. In South Africa, 70 percent of requests were either rejected or ignored. The problem was not simply the "enduring reflex toward secrecy," the report concluded; officials were often ignorant of the law, and agencies often lacked clear procedures for handling requests. The promise of the law had been defeated by failures in implementation.[40] A similar 2004 study of the Moldovan law found that one-quarter of state bodies ignored requests entirely, while another quarter violated deadlines for response.[41]

In the affluent democracies, official recalcitrance is often remedied by an appeal to the courts. But this makes another assumption about governmental capacity: specifically, that the courts are able to make a timely and independent appraisal of bureaucratic compliance with the law. This may not always be the case. In some poorer countries, court systems are overburdened and incapable of handling cases promptly. (In a 2004 assessment, American human rights specialists observed that the Pakistani court system was plagued with backlogs due to "archaic and inefficient court procedures"; the Indian court system was subject to similar criticism.[42]) Court systems may also be subject to political interference or governments may simply fail to comply with judgments – both of which are significant problems in the Ukraine, for example.

Civil society capacity

To say that the right to information is a *citizen*'s right is, in a certain sense, misleading. There are many circumstances in which the disclosure of information helps to protect a citizen's important interests. However, it is unlikely – at least based on the experience of laws already in operation – that individual citizens will, on their own behalf, make requests for information under a disclosure law. Even if they seek personal information (about a health benefit, for example, or an adverse decision on school admission or immigration status), individuals may rely on an advocate to make a request for them. And individuals are even less likely to make requests for other kinds of documents – sometimes known as "general records" requests. Requests such as this might also protect important interests such as the right to be informed about government decision making, but it is more likely that a nongovernmental organization – an advocacy group, media outlet, union, or business – will ask for the information.

The reasons for this are straightforward. Even in countries with long-established disclosure laws, making a request for information requires knowledge about the bureaucratic routine by which information requests are processed and about the legal provisions that should govern decisions on the release of information. Often it is useful to have a good understanding of the organization of files within the bureaucracy – to know where the bodies are buried, so to speak. The act of requesting information also requires a strong sense of political efficacy and persistence, due to the long delays that may arise in the handling of requests. Finally, asking for information may require money, particularly if the request is novel or complex or if the law lacks a mechanism by which appeals can be lodged at little or no cost to the requester.

The practical impediments to the use of any disclosure law are evident in the stories that are told about the use of new disclosure laws. In Rajasthan, it was not the villagers of Kelwara who pursued the request for ration dealers' registers; it was MKSS, an organization created by a former employee of the prestigious Indian Administrative Service (see Chapter 1). In Thailand, the case against the Kasetsart University Demonstration School was brought by a parent who also happened to be a public prosecutor. (In fact, most of the individuals who filed complaints about noncompliance with the Thai law in 2002 were government employees seeking information about disciplinary actions.[43]) It was also lawyers (a high-status occupation in Japan) who constituted the *Zenkoku Shimin Ombudsmen*, the organization that routed out evidence of corruption in Japanese government. Disclosure laws are wielded by knowledgeable, empowered professionals, even if they are used to protect the interests of a larger population.

Expertise and a strong sense of political efficacy, while critical, may not be enough. The U.S. Freedom of Information Act works as it does because the federal government is surrounded by nongovernmental organizations and media outlets with the resources to use the right to information aggressively. Many of these nongovernmental organizations also take a special interest in the principle of openness. These include groups such as Public Citizen ("We fight for openness and democratic accountability in government"), the National Security Archive ("a counter-institution to the U.S. government's secrecy system"), or OMB Watch ("Our objective is to improve access to government decision-makers and energize citizen participation").[44] Others, such as the Reporters' Committee for Freedom of the Press, treat the right to information as one of several issues that are important to their core constituency. This "transparency lobby" depends in turn on contributions from a broad community of philanthropies, as well as favorable treatment under federal tax law.

The affluence of public interest groups within the United States, as well as the country's major media outlets, is remarkable even when compared to other advanced democracies (see Table 2). And it is clear that the health of disclosure regimes in other rich democracies is tied to the health of the community of nongovernmental institutional users. Where the nongovernmental community has limited capacity, requests are either less likely to be made or are poorly drafted and pursued half-heartedly; or, if successful, requests may result in the release of information that is misconstrued or not used at all. All of this tends to discredit the law among policymakers, encouraging their efforts to reverse the law – efforts that, again, are unlikely to be strongly resisted. In Canada, for example, it is common for policymakers to complain that journalists misuse disclosure laws by dwelling on requests for travel and hospitality expenses – requests that are simple and unlikely to incur large charges for the journalists themselves but yield a sensational news report if the expenses are anything other than wholly prosaic. These complaints about the "trivialization" of access help to legitimize efforts to restrict the right to information.

The question in countries that are now adopting disclosure laws is not only whether government has the capacity to fulfill the law, but

Table 2 Washington's Transparency Lobby

A partial list of nongovernmental organizations in the United States that promote governmental transparency and use FOIA actively. Budget data are drawn from IRS Form 990's collected by guidestar.org. Several of these organizations also work on issues other than the right to information. ACLU data excludes state affiliates. Data is for most recent available year, either 2002 or 2003

Organization	Annual expenses
American Civil Liberties Union Foundation	$9,046,534
Center for American Progress	$2,943,509
Center for Democracy and Technology	$1,689,245
Center for Public Integrity	$3,682,146
Electronic Frontier Foundation	$1,523,891
Electronic Privacy Information Center	$917,737
Federation of American Scientists Fund	$2,359,729
Freedom Forum, Inc.	$26,152,357
Judicial Watch	$11,847,367
National Security Archive Fund	$2,508,414
OMB Watch	$1,137,435
People for the American Way Foundation	$7,034,194
Public Citizen Foundation	$8,482,766
Reporters' Committee for Freedom of the Press	$808,151
Total	$80,133,475

whether the nongovernmental sector will have the capacity to use the law effectively. In several countries, cumbersome registration laws – such as Turkey's Law of Associations – discourage the establishment of nongovernmental organizations and sometimes allow government leaders to block the establishment of unfriendly associations.[45] Governments also harass already-established nongovernmental organizations. Ukrainian nongovernmental organizations complained in 2003 that their mail had been opened and their activities monitored by the security service; in Georgia in 2002, a pro-government gang attacked the offices of the Liberty Institute, a nongovernmental group that played a key role in the adoption of Georgia's disclosure law. ("You hit the Liberty Institute, you hit all the NGOs," another association leader said. "The message is the same for everyone."[46])

Funding is also a critical issue for media outlets and nongovernmental organizations. The condition of the independent press in Georgia – constrained by "high printing costs, a lack of advertising, and general poverty" – is typical of many other nations.[47]

Nongovernmental organizations in these countries frequently rely on foreign assistance. The Soros-funded Open Society Justice Initiative said in 2004 that it provided support for freedom of information and expression projects to nongovernmental organizations in about twenty-five countries, and to international organizations such as the International Media Lawyers Association and the new Freedom of Information Advocates Network.[48] Conventional development agencies also provide aid for transparency-oriented nongovernmental organizations. South Africa's Open Democracy Advice Center has received support from Swedish, Finnish, and British development agencies; in the Philippines, the Center for Investigative Journalism has received support for transparency projects from the United Nations Development Programme. However, reliance on foreign assistance carries a price: In the Georgian state of Adzharia, President Aslan Abashidze used the fact of Justice Initiative funding to tar the Liberty Institute as a tool in an alleged Soros-driven plot to overthrow him.[49]

Civil and political rights

For disclosure laws to work well, nongovernmental organizations must also have the capacity to *act* on the information they receive from government agencies. In individual cases of misconduct, we presume that individuals will have remedies against arbitrary or corrupt decisions; but there may be no legal basis for challenging the decision – no equivalent of the Administrative Procedures Act, for example – and it may be impossible, for reasons noted earlier, to obtain a remedy in court. More broadly, information might be used to ensure that political rights can be exercised intelligently, but this assumes that political rights can be exercised at all. Recent elections in several of the countries that have recently adopted disclosure laws – Armenia, Georgia, Ukraine – have been marred (in the antiseptic language of American officials) by "serious irregularities."[50]

The capacity of media outlets to act on information obtained through the law may also face sharp constraints. Many countries still maintain defamation or *desacato* laws that threaten imprisonment for news reports that insult the honor or dignity of public officials. There are, in addition, other methods of suppressing or intimidating independent media. Ironically, one common tactic is deployed in

Zimbabwe's Access to Information Act, adopted in 2002. The law provides a right to government documents, albeit a right that is hedged by broadly drawn exemptions. The law also created a new Media and Information Commission to hear complaints about denial of information. However, a 2004 report found only one instance in which the right to information had been exercised. This was hardly surprising, because the 2002 law also included severe restrictions on press freedom, including fines or imprisonment for media outlets and journalists who were not registered with the Commission. (The penalties were strengthened in 2004.) The principal use of the law was to harass journalists and suppress independent newspapers prior to the country's 2005 election.[51]

There have been comparable restrictions on the media in other countries that have recently adopted disclosure laws. Uzbekistan, which adopted a law in 1997 and overhauled it in 2003, also maintains a registration system that has effectively crushed an independent media, and independent journalists have been harassed in an effort to discourage the distribution of stories critical of the government. Major media outlets are state-owned, and therefore subject to direct political control. Human rights observers reported a comparable situation in Azerbaijan, whose parliament was considering adoption of a disclosure law in 2005.[52] The editor of a prominent Azerbaijani opposition magazine, *Monitor*, was murdered in early 2005.

Initiatives to improve transparency in China will also be hampered by controls on press freedom. Chinese leaders may wish to curb corruption, but their tolerance for "external supervision" of state institutions clearly has firm limits. China's state secrets law, which prohibits "spreading rumors or libel or in other ways instigating subversion of the state regime," is a useful tool for constraining dissent. In 2002 the Chinese government jailed the journalist Jiang Weiping for eight years for violating the state secrets law: Jiang had written a series of articles in a Hong Kong magazine about an alleged cover-up of corruption in Liaoning province in northeast China. (Jiang's sentence was later reduced, and he is now scheduled for release in 2007.[53]) In 2004 Chinese authorities also detained Zhao Yan, a researcher for the *New York Times*, on allegations that he had "divulged state secrets" by providing the *Times* with details about the imminent retirement of President Jiang Zemin; Zhao was already suspect because of his earlier work against corruption in rural areas.[54] Local officials in Guangzhou (which adopted its Provisions on Open Government Information in 2002) jailed editors and journalists from the *Southern Metropolitan Daily*, which had embarrassed the local government with its coverage of corruption and police abuses.[55] Central government officials who had cited their eventual openness on SARS as evidence of a new commitment to transparency later detained Jiang Yanyong, the government physician who first exposed official deception about the extent of the crisis.[56]

A Brave New World?

The editors of the Lagos *Vanguard* were exultant when the Nigerian House of Representatives passed a Freedom of Information bill in September 2004. The government of President Olusegun Obasanjo agreed in 2003 that it would support a disclosure law as condition for a US$17 million aid package negotiated with the UNDP in 2003.[57] Nigeria was in terrible condition, still wrestling with the legacy of sixteen years of military rule and plagued by corruption. The FOI bill, said the *Vanguard*, would allow Nigeria to "join the league of open democratic societies":

> The bill...has removed the shackles from the media for conducting investigative journalism...and would allow the Nigerian media to beam its searchlight on public officials. Henceforth, public service will cease to be attractive to those who in the past have considered public office as a method of self-enrichment....It is a brave new world for the Nigerian media and its people.[58]

That the editors took this view was not surprising. To a small degree the overstatement may have reflected their desperation to find *any* remedy for the overwhelming problems confronting the nation. To a larger degree, the editors had merely accepted what they had been told by many advocacy groups and international organizations: Disclosure laws were powerful instruments for eradicating corruption.

In truth, the actual effectiveness of disclosure laws as corruption-fighting tools in developing countries is largely unknown. Yes, many of the world's cleanest countries have similar laws, but this confuses correlation with causation. Many of these nations had been among the cleanest in the world *before* they acknowledged the right to information. Disclosure laws have been used to uncover abuses subsequently, but it could be argued that disclosure laws did this precisely because the system of governance was, on the whole, already functioning well: officials were usually honest; records were well maintained; courts were efficient and independent; nongovernmental organizations were free to express their opinion about official misconduct; and governments were compelled to pay attention to public outrage.

Now the same instrument is being deployed in a much more hostile environment. It is certainly possible that the right to information could prove useful as a corruption-fighting tool in poorer countries, as the Indian experience seems to show. Right-to-information campaigns in several Indian states have succeeded in giving attention to abuses and prompting promises of reform; furthermore, there is a vibrant national community of professionals, activists, and academics who are committed to the use of disclosure law. On the other hand, India has several advantages over other countries in the group of recent adopters. Within this group, India is perceived to be more committed to the rule of law, and more respectful of civil and political rights. It also has the advantage of an independent high court that has spoken forcefully about the importance of the right to information, and a senior public service that is generally regarded as professional and free of corruption.

Perhaps the Indian case suggests that there must be a certain minimum set of conditions in order to make a disclosure law useful in anticorruption campaigns. But even this may be saying too much: It is still unclear whether Indian government has the budget or administrative capacity to maintain an *active* disclosure system – that is, one that is capable of responding to thousands or millions of information requests every year. In India, as in most other countries in the cohort of recent adopters, statutory recognition of the right to information is an experiment in governmental reform, and the odds are slim that it will quickly corrode old habits of secrecy.

II STRUCTURE

6

OPAQUE NETWORKS

The days before the 2000 election held a moment of drama for advocates of open government in the United States. Two weeks before election day, Congress sent President Clinton the appropriations bill for the CIA and other intelligence agencies – but with a stinger in its tail. The bill contained a new criminal penalty for the unauthorized disclosure of classified information by federal employees.[1] With the country distracted in the run-up to voting day, would Clinton sign the bill?

A last-minute campaign that enlisted the editorial boards of many major newspapers succeeded in persuading Clinton to veto the 2000 law three days before the election. However, proponents of the penalty made another effort a few months later to include it in the intelligence appropriations bill for 2001. The threat of another public campaign eventually persuaded the Senate Intelligence Committee to abandon the proposal – by coincidence, only a few days before the 9/11 attacks.[2]

The campaign against the bill leaned heavily on the claim that there was something profoundly un-American about the new penalty. William Safire of the *New York Times* said the new crime would be like those "used by so many dictatorships . . . to stifle dissent and hide misdeeds."[3] The *St. Louis Post-Dispatch*, like many other newspapers, equated the law with "Britain's loathsome Official Secrets Act."[4] The *New York Daily News* railed against what it called a "Soviet-style secrecy law."[5] "Other nations have long criminalized the disclosure of government information," said former White House counsel John Dean, "but there's a crucial difference between them and us: They lack an equivalent of our First Amendment."[6]

In reality, the distinction between "them and us" was not quite so simple. It was true that the United States had a long tradition of resisting attempts to create criminal penalties for leaking classified information. In 1957, for example, Congress rejected proposals put forward by two special inquiries – the Wright Commission on Government Security and the Coolidge Committee on Classified Information – to establish such penalties.[7] The proposals, said the *New York Times'* James Reston at the time, posed great danger to government accountability and a free press.[8]

Reston could not have appreciated the extent to which the United States was, at that very moment, secretly succeeding in efforts to strengthen criminal penalties for unauthorized disclosure of classified information in other countries. In the spring of 1953, planners within the North Atlantic Treaty Organization became frustrated by a series of compromising leaks of information about NATO military planning. At a secret meeting in Paris in April 1953, the Organization's Secretary General, Lord Ismay, told NATO leaders that "the problem of information leaks" had become grave and that "it was essential to search out the malefactors and to make examples of those who were caught."[9]

Some of the most frustrating news stories had arisen as a consequence of leaks by American sources to C. L. Sulzberger of the *New York Times*. The leaks provoked a three-year effort by the NATO Security Committee, in closed meetings at NATO headquarters at the Palais de Chaillot in Paris, to push for stronger antileaking penalties. Prodded by the Security Committee, several NATO countries strengthened criminal antileaking laws over the next four years. Ironically, the United States – the dominant partner in NATO – was the only major government that did not respond to the Security Committee's call for stronger laws.[10]

The United Kingdom was not then a bastion of open government, and appeals from NATO to maintain a strong antileak law were unlikely to be fiercely resisted. In other respects, however, British policy on the handling of sensitive information was more liberal than that of the United States. British officials protested against American demands for tighter security clearance procedures, arguing that the procedures were likely to be ineffective and that the American standards – which denied clearances based on political affiliation and sexual orientation – went too far in limiting civil liberties. In 1953, the U.S. government made clear it would not share any information about its nuclear defense plans until the British adopted tighter procedures, and the British finally relented.[11] After 1955, these U.S. rules were codified in secret standards that applied to all NATO governments.[12]

There were also other governments that were troubled by the secrecy rules imposed through NATO. Norway and Denmark complained privately in the 1950s that NATO's standards for classifying information were too broad and vague. Other tensions arose as NATO member states began adopting national right-to-information laws. NATO's practice of subjecting all information flowing through its channels – classified *and* unclassified – to the "third party rule" (which gives the originating government absolute control over its distribution) clashed fundamentally with the ethic of disclosure built into the new national laws. Sweden, which has a long tradition of open government, felt this conflict acutely when it began cooperating more closely on military matters with Western European governments in the early 1990s.

In the late 1990s, NATO's influence on national openness policies became evident as it responded to American pressure to incorporate former Soviet bloc countries in Central and Eastern Europe. Following the collapse of the Berlin Wall, countries in this region had been quick to throw off Soviet-era secrecy laws and adopt right-to-information laws on the Western model. Soon, however, governments began adopting new state secrets laws that included rules on the protection of sensitive information, security clearances, and criminal penalties for leaking. The motivation was simple: NATO had made clear that the laws were a prerequisite for joining the alliance.

Nongovernmental organizations throughout the region were frustrated by their 'governments' rush to adopt new secrecy laws. In Romania, legislators successfully launched a constitutional challenge against the government's first attempt at a secrecy law, arguing that it had been compromised by procedural irregularities. (Legislators were eventually persuaded to agree on a law in 2002. A security official "came down like a storm" on members of a Senate committee, a Bucharest newspaper reported: "'This morning we have received signals from Brussels indicating that if the bill on classified information is not passed before 16 April, they cannot exclude adopting a critical attitude regarding Romania. We agree with any form – the colonel added – but please, pass it as soon as possible, or we will be facing huge problems'."[13]) Protests also delayed the Slovak law, while the Polish, Czech, and Bulgarian laws provoked unsuccessful constitutional challenges.

The Bulgarian case provided a vivid illustration of the tensions between the post-1989 spirit of openness and the new emphasis on secrecy. The Classified Information Protection Act adopted in 2002 included a repeal of a 1997 law that allowed citizens to access the files created by Bulgaria's secret police in the Soviet era. Was this a step required by NATO, as the Bulgarian government claimed, or had it simply exploited an opportunity presented by the NATO accession process? This proved difficult to judge, because NATO itself refused to release the unclassified documents that detailed its requirements.[14] In September 2003, the Bulgarian government also proposed more severe criminal penalties for leaking classified information, including sanctions against journalists who repeated the information. Whether NATO had specifically required the measures remained unclear. Bulgarian newspapers reported in the months before accession that NATO sources had become concerned about Bulgaria's capacity to protect secrets,[15] and U.S. Secretary of State Colin Powell, in a meeting with the Bulgarian President, had urged that the government take further measures to protect classified information.[16]

Protecting the network

NATO has been called one of the great military and political alliances in history. In contemporary terms we would call it a model of "networked governance." The ten countries that signed the Washington Treaty in April 1949 faced a common problem that could not be resolved through action by any one state alone. A system for collective action by a number of legally autonomous but interdependent states had to be devised.[17] A critical part of the infrastructure built to sustain this new collective security network was intended to encourage "information sharing" (to use another contemporary phrase) among military staff and diplomats in the network. As it turned out, building an effective information-sharing policy was not easy. In fact, the first ten years of the alliance were punctuated by repeated efforts to overhaul the policy. But by the end of the first decade the NATO countries – heavily influenced by the preferences of the dominant NATO member, the United States – seemed to reach rough agreement on the rules for information sharing.

The deepening flow of information among NATO governments undoubtedly enhanced collective security. However, security came at a price: In the drive to give assurances that shared information would be strongly protected, each government took steps that restricted the ability of its own citizens to gain access to the information – even *unclassified* information – flowing through the network. The network ensured transparency for actors within the network, but opacity for those without.

That the policy should have put so little emphasis on adequate transparency for actors outside the network is not surprising. At the time, the threat posed by the Soviet Union and its satellites seemed overwhelming, and the revolution in popular expectations about governmental transparency had not yet occurred. The dominant actor in the network – the United States – was also indifferent to the costs that NATO policy imposed on legislators and citizens in other states. Furthermore, NATO was aided by the secrecy that was imposed on the policy itself – it was difficult to protest conditions imposed in documents that were themselves withheld from public view.

NATO's own significance may be in question after the collapse of the Soviet Union, but the dilemmas posed by its information-sharing policies have not faded. On the contrary, the restructuring of military and political relationships in the post-Cold War era have led to a proliferation of bilateral and multilateral partnerships among national governments that often include equally problematic rules on the handling of shared information. The burgeoning number of international networks can be divided into three categories: those relating to defense cooperation; cooperation between national intelligence agencies; and cooperation between national police forces.

International defense networks

The U.S.-led expansion of NATO is only the most obvious aspect of the post-Cold War restructuring of military alliances. The United States has also undertaken new bilateral partnerships that involve the sharing of information between military and diplomatic officials – and, as a consequence, negotiation on terms to protect shared information from unwanted disclosure.

The conditions that govern the handling of shared information are laid out in bilateral Security Of Information Agreements, or SOIAs. SOIAs are not new: The United States has been negotiating them with its defense partners for a half-century. In the 1950s, many countries that collaborated with the U.S. through NATO also signed bilateral SOIAs that provided assurances on the flow of information outside NATO channels. The practice of negotiating SOIAs was formalized in the United States in 1971 by National Security Decision Memorandum 119, which prohibits the sharing of military information with a foreign government that has not signed a legally binding SOI agreement.

In 1999, the Australian government created consternation within the U.S. Defense Department when it privately advised that it had never taken the steps required to make their classified 1962 SOI agreement with the U.S. legally binding. U.S. officials began pressing the Australian government to adopt an agreement that would be enforceable under international law. "A gentleman's agreement is not enough," a Defense Department official said. The State Department agreed. Its "biggest concern," an internal e-mail explained, was to get Australia "on the hook legally." Hurried negotiations produced a new, legally binding agreement. Australia's Foreign Affairs minister told the public that the new agreement was negotiated to "account for advances in information technology" since 1962.[18]

Tracking the number of SOIAs that have been negotiated by the Department of Defense is difficult, because the very existence of the agreements themselves may not be acknowledged. For example, the U.S. does not acknowledge an SOIA with Indonesia. It may be that no such agreement exists; alternatively, the Indonesian government might be reluctant to acknowledge the agreement, to avoid stoking domestic concern about military collaboration with the United States. In other cases, an agreement may be publicly acknowledged while its content remains classified. For forty years, the British and American governments refused to divulge the content of the bilateral SOIA signed in 1961. This agreement was finally declassified in 2001, but the details of some other agreements – such as the 1986 U.S.– Turkey SOIA – remain secret.

Despite such secrecy, there is evidence that the number of U.S. SOIAs is growing in the post-Cold War age. The collapse of the Soviet Union led to the negotiation of bilateral SOIAs with former Warsaw

Pact states even before those governments joined NATO. Alliances in other regions – such as the intensified collaboration of the United States with the Indian government – also led to the negotiation of new SOIAs. Roughly one-third of the fifty-four bilateral agreements that have been acknowledged by the United States were negotiated in the decade following the collapse of the Soviet Union.[19]

The content of these agreements seldom varies. At minimum, they entrench the third-party rule, so that a government receiving information covered by the agreement is denied any discretion to make a judgment about the wisdom of releasing shared information with legislators or citizens, or third countries. SOIAs may also require governments to adopt acceptable procedures for security clearances and physical protection of information as well; agreements with countries that are also NATO partners may simply apply NATO standards to all flows of defense information between the two countries.

The right-to-information laws adopted by national governments must be trimmed to accommodate the constraints imposed in these sometimes-secret documents. On the American side, an executive order creates a presumption that *any* information received from foreign governments merits classification, thus protecting it from disclosure under the Freedom of Information Act.[20] Other countries may create a similar blanket exclusion within their right-to-information law, or persuade courts that the release of shared information necessarily jeopardizes national security, regardless of the actual sensitivity of the information that is the subject of an access dispute.

In some instances, there is evidence that agreements have been crafted to anticipate the pressures created by new transparency laws. In 1982, Australia and Canada were among the first eight countries to adopt national right-to-information laws (following the United States, the Nordic countries, and France). Both laws established a general presumption that government-held documents should be publicly accessible and created procedures for an independent tribunal to referee disputes about access to information. These provisions clashed with the arbitrary protection provided by SOIAs. In 1996, diplomats and defense officials in the two countries negotiated a new bilateral SOIA drafted to counter the new legal restrictions. Each government promised to "take all steps legally available" to block disclosure of shared information under its national laws – a direct reversal of the presumption of openness – and also agreed that disputes over disclosure would never "be referred to any third party or tribunal for resolution."[21]

These general agreements on the sharing of defense information may also be accompanied by bilateral agreements on information sharing that are tied to specific projects. Since 2001, the Bush administration has undertaken negotiations with at least three countries[22] on agreements to protect information relating to the development of its controversial ballistic missile defense program. The information-sharing agreement with the United Kingdom was finalized in 2003; however, the British government refused requests made by opposition legislators under its own open government code to make the document public. A leaked copy of the agreement showed that British officials had committed to taking "all lawful steps" to avoid disclosure of classified *and unclassified* information, and promised to give immediate notice to U.S. authorities if it became probable that the British government would be compelled to disclose the information – presumably so that American officials could ask for the return of the disputed information before it was released.[23]

The restructuring of American defense relationships in the post-Cold War years has also had other consequences in Europe. The European Union's decision to begin cooperation among its member states on defense matters – a step often justified as a way of counterbalancing U.S. dominance after the fall of the Soviet Union – resulted in the adoption of similarly restrictive information-sharing rules. In July 2000, the Council of the European Union executed what critics called a "summertime coup" against transparency by adding severe limits to its own right-to-information code. It was not publicly known until later that the Council had signed a SOIA with NATO on the same day; the Council's revisions were intended to provide assurances to NATO that shared information would be protected from disclosure. (Similar restrictions were included in an overhauled right-to-information policy adopted by the European Union the following year.) In 2001, the European Union adopted new rules to govern the sharing of sensitive information among its own member states that barred any government from making an independent decision about the disclosure of shared information. The EU also considered requiring its member states to establish criminal penalties for the unauthorized disclosure of shared information.[24]

International intelligence networks

Relationships among national intelligence agencies have also become more complex in the post-Cold War era. Canadian intelligence agencies, as relatively small players in the global intelligence community, have been particularly sensitive to changes in the structure of that community and the constraints those changes appear to impose. Canadian intelligence professionals have spoken about the emergence of a "New Intelligence Order" characterized by a deeper flow of information among a much larger network of national agencies.

In a confidential internal memo written in May 2001, senior Canadian officials explained that:

> The end of the Cold War heralded changes in intelligence activities and targeting. This had concurrent effects on intelligence relationships. . . . One impact has been the development of more bilateral relationships, and arguably, a more complex set of sensitivities regarding the protection of information provided in confidence.[25]

In February 2004, the former head of Canada's Security and Intelligence Service explained the new realities in more concrete terms. Giving evidence before a public inquiry into the conduct of the intelligence community, Canada's former intelligence chief explained that the Service now had about 250 information-sharing arrangements with foreign intelligence services – compared to only fifty in the late 1980s. An exact accounting of the change is complicated by the informality of some arrangements and the practice of keeping the details of all arrangements confidential.[26] (American officials have also refused to release details about the full extent of their agreements with other intelligence services.)

This trend was in place well before the terror attacks of September 2001. In the eyes of Canadian intelligence staff, it also created a growing tension with Canada's own transparency laws. Under Canada's Access to Information Act, there is no obligation to disclose information received in confidence from other governments. However, officials are expected to ask other governments whether they will consent to disclosure, and also to release parts of documents that are not covered by the promise of confidentiality.[27] Canadian officials argued that it was becoming increasingly difficult to honor these obligations, for several reasons: There was more shared information; it was harder to disentangle the sources of information that had been combined in some analyses; and many of Canada's new partners did not share its own "open government values."[28]

Even before September 2001, Canadian intelligence staff had concrete ideas on how to deal with these concerns. Internal documents from April 2001 suggested that the public's right to information should be loosened by eliminating the government's obligation to release domestic information that had been mixed in documents with foreign government information, or to consult with other governments if the act of consultation would itself "affect the relationship of trust."[29]

Months later, intelligence officials had an opportunity to address these concerns. The Anti-Terrorism Act adopted by the Canadian government in the wake of the September 11th attacks included a powerful new restriction on the right to information. Under the new law, Canada's Attorney General is permitted to issue certificates that conclusively bar the disclosure of information obtained from other governments in the name of national security. The nation's independent Information Commissioner is prevented from investigating cases in which certificates are issued.[30] "One gathers intelligence, one shares intelligence," the Justice Minister told Canada's Parliament in 2001. "Unless we can guarantee to our allies that this type of limited, exceptionally sensitive information will not be subject to public disclosure, we will not get that information."[31]

Two years later, Canada's Arar Inquiry provided a harsh illustration of the "New Intelligence Order" at work. Maher Arar was born in Syria but immigrated with his family to Canada as a teenager. He acquired Canadian citizenship and worked as a technology consultant in Ottawa. In September 2002, Arar vacationed with his family in Tunisia, and took a return flight to Canada that required a change of planes at New York's Kennedy Airport. When he landed at Kennedy Airport, Arar was detained by American authorities, held for ten days, and deported – not to Canada, but to Syria, where he was imprisoned for ten months and tortured by Syrian military intelligence. American authorities defended their decision by alleging that Arar was a member of al Qaeda; Arar said that he had been targeted because of an innocent connection to other Syrian-Canadians who had aroused the suspicion of security agencies. Growing popular protests in Canada led to Arar's release in October 2003, and to the set-up of a special inquiry into the role of Canadian security officials in Arar's deportation and imprisonment.

The inquiry hinged largely on information-sharing practices among intelligence and security agencies. Canadian officials conceded that after the September 2001 attacks they had worked to assure "open information sharing" and "a climate of trust and cooperation" with security organizations in other countries.[32] They boasted in particular about the "seamless exchange" of information with U.S. security agencies.[33] Leaks to Canadian media also made clear that Canadian officials had exchanged information with Syrian intelligence.[34] Arar's lawyers wanted to know whether information sharing had made Canadian security agencies complicitous in his mistreatment: Did information received from other security services lead Canadian officials to make Arar a target of investigation? What information did Canadian authorities provide to U.S. officials prior to their decision to detain and deport Arar? Did information received later from other services predispose Canadian officials against helping Arar once he was in American and Syrian custody?

The inquiry, still underway in 2005, was hobbled by the reluctance of Canadian security agencies to reveal details of their information-sharing practices. Security officials insisted that any disclosure of information received from other security forces would lead to a damaging "loss of credibility."[35] "Confidentiality is a fundamental and necessary characteristic of sharing information," Canada's Attorney General told the inquiry. "Any perceptions of a relative weakening in Canada's ability to ensure protection of information" threatened to undermine critical security partnerships.[36] Looming over the investigation was the possibility that the Canadian government might invoke the new powers to withhold information contained in the Anti-Terrorism Act of 2001. The judge running the investigation complained that these new powers "do not appear to sit well with the whole idea of a public inquiry."[37] In December 2004, government officials refused to allow the publication of evidence that the commission said "could not conceivably relate to national security confidentiality"; a few months later, a commission advisor warned that the commission's report "may never see the light of day because of continued national security claims."[38] (A parallel effort by Mahar's lawyers to obtain documents from the American government was also stymied in 2005 when the U.S. Attorney General invoked its "state secrets privilege" to "protect the intelligence, foreign policy and national security interests of the United States."[39])

Law enforcement

Collaboration is also deepening among national law enforcement agencies. One of the key markers of this trend is the proliferation of multilateral legal assistance treaties (MLATs) that define the terms on which law enforcement agencies will work with one another. The United States signed its first major MLAT with Switzerland in 1973; by 2002, the number of bilateral agreements to which it was party had increased to forty-eight. In 2003, the United States added new MLATs with the European Union, covering all of its member states, and also with Japan, India, Russia, and three other countries.[40] (The European Union has also developed its own understandings on cooperation among EU member states, recently codified in the 2000 Convention on Mutual Assistance in Criminal Matters.)

The growth in the number of MLATs is the product of a sustained effort to improve governments' ability to fight transnational crime – an effort that again predated the collapse of the Cold War but gained new momentum afterward. In 1988, forty-three countries signed a new United Nations convention that committed them to closer cooperation in fighting drug trafficking and encouraged governments to negotiate bilateral MLATs.[41] In 1989, the G-7 countries set up a special task force on money-laundering that also encouraged the negotiation of new agreements.[42] (The task force also publishes a list of "non-cooperative" states.) In 2000, U.S. Attorney General Janet Reno said that the Clinton administration was attempting to build up an "effective matrix" of MLATs to combat transnational criminal rings engaged in software and music piracy.[43] After 2001, the Bush administration identified terrorism as its foremost reason for negotiating more MLATs.[44]

The sharing of information between law enforcement agencies creates special challenges, because shared information might have

to be publicly disclosed as part of a criminal prosecution. Nevertheless, MLATs are often drafted to minimize the probability that shared
information will be revealed. An agency that is asked to provide information needed by investigators in another country can request that
the records they provide be kept confidential. (Those investigators can
also ask for the request itself to be kept confidential.) If investigators
anticipate that they may be required to disclose information as part
of a criminal prosecution, they must warn the agency providing the
information. The agency then has the option of refusing to cooperate
if doing so would prejudice the country's "sovereignty, security, public
order or other essential interests."[45]

A new security architecture

Amitai Etzioni has argued that patterns of cooperation among security and intelligence agencies born out of the "global war on terrorism" are now so routine and institutionalized that they can be
described as "a new global architecture, . . . a de facto Global Antiterrorism Authority, formed, led, managed and largely financed by the
superpower."[46] Etzioni is probably mistaken to put so much emphasis on the influence of the "war on terror"; there is good evidence
that the movement toward this new "Authority" began soon after the
collapse of the Soviet Union. But there undoubtedly is a new global
architecture – a new set of networks among national security and
intelligence agencies – and this architecture includes a set of rules
on the exchange of information that is intended to ensure that work
within the networks cannot be easily observed by people or organizations outside the networks. Transparency *within* the network is
matched by opacity *without*.

There is also an aspect to this emerging "security architecture"
that is overlooked by Etzioni. This architecture does not consist only
of a thickening web of relationships between the security and intelligence agencies of different countries. There is a domestic component
as well. Within national borders, new networks are being formed that
connect national and subnational security agencies – and that rely on
equally problematic rules about the handling of shared information.

In the United States, the emergence of these domestic networks
has clearly been spurred by the new concern for homeland security.
Their growth is a product of the widely held view that the terror

attacks of September 2001 could have been averted if government agencies had been more effective in sharing information about potential threats. There were other possible diagnoses of the events that led to September 11, such as the unwillingness of political leaders to bear the cost of tightening security before the attacks. The emphasis on weaknesses in information sharing had the advantage of pinning responsibility for the failure to deter the attacks on bureaucratic pathologies rather than indifferent leadership.

Having said this, there was substantial evidence that the security and intelligence community *had* failed to share information fully, and that its capacity to "connect the dots" and see the looming threat had been compromised. Federal agencies (said the Joint Congressional Inquiry into September 11 in its 2002 report) "did not bring together and fully appreciate a range of information that could have greatly enhanced its chances of uncovering and preventing Usama Bin Ladin's plan to attack these United States."[47] The Central Intelligence Agency had not shared leads with the Federal Bureau of Investigation. Regional offices of the FBI had not shared information about investigations of related terrorist threats. The CIA and FBI both failed to warn the Immigration and Naturalization Service that newly discovered al Qaeda associates should be added to its border watch list.[3] In 2004, the 9/11 Commission reached a similar conclusion: Most of the "missed opportunities" to thwart the 2001 attacks arose because of the failure of federal agencies to share information.[48]

New awareness of the United States' domestic vulnerabilities also led to complaints about the federal government's limited efforts to share information with state and local officials. In the months following the attacks, mayors and police chiefs criticized the FBI and newly appointed homeland security staff for their unwillingness to trust state and local agencies with details about investigations and potential threats.[49] (A study of the New York Police Department's response to the World Trade Center attacks by McKinsey & Company found that it undertook "minimal intelligence sharing with federal agencies" before September 11.[50]) The federal government's capacity to coordinate with public health agencies and emergency responders in lower levels of government, and the capacity of state and local agencies to exchange information laterally, was similarly weak.

Governmental failures in information sharing were contrasted with the presumed strengths of al Qaeda itself. The terrorists "worked together," wrote the journalist John Miller, who had tracked al Qaeda for a decade. "That was one of the terrorists' great strengths. . . . They shared critical tactical information across units."[51] Al Qaeda seemed to be structured as an "all channel" or "full matrix" network, in which each cell was able to communicate easily with all others. This "all channel data flow" made al Qaeda more agile and resilient. To fight the terrorists, government agencies would have to learn from its example. Sharing information with partners in the terror-fighting network would have to become the norm.[52]

The need for improved communication between agencies soon became one of the mantras of reform. The 9/11 Commission urged federal agencies to develop a "decentralized network model" in which information would be "shared horizontally" across agency boundaries.[53] Federal homeland security officials called information sharing one of the "four foundations" of improved security, and promised to build

> . . . a national environment that enables the sharing of essential homeland security information. . . . Information will be shared 'horizontally' across each level of government and 'vertically' among federal, state, and local governments, private industry, and citizens. With the proper use of people, processes, and technology, homeland security officials throughout the United States can have complete and common awareness of threats and vulnerabilities as well as knowledge of the personnel and resources available to address these threats.[54]

"Sharing information," Homeland Security Secretary Tom Ridge told governors in August 2003, "is at the heart of what we do as a country."[55]

Information sharing requires a set of ground rules on the handling of sensitive information. One response to the new demand for better networking in the months following September 11 was an adaptation of the rules already established for the circulation of classified national security information. In March 2003, the Bush administration amended the executive order that governs the classification system so that it could accommodate information relating to homeland security concerns.[56] The list of agencies with authority to classify information was also broadened to include some – such as the Department of Health and Human Services, the Department of

Agriculture, and the Environmental Protection Agency – that traditionally were not counted within the national security community.[57]
By early 2004, roughly 3,000 state and local officials had been given
the security clearances needed to receive classified information from
the federal government.[58]

Many observers saw these developments simply as more evidence
of the Bush administration's bent toward secretiveness. There was
truth to this, but it also neglected the extent to which new security
threats were causing a qualitative change in the classification system
itself. The system – built to accommodate information flows among
U.S. national security bodies and with the national security agencies of other countries – was being domesticated, to permit the flow
of a broader range of information among a wider range of federal,
state, and local officials. By domesticating the classification system,
transparency might actually be improved for those officials who had
an appropriate clearance and a "need to know" the information contained within the system.

However, the improved flow of information came at a price: the
extension of the disclosure restrictions already embedded within the
classification system. Under federal classification rules, state and
local officials are prohibited from declassifying or disclosing classified information without the approval of the agency that classified
the information. As part of the clearance process, these officials must
sign a nondisclosure agreement that reminds them of the penalties
for the release of information without federal approval.[59] The agreement asserts that shared classified information remains the property
of the federal government, and must be returned to the federal government on its request – a legal gambit intended to further reduce the
risk of disclosure under state and local laws.[60] (The probability that
information will be accessible under federal law is also dramatically
reduced once it has been classified.)

These restrictions on disclosure might seem less problematic if
we believed that the individuals responsible for determining whether
information should be classified were limiting themselves to cases
where disclosure seemed likely to cause real harm. Unfortunately
there was little evidence that this was the case. In August 2004 the
Deputy Undersecretary of Defense for Counterintelligence and Security, Carol Haave, estimated that perhaps 50 percent of all classified

information was improperly classified.[61] There are strong incentives for federal officials to classify information and few checks to ensure that their discretion to classify is not overused.

Other programs aimed at improving information flows put a similar emphasis on the need to prevent the disclosure of information to actors outside the network of government agencies. One of the most prominent of these efforts was the creation by the Federal Bureau of Investigation of dozens of new Joint Terrorism Task Forces (JTTFs). JTTFs are investigative teams established by field offices of the FBI that include personnel from the FBI, other federal agencies, and state and local law enforcement agencies. The first JTTF was established in New York City in 1980. In the late 1990s, federal concern about terrorist threats led to quick growth in the number of JTTFs – from eleven in 1996 to twenty-nine in March 2001. After September 11, all FBI field offices established a JTTF, as did ten smaller FBI offices. By 2004, over eighty task forces were in operation.[62]

After 9/11, JTTFs were frequently presented as one of the federal government's most important techniques for sharing information with state and local law enforcement agencies. The head of the FBI's new Information Sharing Task Force told Congress in 2002 that JTTFs "have proven to be one of the most effective methods of unifying federal, state and local law enforcement efforts to prevent and investigate terrorist activity by ensuring that all levels of law enforcement are fully benefiting from the information possessed by each."[63] The Bush administration's 2002 National Strategy for Homeland Security, and the Joint Congressional Inquiry's report on the September 11th attacks, also presented JTTFs as a major tool for information sharing.[64]

Discovering the terms on which information is shared within a JTTF has not been a simple matter. The rules that regulate the flow of information are contained in a memorandum of understanding that is signed by each local police department and the FBI, but these MOU's – like many international agreements on information sharing – are rarely made routinely available. The Los Angeles Police Department, like other major police forces, declined in 2003 to release its MOU, arguing that disclosure might "result in a penalty or corrective action" by the FBI.[65] The Colorado chapter of the American Civil Liberties Union resorted to litigation to obtain a copy of the JTTF MOU signed by the Denver Police Department.[66] The University of Massachusetts at Amherst and the City of Springfield, MA, also refused to disclose their agreements to the ACLU after the Boston office of the FBI warned that they had no authority to release "FBI property."[67]

The FBI finally released its template JTTF MOU in 2004.[68] The document showed that the FBI imposes strict controls on its JTTF partners. Records for JTTF investigations are kept in an FBI field office. Local police who are assigned to a JTTF agree not to disclose sensitive information to non-JTTF members without the express permission of the FBI, and may be required to sign nondisclosure agreements by the FBI as well.[69] (In addition, there is a more detailed ban on discussions with the media unless approved by the FBI.) Local officers are sworn as federal marshals, making them subject to federal laws that prohibit the unauthorized disclosure of investigative information.

The restrictions imposed by the FBI are so demanding that it lays the initial proposition – that the JTTF is an exercise in information *sharing* – open to question. There is no sense in which information has been given to local authorities at all; the only local officials who handle JTTF information are those who have been deputized as federal employees, working on FBI files under FBI supervision. It might be more accurate to say that JTTFs extend the reach of the FBI by incorporating state and local officials into the FBI's own structure. From this point of view, the local police departments that balked at releasing their MOUs understood the spirit of the exercise exactly: They were not expected to exercise their own judgment about the release of JTTF information.

The arrangement has the effect of enlisting local police forces in a federally led security network while undercutting mechanisms traditionally used to maintain the accountability of local police forces. This was a particular concern for the Colorado ACLU, which, in early 2003, negotiated a settlement with Denver police following the revelation that its intelligence bureau had systematically monitored the legal activity of local protest groups. Weeks after the notorious "spy files" case was settled, a new question arose: Would local police assigned to the Denver JTTF be bound by restrictions on surveillance just negotiated with the ACLU?

Within months, the ACLU's question proved to be more than hypothetical. In November 2003, the *New York Times*, drawing on a leaked

FBI memorandum, reported that the agency appeared to have undertaken a "coordinated, nationwide effort" to monitor protest activity that enlisted local law enforcement officials participating in JTTFs.[70] The FBI's new emphasis on monitoring, which it said was aimed at deterring violent protests, was confirmed in another memorandum leaked to the *Times* in August 2004.[71] The influence of the nationwide program was evident in Colorado, where the FBI acknowledged that local police officers assigned to the Denver JTTF were interviewing activists about protests tied to the 2004 election.[72] City officials claimed that the ACLU's 2003 settlement did not apply to the JTTF,[73] and the ACLU's ability to determine precisely what local officers were doing was undercut by the terms of the city's agreement with the FBI.

Concern about oversight of the JTTFs was not limited to nongovernmental groups. In April 2005, Mayor Tom Potter of Portland, OR, announced that the city would withdraw from its partnership with the FBI. Mayor Potter said that his main reason was the FBI's refusal to provide the mayor with the same security clearance given to the two local police officers participating in the task force. In Portland, the mayor is also police commissioner, and Potter said that the FBI's refusal would undercut the local government's "oversight process."[74]

Another federal information-sharing initiative, the Joint Regional Information Exchange System (JRIES), also imposed restrictions on local officials. JRIES was created in 2002 by the Joint Intelligence Task Force, Combating Terrorism (JITF-CT), a unit of the Defense Intelligence Agency. The JITF was established following the 2000 attack on the USS Cole as an "all-source intelligence fusion center staffed, equipped, and directed to support an aggressive, long-term, worldwide campaign against terrorism."[75] After the 9/11 attacks, the JITF sought to create a domestic component to its information-gathering network. By 2003, JRIES included ten state and local law enforcement agencies and several federal defense and security agencies, all of whom agreed to share information relating to terrorist threats within the United States, including "strategic analysis" on threats and "pre-incident indicator data."[76] In 2004, lead responsibility for JRIES was moved to the Department of Homeland Security, which announced its intention to expand the network to include all fifty states and fifty major urban areas.[77]

As in the other cases, participation in JRIES is governed by a memorandum of understanding between the state or local agency and the lead federal agency. In 2003, major police forces such as the New York City and Chicago police departments refused to disclose their MOU; the Chicago police department argued that the agreement was federal property and that requests for the agreement should be sent to the federal government.[78] The Houston Police Department was more forthcoming, however, and released its 2003 agreement with the JITF. The agreement affirms that "to the greatest extent possible, there should be transparency between and among" members of the JRIES network. But JRIES members also promise that received information will be treated as "the property of the originating agency" and that requests for such information under state or local laws will be denied.[79]

This limitation on transparency is potentially troubling. Critics have already expressed concern that JRIES will provide the Department of Defense with a way of circumventing restrictions on the collection of domestic intelligence, and the MOU's conditions will complicate efforts to determine whether this new capacity is being abused. Other JRIES members have also been criticized for the misuse of network capabilities. One of the three founding members of JRIES, the California Anti-Terrorism Information Center (CATIC), is itself the hub of an information-sharing network of law enforcement agencies within California. In 2003, CATIC was reorganized following the revelation by the *Oakland Tribune* that it had spread information on the activity of nonviolent political groups to local police.[80]

The restrictions contained in the JRIES agreement are replicated in several other new information-sharing schemes. The Homeland Security Act of 2002 authorizes the Department of Homeland Security to develop a new policy for the distribution of "sensitive homeland security information" to state and local officials that also blocks the disclosure of shared information. The law stipulates that information sent to state and local governments remains under the control of the federal government, and that state or local open government laws will not apply to it. For added protection, the law anticipates that state and local officials will sign nondisclosure agreements before receiving information under the policy. New policies for the sharing of "critical infrastructure information" with state and local officials also include provisions to override state and local transparency laws.[81]

Intractable secrecy

Conventional wisdom tells us that the twentieth century was the age of strong states and large bureaucracies. Governments managed their own problems, largely without intensive interaction with neighboring governments; and they did this work through large departments or agencies over which they exercised total control. By the end of the twentieth century this mode of governance was dying. Many problems require now the combined efforts of agencies in many different jurisdictions. In a real sense, the administrative capability of one state – its organizational ability to diagnose and solve problems – is determined in large measure by the capabilities of departments or agencies in other sovereign states.

We had begun to shift from the age of bureaucracy to the age of networks. "Networks," said the noted analyst Manuel Castells in 1996, "are the fundamental stuff of which new organizations are and will be made."[82] (Similarly, Ronald Diebert and Janice Gross Stein suggest that the network will be "the dominant form of social organization in postindustrial society."[83]) Increasingly, Castells argues, work will be accomplished through "network enterprises" whose "system of means is constituted by the intersection of autonomous systems of goals" – in other words, by the collaboration of units that are independent and formally integrated in other organizational structures that may well have distinct priorities. The expansion of security networks – the new "security architecture," in Etzioni's terms – may be a harbinger of how governing structures will evolve in other areas of government, just as the emergence of large defense and police forces marked the advent of the age of bureaucracy a century earlier.

The threat to open government is straightforward. As networks become larger, and information flows among network members become deeper, the inventory of information held by any one agency at a particular point in time will change. That inventory of information will increase; but the proportion that has been received from agencies in other jurisdictions will also increase, and the number of agencies whose information is represented in that inventory will increase as well. We expect that agencies with a larger and more diverse inventory of information will make better decisions. But sometimes they will make mistakes, and when they do, we will want to know what information they had available when they made their decisions.

Unfortunately, conventional open government laws will do little to reveal what information was available to decision makers in a particular jurisdiction. The stock of information that was produced by an agency on its own might be subject to the usual test on disclosure, balancing the benefit and harm from release of information. But the increasing proportion of information that is received from other agencies will not be subject to this test. This shared information will be subjected to confidentiality rules; the agency that provided the information will continue to "own" – and therefore control – it. The public record (and perhaps even the archival record[84]) will have a large hole where the shared information once had been.

There might seem to be a simple solution to this problem: Have the resident of jurisdiction A (which received the information) simply ask jurisdiction B (which sent the information) to provide it directly. There are several reasons why this will not be an effective remedy. Jurisdiction A may be unwilling to reveal the source of its information, or may have received its information from so many sources that further searching is impractical. Or the citizen in jurisdiction A may have no right to the information from jurisdiction B. (A resident of New York cannot use Pennsylvania's public records law, and a resident of the United States cannot use the European Union's.) Or there may be no *effective* right to information. (A citizen of the United Kingdom who applies to the FBI for information will find that a complex request will require more than a year for a decision.[85]) Underlying all of this is a more fundamental question: Why should a citizen's capacity to hold his *own* government accountable hinge on the transparency rules adopted by *another* government?

There is an alternative approach, one that acknowledges the right of agencies within a network to make their own judgment about the release of shared information, or that (a variation on the theme) establishes effective procedures to ensure that intergovernmental information-sharing agreements conform to the spirit of domestic transparency laws. The ease with which this might be done should not be overestimated. As networks grow larger, the difficulty of coordinating practice on the disclosure of information by network members increases. Current practice – essentially a flat rule against disclosure of shared information – has the virtue of being easily applied.

Another difficulty is political. The challenge of renegotiating information-sharing rules also increases as the population of agencies within a network increases, and existing rules become entrenched in practice. Outsider agencies face the reality that the benefits of joining an established network are large, while the prospects of successfully persuading existing members to redefine the terms on which the network operates are very poor. This is the predicament that confronted the countries of Central and Eastern Europe, whose leaders saw the substantial benefits of joining NATO and the futility of attempting to engage NATO about the reasonableness of its information-sharing policy. The same predicament will be confronted by other states on the edges of emerging transnational and domestic security networks. Opaque networks tend to stay opaque.

7

THE CORPORATE VEIL

"The era of big government is over," President Bill Clinton told Americans in his 1996 State of the Union Address, promising a "smaller, less bureaucratic government in Washington."[1] This was both true and untrue, depending on how one thought about the question. The number of employees working within the federal bureaucracy had undoubtedly declined substantially during Clinton's first term as President. On the other hand, the level of government spending had not radically changed, nor had the catalogue of functions for which government was responsible been reduced. What had certainly changed was the Clinton administration's attitude toward the *means* by which government work was to be done. The volume of work that was being transferred to private contractors and nonprofit organizations was growing steadily.

Clinton's statement represented a liberal concession to the new realities of governance. Almost two decades earlier, rising conservative forces began to threaten the structure of government as it had developed in most advanced democracies in the preceding half-century. The conservative challenge was pointed: State-owned businesses were to be divested – or *privatized*, to use a phrase popularized by the *Economist* magazine. The power of regulatory agencies would be sharply reduced. Government agencies would retreat from the business of directly producing health, education, and other social services. Private enterprise, working in lightly controlled markets, would take up responsibility for producing these services instead.[2]

In the 1990s, many liberal policymakers attempted to absorb this conservative challenge by proposing a new way of thinking about government. Liberal purposes, they conceded, might not necessarily mean the expansion of bureaucracy. Governments had to be clever in finding other ways of achieving their goals, which might include the use of contractors, or the delegation of functions to nonprofit organizations, or the creation of new markets for the production of services. Americans called this "reinvented" government, in which policymakers retained the responsibility for "steering" the ship of state but were indifferent about the means by which the "rowing" was accomplished.[3] British activists called this a "third way" of thinking about the role of the state, with a point of view that could be described as "structural pluralism": bound neither to the monisms of bureaucracy or market, and pragmatic in the choice of methods for advancing the public interest.[4]

The result of this debate over the role of government – of conservative thrust and liberal parry – is, in most advanced democracies, a public sector whose structure has been fundamentally transformed. Large state-owned industries have been transferred to private hands. Major utilities – responsible for the provision of water, electric power, telecommunications, and other services – have been sold off. Private enterprise has entered areas that were once regarded as the core of the public sector.

In the United States, one company, Edison Schools, boasts that it operates so many elementary and secondary schools that it could be counted as one of the largest school systems in the United States. Around the world, the business of providing water and sewer systems is now dominated by three French and German firms – Ondeo, Veolia, and RWE Thames Water. A Danish firm, Group 4 Falck, operates a network of prisons and detention centers spanning four continents. An Australian business, Macquarie Infrastructure, has developed a lucrative business in building and operating toll highways and bridges around the world.[5] Britain's Labour government, once the main proponent of an expansive state sector, now has a policy of encouraging private businesses to build hospitals and schools on its behalf.

Even the defense sector – surely the most basic state function – has been laid open for business. It is estimated that the private military industry earned $100 billion in global revenue in 2003.[6] So many contractor employees were at work in occupied Iraq in 2004 – by some estimates, 20,000 or more – that analysts suggested it was the private military industry, and not the United Kingdom (with only 10,000 troops in the field), that should be counted as the second-largest contributor to the war effort.[7] Contractors engaged in combat in Iraq, took heavier casualties than some regular combat forces, and played a controversial role in collecting intelligence.[8]

Blurred boundaries

The transformation of the architecture of the public sector over the last two decades has caused confusion about the applicability of disclosure laws, most of which were drafted with the purpose of improving transparency within government agencies staffed by government employees. As work left government departments – to go to contractors, privatized utilities, and nonprofit organizations – the principle of access to government documents began to break down.

The simplest problem was that of gaining access to the contracts that governments signed when they decided to shift functions (the operation of a prison, for example) to a private operator. The terms of a prison contract are critically important: This single document defines the conditions under which prisoners will live, as well as the incentives that shape the behavior of their keepers. The contract can be very specific on these points. One prison contract between the state of Western Australia and Corrections Corporation of Australia, a subsidiary of the American Wackenhut Corrections Corporation, tied payment to twelve performance targets, including a maximum number of attempted suicides (twenty-five) or prisoner-on-prisoner assaults (thirty) each year, and imposed a flat $100,000 fine for each escape or death in custody from unnatural causes.[9]

In principle there is no reason why contracts such as these cannot be put in the public domain. Because a copy of the contract is held by a government agency, it is unambiguously a government record. In practice, however, many governments who began relying heavily on contractors throughout the 1990s also resisted demands for disclosure of contracts. Contractors pressured policymakers to keep the documents secret, to avoid disclosure of information that would have been valuable to competitors and other prospective clients; but governments also had their own reasons to keep contracts secret – for example, to obscure evidence that might compromise their claims about the success of highly controversial privatization programs.

In Australia – the first country after the United States to actively pursue a program of prison privatization – details about contracts were often hidden from public view. (The state of Western Australia's decision to publish its contract with the Corrections Corporation of Australia on the internet was an exception – a "world first," according to its officials.[10]) In the state of Queensland, officials promised the Corrections Corporation of Australia that they would not disclose prison contract documents without its consent; while CCA and government officials publicly promoted the success of the privatization effort, requests for contract information needed to evaluate the project were rebuffed. ("As the contract is still in existence," one researcher was told, "it can be assumed that Borallon [one of the state's privately run prisons] is meeting the standards required."[11]) In the state of Victoria, which in the late 1990s held a larger proportion of its convict population in privately run prisons than any other jurisdiction in the world,[12] officials steadfastly refused to release contract details until forced to do so by the courts.[13] One result was that prisoners and their advocates did not know what requirements had been imposed on prison managers, and could not say whether those conditions were being met.[14] The stakes were not inconsequential: As editorialists noted, eleven prisoners died within Victoria's private prisons while the government fought against disclosure of its contracts.[15]

Other governments have wrestled over the release of contract documents for major privatization projects. Efforts to assess a new privately operated toll highway in the Canadian province of Ontario were complicated by the government's refusal to disclose the tolling contract.[16] In another case – a complex project in which the consulting firm Accenture was hired to overhaul Ontario's social services system – disclosure of the contract was successfully blocked on the grounds that the relationship was so innovative in its design that the contract details constituted a valuable form of intellectual property.[17] In Scotland, the advent of a new Freedom of Information Act was marked by controversy over the government's refusal to release a contract with a private security firm that had mistakenly released several prisoners in its custody.[18] In South Africa, the Johannesburg Water Authority resisted the release of documents relating to a contract under which a consortium led by the French firm Suez undertook to manage the municipal water system.[19]

The struggle over contract documents already in the hands of government officials is relatively simple when compared to the contest over documents held by contractors alone. When documents are held by government officials and a disclosure law is in place, the right of appeal to a court or ombudsman is recognized, and claims of commercial confidentiality can be scrutinized and perhaps rejected. When documents are held only by contractors, the law is less helpful. Only a small number of disclosure laws establish a right to obtain documents created by a contractor while doing work for a government agency, if the documents remain only in the contractor's hands.[20] (Governments could also draft contracts to confirm public right of access to contractor files, but usually do not.) More often, there is no right to contractor records at all. Added to this is a strong resistance to the idea of transparency on the part of contractors themselves. "As long as water is coming out of the tap," one water company executive told an international conference in 2000, "the public has no right to any information as to how it got there."[21]

This creates the potential for inconsistencies in accountability, illustrated brutally by the scandal over abuse of prisoners in Iraq. Contractors were deeply implicated in the controversy over prisoner abuses. In May 2004 the *Houston Chronicle* – relying on documents obtained through the Freedom of Information Act – reported that the U.S. Army had investigated almost thirty cases of alleged abuse by contractors over the preceding year.[22] A series of government reports also acknowledged the role played by contractors, sometimes in graphic detail. "The first documented incident of abuse with dogs occurred on 24 November 2003," the Fay-Jones report said:

> MA1 Kimbro went to the top floor of Tier 1B, rather than the MI Hold area of Tier 1A. As he and his dog approached a cell door, he heard yelling and screaming and his dog became agitated. Inside the cell were CIVILIAN-11 (CACI contract interrogator), a second unidentified male in civilian clothes who appeared to be an interrogator and CIVILIAN-16 (female contract interpreter), all of whom were yelling at a detainee squatting in the back right corner. MA1 Kimbro's dog was barking a lot with all the yelling and commotion. The dog lunged and MA1 Kimbro struggled to regain control of it. At that point, one of the men said words to the effect "You see that dog there, if you don't tell me what I want to know, I'm gonna get that dog on you!"[23]

The Taguba report concluded that four individuals were "directly or indirectly responsible" for abuses at Abu Ghraib: Two were government employees, and two were contractor employees.[24] There was a neat symmetry in this finding of fault, but no comparable symmetry in terms of accountability. In the months following the Abu Ghraib revelations, public interest groups pressed federal agencies to provide documents that detailed the role that government employees had played in the abuses. The American Civil Liberties Union played a key role in pushing for disclosure, aided by a court decision that chastised the Defense Department for forgetting that FOIA "was intended to provide a means of accountability, to allow Americans to know what their government is doing."[25] At the same time, CACI denied that its employees had participated in abuses at Abu Ghraib, and claimed that its training had met all military requirements.[26] FOIA could do nothing to check the veracity of CACI's claims – to determine what training or direction it had provided to its employees, or how thoroughly it had investigated abuse allegations. CACI was not subject to the law.

Coincidentally, Abu Ghraib had been selected for use as the main American prison in Iraq by another contractor, the Management and Training Corporation, a private prison operator based in Utah. Shortly before, the Corporation had been sharply criticized for serious faults in a New Mexico prison that led to the death of an inmate.[27] The inmate's family later complained about their inability to obtain records about the prison's operations at the time of the suicide. ("When asked what the company's policy is regarding the release of information regarding an inmate's death," the *Albuquerque Journal* reported, a company spokesman "said he was not exactly sure."[28]) The eventual settlement of the family's suit contained a confidentiality clause that restricted discussion of the case.[29] New Mexico, with a larger proportion of its prisoners in private facilities than any other state, illustrated the inconsistency of treatment within the restructured public service: In 2003, roughly half of its inmates were held in public prisons that were subject to the state's disclosure law, while the remainder were held in private prisons that were not.[30] Some private prisons in the state even questioned their obligation to disclose the identity of inmates in their facilities.[31]

The conflict in Iraq heightened awareness of questions about the accountability of U.S. military contractors more generally. The exclusion of contractors from the Freedom of Information Act made a close study of their work difficult, said Peter Singer, author of *Corporate Warriors*, in 2003.[32] Nevertheless, Singer argues, three difficulties in military contracting are evident: minimal oversight of contractors by government personnel; contracts that are not drafted to provide information needed for official oversight; and disincentives to enforcement of contract terms that arise because of bureaucratic dependence on the contractor.[33]

In fact, the problem of inadequate oversight pervades every part of the federal bureaucracy. The "presumption of regularity," as Daniel Guttman calls it – the presumption that officials exercise continuing control over their contractors – cannot be sustained in practice.[34] A 2000 report found that the Defense Department had cut its contract oversight staff by half over the preceding decade; by 2004, the department's oversight capacity had deteriorated so far that it was reduced to hiring contractors to monitor other contractors.[35] (Indeed, a 2005 investigation by the Government Accountability Office found that Defence Department officials had "effectively abdicated" their responsibility to oversee CACI's interrogation contract at Abu Ghraib.[36]) Whistleblowing employees within contractor firms have revealed many abuses by those firms in Iraq,[37] but the risk of punishment means that whistleblowers cannot be relied upon to do the monitoring work that ought to be shouldered by bureaucratic overseers. Whistleblowers who revealed that employees of Dyncorp, a U.S. military contractor in Bosnia, had been involved in sex crimes and illegal arms trading were subsequently fired by the firm: In one case a court found Dyncorp's subsequent explanation for the dismissals "completely unbelievable."[38]

The reshaping of the public sector is also producing situations where there is no pretense of contract monitoring at all, because there is no contractual connection between the private actor and the government of the jurisdiction in which it operates. In 1995, neighbors of a prison operated by Corrections Corporation of America in Mason, TN, were alarmed by a riot by 100 inmates that caused $2 million in damage and required response by state law enforcement officers. A state legislator complained about CCA's slowness in providing information about the riot, but the state had no contractual relationship with the prison: The riot had broken out among prisoners held by CCA for the state of North Carolina.[39] In Ohio three years later, state legislators also complained that they were "stonewalled" by CCA following a mass escape from its new prison in Youngstown. The legislators' ability to exercise oversight was again compromised by the lack of a contractual connection: The escapees had been transported to Youngstown by the District of Columbia.[40]

A comparable difficulty arises when governments retreat entirely from service production, either directly or through contractors, and instead encourage citizens to consume services from independent private actors. One example is the growing popularity of educational reforms that allow parents to send their children to private schools that may be approved by government authorities but are not subject to state law.[41] It is conceivable that a school system could include three types of schools, each doing similar work but with a distinct legal status: publicly operated schools subject to disclosure rules; contract-run schools whose obligations are ambiguous; and private schools not subject to disclosure rules at all. Comparable reforms in health and welfare services could produce the same result.

The privatization of utilities over the past two decades has also posed a challenge to transparency. The practice of selling off government-run utilities has been a worldwide phenomenon, popular in both the developed and developing worlds, and often encouraged – over strong local protests – by international institutions such as the World Bank and the International Monetary Fund. Where governments had already adopted disclosure laws, newly restructured utilities did their best to escape them. In the United Kingdom, an array of newly privatized utilities – in electricity, water, rail, and telecommunications – persuaded the Blair government to abandon its early proposal that they should be covered by the new Freedom of Information Act, arguing that they would otherwise be at a competitive disadvantage to other firms entering the power market.[42] In Canada, components of Ontario's newly restructured electric system – including the operator of its extensive nuclear facilities – also lobbied successfully to be removed from the province's disclosure law, arguing that the requirements would undermine their competitive position.[43] (The disclosure law had embroiled the provincial utility in controversy several times: In 1990, an internal document considered how brownouts might be an effective method for "selling need" for additional generating capacity.[44]) South Africa's major utilities, Eskom and Telkom, sought to escape from the country's disclosure law as well. In Australia, legal analysts could not agree on the proper treatment of the nation's telecommunications company, Telstra, a candidate for privatization: Some saw the risk of competitive disadvantage, while others worried about the lack of other mechanisms for ensuring transparency in the deregulated industry.[45]

The Australian analysts had spotted the central issue. By selling their utilities, many countries appear to be following the example of the United States, where private ownership of utilities is the norm. However, the comparison is imperfect: Many foreign policymakers have not, at the same time, adopted the American approach to *regulation* of private utilities – which, as some observers have pointed out, involves a high level of transparency. "In the U.S.," say Greg Palast, Jerrold Oppenheim, and Theo McGregor, "the right to information from a monopoly utility is virtually without bounds."[46] A range of stakeholders – competitors, unions, major consumers – aggressively exercise this power to obtain information in an effort to check utilities' profit seeking. The American approach to regulation, Palast and his colleagues argue, creates a forum in which the limited oversight capacity of the regulator is complemented by the much more extensive capacity of these other groups. By contrast, overseas regulators negotiated secretly with utilities and allowed them to avoid public disclosure of information on the grounds of commercial confidentiality. The twin pathologies of bureaucracy – paternalism and a preference for quiet accommodation – tainted efforts at regulation.

Many notorious cases of regulatory failure have been blamed on the failure to adopt regulatory processes that allow adequate transparency. British consumers of water, gas, and electric services have paid a premium because of regulators' inability to adequately scrutinize utilities' financial plans and monitor their actual behavior. Failed efforts to privatize Brazilian and Indian electric systems and Bolivian water systems – three cases routinely invoked by opponents of privatization – are more precisely described as failed efforts at *regulation* of privatized entities, rooted in the unwillingness of regulators to disclose the calculations underlying the arrangements made with private utilities.[47]

(Attempts to introduce market mechanisms as an alternative method of disciplining utilities also proved unsuccessful. In California, the Enron Corporation devised a broad range of schemes designed to hide its internal efforts to manipulate the deregulated electricity market. Enron's games were given distinct nicknames – Death Star, Fat Boy, Perpetual Loop, Black Widow, Red Congo – but shared the common goal of secretly abusing market rules.[48] When the California market finally collapsed in 2001, state policymakers strengthened their regulatory capacities, and Enron came under intense scrutiny. In a belated but nonetheless extraordinary effort to promote transparency, the Federal Energy Regulatory Commission created an online database of one million internal e-mails written by Enron employees over the previous three years. Some Enron employees complained, with justification, that FERC's disclosure had compromised their personal privacy. One e-mail, with author and recipient identified, asked: "So . . . you were looking for a one night stand after all?"[49])

Even in the United States, however, enthusiasm for vigorous public sector regulation waned over the quarter-century. Government sought less burdensome ways of achieving regulatory objectives, often passing regulatory functions to quasi-governmental or non-governmental organizations within which industry representatives could formulate and enforce regulatory standards. This sort of self-regulation was not novel: Some prominent self-regulatory organizations – such as the Joint Commission on Accreditation of Healthcare Organizations and the New York Stock Exchange – have operated for decades. Recently, however, this corporatist model of self-regulation has been extended into other sectors, as a way of lowering the regulatory profile of government itself. For example, authority for safety within nuclear plants is shouldered by a private regulatory bureaucracy, the Institute for Nuclear Power Operations, while authority for regulating the internet has been passed from the U.S. Department of Commerce to the Internet Corporation for Assigned Names and Numbers, set up as a nonprofit corporation under California law.[50] Neither the old nor the new self-regulatory organizations were subject to federal or state disclosure laws.

Other countries also adopted similar industry-run structures for delivering public services. Canada transferred national air traffic control functions from a government department to an industry-led nonprofit corporation, NavCanada, which operated outside Canada's Access to Information Act. (Because Canadian and U.S. air traffic is so tightly intermingled, this meant that many U.S. airline passengers, flying on what they imagine are purely domestic flights, are being directed by a foreign and private air traffic control service.) The United Kingdom adopted a similar model for its air traffic control service and for Network Rail, the organization that now oversees the country's expansive rail system; neither is covered by the UK's Freedom of Information Act. Other countries, including the United States itself, have also contemplated using nonprofit structures to deliver air traffic control and other transport services.

A conceptual muddle

The process of restructuring the public sectors of the advanced democracies is still underway. When it is done, the public sector will look radically different than it did twenty or thirty years ago. Indeed, it may be difficult to speak intelligently about a "public sector" at all. Functions that traditionally have been performed by government employees working within government agencies will be spread across a heterogeneous mix of new organizations. Some will still look like traditional government departments; but others will be nonprofit organizations, or for-profit enterprises, or partnerships of all three of these forms. There may be no tight correlation of functions and organizational forms: Different institutions may work beside each other within one jurisdiction, doing essentially the same work; or different countries may choose different structures for doing the same work. This is the inevitable result of the pragmatism that is characteristic of new thinking about the delivery of services to the public.

This process of restructuring has already posed a substantial threat to existing disclosure laws, and this threat will grow in coming years. The threat arises because of a weakness in our traditional thinking about governmental openness. Most disclosure laws build on a classical liberal conception of the social and political world, which draws a sharp distinction between public and private spheres of activity, and which regards one of the main aims of political action as being the defense of the private sphere from incursions by the public sphere.[51] Disclosure laws typically articulate the distinction by establishing rights to information held by organizations in the public sphere. Indeed, these laws are often justified as a tool for maintaining a sharp distinction of public and private spheres by preventing an overreach of governmental power. This is particularly true in the United States, where James Madison's warning – "A people who mean to be their own governors, must arm themselves with the power which knowledge gives" – is routinely invoked in calls for stronger disclosure laws.

Because disclosure laws are built on the premise that the aim is to curb abuses of *governmental* power, the question for legislative draftsmen is to determine where the boundaries of government lie. Some disclosure laws draw the border tightly, including only departments and agencies at the heart of government. Others may draw the border more expansively – perhaps including organizations created by government, owned by government, primarily funded by government is, effectively controlled by government agencies, or performing functions traditionally undertaken by government agencies.[52] The language of these more expansive approaches varies, but the theme is consistent: If a right to documents is to be acknowledged, the organization holding the documents must have a structure or mandate that makes it appear governmental.

In all, these approaches to disclosure law are restrictive. At best – but still rarely – they include some government contractors and other organizations that closely resemble conventional government agencies while excluding (for example) privatized utilities or self-regulatory organizations. This narrow approach creates inconsistencies. Why is it, as one American commentator has recently asked, that a journalist can review immigration records at the federal government's Krome Avenue Processing Center in Miami, but not at its contractor-run El Centro Detention Center in El Centro, CA?[53] Why should a parent's ability to obtain information about admission standards at an elite school – the subject of Sumalee Limpa-ovart's complaint under Thailand's Official Information Act (see Chapter 1) – evaporate when the school is privately owned?[54]

These inconsistencies are amplified across jurisdictions. Why do residents of Ohio have the right to information from their local nonprofit fire company, while residents of the neighboring states of Pennsylvania or West Virginia do not?[55] Why is a British doctor in private practice, providing medical care that is paid for with government money, subject to disclosure requirements while an American doctor in a similar situation is not? Why do hemophiliacs who are dependent on New Zealand's national blood service, which is set up as a government-owned corporation, have a statutory right to information about its operations, while Canadian hemophiliacs have no comparable right to information from their national blood service, which is set up with government approval as an autonomous charitable corporation? Some variation in policy across jurisdictions is, of course, inevitable – but this variation is also symptomatic of an underlying intellectual predicament. As the old public sector has broken up, policymakers around the world are unable to articulate a clear explanation of the standards that should be used to determine when an organization must be subject to disclosure rules.

Preventing harm to basic rights

Of all the new disclosure laws adopted in the last two decades, there is only one – the South African Promotion of Access to Information Act – that does not rely on the liberal dichotomization of public and private spheres. The logic of the South African law unfolds differently, providing (as a matter of law, if not practice – there have been difficulties in achieving compliance[56]) a much broader right to information.

In July 1993, South Africa's apartheid government and the main opposition force, the African National Congress, reached agreement on a plan for transition to majority rule. In the interim constitution that governed South Africa for two years after free elections in 1994, access to government information was recognized as a fundamental right. The constitutional assembly that was charged with drafting a permanent constitution was also directed to ensure that the new text made provision for "freedom of information so that there can be accountable administration at all levels of government."[57] These provisions were not unusual; several other countries that were moving to democratic rule at that time also recognized a constitutional right to government information. The 1994 provision, like others, relied on the classical separation of public and private sectors.

However, South Africa soon went further. Activists pressured the constitutional assembly to recognize a right to information held by *nongovernmental* organizations as well. The country's main labor organization, the Congress of South African Trade Unions, made the extension of information rights one of their foremost demands, arguing that the "veil of secrecy" that had covered the private sector during the apartheid years had "enormously prejudiced' the human rights of workers and consumers.[58] The appeal resonated with influential members of the African National Congress, who were "acutely aware of the immense wealth and power of both South African corporations and transnational companies."[59] The new constitution adopted in 1996 included in its Bill of Rights the now-familiar assurance of a right to government documents – and the added promise of a right to any information held by another person or organization "that is required for the exercise or protection of any rights."[60] This caused alarm in the business community, and the first draft of legislation required to implement the guarantee retreated from the language of the constitution, providing only a limited right of access to *personal* information in private hands, justified as a safeguard for privacy rights. Critics of the proposed bill successfully argued that it would not survive a constitutional challenge, and the final draft of the law – the Promotion of Access to Information Act (PAIA), adopted in 2000 – restored the constitutional language.[61]

The PAIA was not wholly inattentive to differences between the public and private sphere. The right to request information from private bodies required an explanation of need, while no such explanation was required when information was sought from public bodies. Once this hurdle was overcome, however, the requirements imposed on public and private organizations were substantially the same: The law specified comparable procedures for handling requests and described the limits of the right – the grounds on which information might be withheld – in roughly equivalent terms.

Early cases under the PAIA gave an intimation of its potential usefulness. The threat of litigation under the law prompted many major South African businesses, including a subsidiary of the powerful conglomerate Anglo American, to disclose their contributions to the country's major political parties. A public interest group claimed that the information was needed so that citizens could exercise their voting rights on an informed basis. In other cases, minority shareholders in privately held companies succeeded in obtaining information about corporate practices. In one of these cases, the documents revealed that a firm's controlling shareholders had manipulated government rules designed to encourage black entrepreneurship. The prospect of litigation also prompted a major South African bank to disclose its reasons for denying a mortgage application.[62]

By the standards of advanced democracies, the *kind* of information being disclosed in these cases was not surprising, but certainly the *process* by which it was being disclosed was distinctive. In countries such as the United States, for example, there are also rules about the disclosure of information about political contributions, the conduct of majority shareholders, or bank lending practices.

However, these rules are contained in discrete statutes (the Federal Election Campaign Act, state corporation laws, or the Equal Credit Opportunity Act), each crafted through a legislative struggle aimed at resolving a discrete policy problem. South African law, by contrast, articulates a general principle that courts then apply in particular contexts, perhaps spurring later legislative action to elaborate rules in that context. Furthermore, the application of the principle is not affected by "structural formalisms"[63] – such as the extent to which an organization is connected to or controlled by a government agency.

The potential reach of the South African law may be dictated by the breadth with which courts are prepared to interpret the phrase "required for the exercise or protection of any rights." If "any right" is interpreted narrowly, to include only those rights recognized under statutory or common law, then disclosure obligations might be no more broad than those already recognized under discovery rules for civil suits in some Western countries.[64] On the other hand, the language could be interpreted to include all of the rights articulated in the national constitution's Bill of Rights, which is broadly drafted and includes rights of access to housing, healthcare, food, and water; a right to a safe and protected environment; and a right to fair labor practices. The South African Bill of Rights is clearly more expansive than the Bill of Rights in the American Constitution, but its language is not idiosyncratic. It enumerates the same basic rights contained in many contemporary declarations, such as the Universal Declaration of Human Rights. When harnessed to this array of entitlements, the right to access privately held information could itself be expansive.[65]

Conservatives in the established democracies will balk at the notion of giving constitutional status to the whole range of human rights, but it can be argued that the logic of the South African PAIA is already followed, imperfectly, even in these countries. A right of access to information held by nongovernmental organizations is recognized when the information is needed to protect one of the fundamental interests typically described as basic human rights. For example, it is common in advanced democracies to impose an obligation on health professionals in private practice to disclose information about a serious danger of violence by one person against another.[66] Commercial enterprises have an obligation to provide communities with information about the release of toxic chemicals by their facilities.[67]

Private employers have an obligation to provide their workers with information about hazardous materials used in the workplace, and manufacturers have an obligation to provide information to consumers about hazards posed by defective products.[68] Individuals in private firms may also be permitted to disclose privately held confidential information if it would reveal a threat to health or safety.[69] Although all of these disclosure rules have evolved in an ad hoc fashion, they share a common logic: The veil that ordinarily surrounds the private sector is lifted to protect a fundamental interest – namely, the right to personal security.[70]

Policymakers have imposed disclosure requirements on private actors to protect other basic rights as well. In almost all OECD countries, a right of access to personal information held by nongovernmental organizations is recognized, as a way of protecting each citizen's right to privacy. In the United States, disclosure requirements have been imposed on many private schools, out of an appreciation of the critical importance of education to the development of human capacities.[71] Students and parents have a right to their own educational records, and under the Student Right To Know and Campus Security Act, a right to information about a broad range of operational matters, including an institution's fee policies, graduation rates, accreditation, and policing practices.[72]

Individuals also have a right to economic security that may lead to the establishment of disclosure requirements for the private sector. Many jurisdictions require businesses to disclose information about plans for plant closings or mass layoffs.[73] Some jurisdictions create a right of access to records pertaining to disciplinary hearings undertaken by private firms.[74] The ability to obtain work and borrow money is also protected by obligations imposed on businesses to disclose information they have collected about the character or health of applicants for employment or credit.[75]

It is sometimes argued that access provisions such as these are only specific applications of a very narrow principle: that individuals should have a right of access to personal information held by public or private organizations, because individuals have a property right in this information – that is, they *own* it – and consequently should be entitled to control its use.[76] However, this explanation does not fit the realities. In many instances, disclosure laws compel the release of information that is not "personal" at all. The information that is accessible under the United States' Student Right To Know and Campus Security Act, describing accreditation and graduation rates, is not personal data. Similarly, much of the information that would be disclosed under many of the "bills of rights" that have been proposed for consumers of health services in the United States – such as information about internal procedures for making treatment decisions, the handling of grievances, and physician qualifications and compensation – is not personal information either. However, it *is* information that relates directly to a fundamental citizen interest, either in good health or education, and this is the factor that drives pressure for disclosure.

The right of access to information is often presented by advocates of transparency as being itself one of the basic human rights.[77] This is not a universally accepted point of view. Furthermore, it is different than the logic proposed here. The line of reasoning pursued in the South African PAIA, and that implicitly drives policy in other countries, regards access to information as a critical tool in protecting those basic interests that are typically described as fundamental human rights – such as the interests in physical security and economic security. The right to information is, therefore, a derivative right: It arises as a natural consequence of our commitment to a range of basic human rights. Although it is a corollary, it may nonetheless be critically important as a tool for ensuring that basic interests are protected.[78]

Take, for example, the question of access to information held by the operator of a privately run prison – perhaps the Diamondback Correctional Facility in Watonga, OK, a CCA prison that in 2004 held over 1,000 prisoners under a contract with the Arizona Department of Corrections, and another 800 prisoners under a contract with the Hawaii Department of Public Safety, but had no contract with the State of Oklahoma itself.[79]

In principle, several different groups could make a legitimate demand for information about the Diamondback facility. Advocates for the prisoners had a right to information held by CCA about internal conditions in the prison, as well as information about disciplinary procedures; these informational claims could be grounded in the basic rights to security and fair treatment, which persist even for prisoners. The citizens of Arizona and Hawaii also had a claim to this information, and to information about work and educational opportunities provided by CCA, so they could exercise their right to participate intelligently in political debate about the wisdom of their states' correctional policies. The 5,000 residents of Watonga, OK, had a right to personal security that could be jeopardized by riots or escapes at the prison, and that entitled them to information about the potential risk, including data about the number and risk profile of inmates, the number and qualifications of staff, and emergency response procedures.[80] Other residents of Oklahoma also had a right to information about internal conditions in the prison, so that they could make an informed judgment about the wisdom of a state policy that allowed the importation of prisoners from other jurisdictions.[81]

In short, there were many groups that could make a reasonable claim to information held by CCA, so they could ensure that an array of basic rights were adequately protected. Unfortunately, existing disclosure law did not follow this logic. The Diamondback prison was not affected at all by Oklahoma's disclosure law, as it was not tied to the state corrections department by a contract. Although CCA had an agreement with the state of Arizona, Arizona's state disclosure law does not recognize a right to information held by contractors. By contrast, Hawaii's disclosure law *might* recognize a right to contractor information, but only if the documents could be shown to be "government records" – a phrase not yet defined by Hawaiian courts. Furthermore, a Hawaiian court would have to be persuaded that the requested documents were *Hawaiian* government records; Oklahomans could not use Hawaiian law to obtain information about Arizonan prisoners in the nearby Diamondback prison.[82] This was the predicament created by reliance on the traditional approach to information rights.

Of the claims that might be made against the Diamondback prison, the demand for information needed to make an informed assessment about the wisdom of prison contracting (or interstate prison contracting) likely seems weakest. This is one of the paradoxes of contemporary attitudes toward disclosure of information. Among specialists who study human rights it is common to make a distinction between two "generations" of rights – the first including basic civil and political rights, and the second including economic, social, and cultural rights.[83] Older documents such as the American Bill of Rights emphasize the first generation of rights, and many critics argue that these rights are more important than second generation rights, which include matters of economic security.[84] It could be argued, however, that this view is reversed when we begin to contemplate the question of imposing transparency obligations on nongovernmental actors. We readily agree that it is necessary to impose disclosure obligations on corporations to protect the economic interests of shareholders, employees, and consumers; the proposition that disclosure obligations might also be justified so that citizens are able to exercise political rights – for example, to allow informed decisions about the wisdom of prison contracting – seems more problematic.

There is, nevertheless, a strong argument in favor of recognizing a right to information held by private organizations that is tied to fundamental political rights. Some tasks – such as the counting of votes, the education of children, or the handling of prisoners – are clearly central to civic life; furthermore, there is rarely consensus on the best way of handling these tasks. Decisions about educational or correctional policy – including the decision to delegate to a private body – may be made despite substantial disagreement and uncertainty about the likely impact of those decisions. Communities need information about the *actual* effect of their decisions in order to improve future decisions and build consensus on community goals. Organizations that perform those functions should not be permitted to maintain informational monopolies that compromise the ability of communities to deliberate effectively about critical policies.[85]

The realities of reform

Principle is one thing, and practice is another. The South African PAIA might articulate a sensible way of thinking about transparency in the private sector, but the probability that any other nation will adopt comparable legislation is negligible. The PAIA is the product of very unusual circumstances – the accession to power of a well-organized popular resistance movement, dominated by a left-wing political philosophy, strongly supported by a mass labor movement, and determined to undercut a white elite that controlled both politics and commerce. These were the conditions that led to the adoption of a provision in the 1996 constitution that assured a right of access to information in private hands; and even under these conditions, the new African National Congress government soon began to reverse course, at first proposing legislation that substantially restricted that right.

We know that any attempt to introduce comparable legislation in an established democracy would be doomed to failure. The essential elements for such a change – a broad suspicion of the private sector, a dominant popular movement, an opportunity for quick and radical change in policy – are not present. On the contrary, the mere contemplation of such a policy would trigger a well-organized and broad-based lobby by businesses and other organizations who would be subject to the law. It would be regarded as an unwarranted attack on the integrity of the private sector. Businesses would also argue – with some justification – that a push to entrench a *general* principle of access ignores the *specific* mechanisms that have evolved to encourage transparency in particular sectors, such as reporting requirements imposed by securities exchanges for publicly traded corporations, or imposed by tax authorities for charitable organizations. (A 1995 proposal to extend the Australian Freedom of Information Act to the private sector was rebuffed for this reason.[86])

In the United States, the difficulties that would beset an attempt to establish a general right to information are illustrated by the prolonged failure to establish a more limited right to personal information held by private organizations. By the turn of the century, many OECD countries had adopted privacy laws (also known as data protection laws) that control the use of personal information in the private sector, and include a right to access personal information held by nongovernmental organizations. The United States, by contrast, has faced intense resistance from business leaders to the adoption of a comprehensive privacy law. As a result, privacy advocates have been compelled to fight a series of smaller battles for legislation on the handling of specific types of personal data held in certain sectors – such as credit, educational, or health information.[87] Even in these smaller battles, privacy advocates have faced fierce resistance from industry lobbies.[88]

This is the future confronting transparency advocates. It is practically impossible to do to the private sector what most democracies have in the past done to their public sectors – that is, impose a general statutory scheme providing for access to information. The fragmentation of the public sector has had the effect of breaking up the old coalition that could once be relied upon to push for stronger transparency rules. It may be true that businesses often resist the disclosure of information they have provided to government agencies; but it is also true that businesses are the dominant users of disclosure laws in many countries.[89] So long as government had an expansive role in regulation and provision of services, businesses had an interest in assuring their own ability to access government information quickly. The commonality may not have been appreciated, but General Motors and Ralph Nader had a shared interest in ensuring that the United States government was bound by disclosure rules.

The transfer of public functions to nongovernmental organizations will break up this commonality of interest – and put in its place new conflicts between citizens and the new private providers of public services. If the principle articulated in the South African law is to be carried forward in other countries, it will be done incrementally, through a succession of battles to establish information rights for specific types of information or for specific sets of organizations. The work of mobilizing coalitions to establish information rights will be difficult. The general principle at stake – access to information to protect fundamental rights – will often be obscured by the details of substantive policy in a particular area. Furthermore these new coalitions will often face well-organized and better-funded industry resistance.

8

REMOTE CONTROL

The restructuring of public services over the past two decades reminds us that power is fluid: It flows easily from one place to another. For the preceding thirty years, the main preoccupation of legislators and nongovernmental organizations had been finding ways of maintaining control over growing national bureaucracies. A number of devices – including disclosure laws that allowed citizens to share in the task of oversight – were invented to provide a check on bureaucratic power. But just at the moment when these checks had been established – and in part, *because* these checks had been established – the locus of power began to change. Authority flowed from public bureaucracies to purportedly private actors, whose work began to provoke, in some quarters, the same complaints about abuse and opacity that had once been lodged against the bureaucracy itself.

This is not the only sense in which power has diffused away from the traditional structures of governance. Increasingly, decisions over a broad swath of national policies are influenced by decisions taken within supranational institutions – new structures for the negotiation and enforcement of multilateral agreements on matters once resolved by national or subnational governments alone. Britain's "metric martyrs" – storekeepers arrested for selling produce by imperial weight rather than by the metric weight required by the European Union – were contending with the influence of new supranational institutions.[1] So, too, were U.S. environmentalists who protested the weakening of American "dolphin safe" labeling rules for imported tuna – which, if unchanged, were likely to be challenged by the Mexican government through the World Trade Organization's dispute settlement system;[2] the Ugandan activists concerned about the economic and social risks created by the Bujagali hydroelectric project promoted by the World Bank;[3] and the Argentine policy makers pressured by the International Monetary Fund to grant rate increases to troubled utilities that had been sold to European multinationals in the 1990s.[4]

In cases such as these it was common to complain that critical decisions were being made by remote control – and the locus of decision making often was remote, in the geographical sense: in Brussels rather than in London; in Geneva rather than in Washington; or in Washington rather than in Kampala or Buenos Aires. But the sense of remoteness was aggravated by the secretiveness with which decisions were being made in Brussels, Geneva, or Washington, and complaints about opacity often undergirded challenges to the legitimacy of decisions made in supranational forums. The critics had a point. Activists were contending against another durable barrier to transparency in government – the ethos of diplomatic confidentiality, which has traditionally dictated that governments should be allowed to conduct their relations with other states in strict privacy.

That there is a long-established norm of diplomatic confidentiality is beyond dispute. A rule of complete secrecy was one of the main characteristics of the system of diplomacy constructed to manage relations among European states after the Renaissance;[5] and J. H. H. Weiler observes that the "ethos of confidentiality" continues to be a "hallmark" of modern diplomacy.[6] It is "longstanding custom and accepted practice in international relations," the U.S. Justice Department told a federal court in 1999, "to treat as confidential and not subject to public disclosure information and documents exchanged between governments and their officials."[7] For many years, executive prerogatives in the field of diplomacy were so fiercely protected that they were said to have produced systems of "bifurcated" government – with one part dealing with domestic policy and subject to strict rules for popular control, and another part dealing with foreign policy and largely exempt from those rules.[8]

The ethos of diplomatic confidentiality is typically defended on realist grounds. To realists, the ability of diplomats to resolve disputes hinges on their ability to manage the number of parties to the conflict.[9] More open discussion of interstate conflicts might also increase pressure on government leaders to articulate basic principles or emphasize doctrinal differences, complicating the process of conflict resolution.[10] (Hans Morgenthau famously warned against the "vice of publicity" in diplomacy, observing that "it takes only common sense derived from daily experience to realize that it is impossible to negotiate in public on anything in which parties other than the negotiators are interested."[11]) Realists also suggested that the mass public was too shortsighted and ill informed to make sound decisions on foreign policy.[12] Furthermore, the costs of poor decision making in the field of international relations could be extraordinary, bearing as they traditionally did on matters of war and peace. The institutions and conventions of diplomacy emerged at a time when the state system was fragile and "the risk of resort to force of arms was inevitably and always present."[13]

Supranational institutions, as products of diplomacy, are imbued with this deeply rooted ethos of confidentiality. And yet the expanding role of such organizations has seemed, to many observers, to create new reasons for challenging the ethos. In many cases, the disputes being resolved through intergovernmental processes do not relate directly to the stability of the state system. On the contrary, they address problems of economic organization or social welfare that might otherwise have been addressed under the more liberal rules on popular participation that govern the "domestic" half of our bifurcated governments. The relocation of these responsibilities into the sphere of intergovernmental relations – the blurring of the line between domestic and foreign affairs – has consequently produced strong challenges to the restrictions on transparency and participation that have traditionally prevailed in that sphere.

Many supranational institutions have attempted to grapple with these challenges over the past two decades. Some have claimed a radical change in practice. The realities, however, are more complex. Many institutions have confronted crises of legitimacy, but their reactions have been varied and usually limited. Only one supranational institution – the European Union – has acknowledged a *right* to information; new policies adopted by other institutions are much more restrictive. In a sense, the shift of power to supranational institutions has created a predicament much like that created by the shift of power to private actors within national borders: The struggle for openness has broken into a series of smaller and often arcane battles against a broader mix of institutional targets.

Eurocrats

Policy governing access to information within the European Union was born out of a crisis of legitimacy that confronted the project of European integration in the late 1980s and early 1990s. Efforts to increase the pace of economic and political integration – through the signing of the Single European Act (SEA) in 1986 and the Treaty on European Union (TEU) in 1992 – were supported among policy elites but regarded more skeptically by electorates.[14] The implementation of the SEA was delayed when Ireland's Supreme Court ruled in 1987 that a referendum was needed. Although Irish voters eventually endorsed the law, the ensuing debate aired public anxieties about the shift of power to EU policy makers in Brussels. A few years later, the TEU was repudiated in a Danish referendum, while a ratification vote in France in September 1992 almost produced a second defeat. Opinion polls in the United Kingdom and Germany showed that referenda in those countries on the TEU would have failed as well, had they been required.[15]

Popular resistance to integration was often expressed as a complaint about the secretiveness of EU institutions. During negotiations over the TEU, the Dutch government proposed to address this complaint by creating a right of access to information held by EU institutions, but other governments balked and the treaty promised only a study of methods to improve access to documents.[16] This tepid commitment proved inadequate during the Danish referendum on the TEU, in which complaints about EU secrecy resonated among voters. Denmark's foreign minister conceded that the Danish referendum defeat "taught us all a lesson" about the need for transparency, and the Danish government reacted by promising that it would unilaterally declassify documents received from the EU.[17] EU leaders also responded with assurances on openness, and in a second referendum in May 1993 Danish voters approved the TEU.[18] In December 1993, two key EU institutions – the Council of the European Union and the European Commission – adopted a Code of Conduct that established new procedures for obtaining access to documents.[19]

The 1993 code had severe limitations. One was the number of specialized organizations set up by the EU that were completely excluded from its requirements, including the European Central Bank, the European Investment Bank, the European Police Office, the

European Agency for the Evaluation of Medicinal Products, and the European Environment Agency.[20] (The EU's independent ombudsman, Jacob Söderman, eventually prodded several of these organizations to develop their own disclosure codes.[21] Occupying a position created by the TEU and appointed by the European Parliament, the ombudsman would prove to play a critical role in promoting openness. Söderman had previously served as Finland's ombudsman.) Nor did the code apply to any document an EU institution had received from a member state or any other organization. Information received from other governments but contained within an EU document would also be withheld if the other government requested confidentiality.[22] These were severe restrictions for institutions that dealt principally with problems of multilateral policy coordination.

The major EU institutions also insisted on strict interpretation of the code. In 1997, the European Commission argued that the code did not apply to its "comitology committees" – influential committees composed of experts appointed by member governments that are given a formal role in guiding the implementation of Commission policy.[23] The commission argued that the committees were completely independent, even though commission staff prepared minutes for committee meetings. After two years of litigation, the commission was compelled by the European Court of Justice to abandon its position.[24]

The EU Council made similar efforts to restrict the code. Its Legal Service argued that the code did not apply to documents produced by officials in the Council secretariat that had not been distributed to all member states, but this interpretation was eventually rejected by the ombudsman.[25] The ombudsman also rejected a claim by council lawyers that the code did not apply to documents produced by the government holding the presidency of the council.[26] (Member states hold the presidency in rotation for six-month periods.) As a fallback, the council argued that documents the presidency had authored jointly with institutions outside the EU (such as agendas for meetings of the EU–U.S. working groups set up to implement the 1995 New Transatlantic Agenda) could not be considered council records. This position was abandoned following criticism from the ombudsman.[27]

The council also argued that the 1993 code did not apply to documents relating to multilateral cooperation in law enforcement, justice, and immigration – a new field for collaboration established by the TEU. In 1995, the council's refusal to provide Britain's *Guardian* newspaper with minutes and voting records of a council of justice and interior ministers was reversed by the European Court of Justice.[28] The following year, the council denied that the code applied to documents of the K4 Committee (a coordinating committee of senior justice and interior officials) but was overruled by the ombudsman.[29] In 1998, two EU governments – the United Kingdom and France – attempted to persuade the Court of Justice that the code did not provide Swedish journalists with any enforceable right to documents relating to Europol, the European Police Office. The court rejected the argument.[30]

At the same time the council attempted to block access to documents relating to another new field of cooperation established by the TEU: foreign and security policy. When a Finnish member of the European Parliament, Heidi Hautala, sought an internal report on the control of arms exports by EU countries, the council denied that there was any enforceable right to the document; it was again overruled by the Court of Justice. [31] The council responded by arguing that it had no obligation to review the report and determine whether parts of it could be safely released (a standard practice under national disclosure laws), but the council was finally compelled to do so by the court.[32] In 2000, the council took more drastic measures to protect information relating to defense cooperation: Quickly and without notice, it altered the code to broaden the circumstances in which documents could be withheld in the interests of collective security.[33]

The EU Council made decisions on disclosure by a vote of member states, and decisions to deny access often frustrated the Danish and Dutch governments.[34] However, the position of the dissenting minority was strengthened as the EU negotiated over the accession of three Nordic countries – Sweden, Norway, and Finland – with long-standing commitments to open government. The potential for erosion of transparency became a major issue during Sweden's closely fought referendum on accession. The EU allowed the Swedish and Finnish governments to add caveats to their accession agreements stating that access to documents was a matter of "fundamental importance."[35]

At the same time, the position of the French and German governments, whose representatives almost always voted against disclosure, was compromised by their desire for treaty reforms that would bolster the EU's authority. EU officials conceded that there was lukewarm public support for more reform in many countries, and a need for actions to "regain the commitment of citizens" so that an agreement could be ratified – an especially difficult proposition in Denmark where a referendum would again be required.[36] Acknowledging the realities, France and Germany finally acquiesced to demands that a new agreement recognize a right of access to information held by EU institutions.[37] The Amsterdam Treaty of 1997 required that a new disclosure regulation be adopted by 2001.[38]

The new regulation provided a qualified improvement in transparency. In some aspects, the policy closed conflicts of the preceding eight years. For example, it clearly applies to all of the policy areas in which the EU now works, and to the documents produced by the commission's expert committees. On the other hand, the new regulation still contains a major restriction held over from the earlier code. At the insistence of the French government, the Amsterdam Treaty included an assurance that the new disclosure policy would continue to give governments the right to request that documents given to EU institutions not be disclosed.[39]

A change in procedures for adopting a new disclosure policy also handicapped efforts to maintain secrecy. The 1993 code was adopted by a simple majority vote of states represented in the European Council, and had been changed in 2000 in the same way. However, the Amsterdam Treaty required that a new policy be approved by the EU Parliament as well as by the council. The Parliament conceived of itself as a check against executive misconduct, and only a year before dispatched several senior EU officials who had resisted a parliamentary inquiry into allegations of corruption.[40] When the European Commission unveiled a draft regulation in 2000 that included broad restrictions on disclosure – such as a ban on release of "texts for internal use"[41] – the ombudsman protested in the *Wall Street Journal* against "a list of exemptions from access without precedent in the modern world."[42] Bolstered as well by complaints from nongovernmental organizations and national legislators, the Parliament succeeded in reversing many of the commission's proposed restrictions.[43]

By 2001, the European Union had acquired the distinction of being the first system of supranational governance that was subject to a disclosure policy that provided enforceable rights roughly comparable to those in national laws. However, a combination of unusual circumstances had led to that result. Treaty and accession negotiations had made otherwise dominant states susceptible to pressure for increased openness. The elaborate EU architecture also created counterweights – such as the European Parliament, the Ombudsman, and the Court of Justice – that had incentives and authority to check the impulses of the European Council and Commission. And even the most resistant states were not, in the end, profoundly opposed to the principle of transparency: France, after all, had a national disclosure law; and while Germany had no national law, many of its *Bundesländer* had disclosure rules. Perversely, the acknowledgement of a right to information also had the effect of consolidating a proposition close to the hearts of French and German policy makers – that citizens of member states were also citizens of the European Union, with rights they could pursue on their own account against EU institutions.

Closed doors in Geneva

The drive to liberalize international trade in the 1980s and 1990s provoked anxieties in many countries, as businesses and workers worried that cheaper imports would threaten their livelihood and activists worried about the erosion of national consumer and environmental protection rules. The World Trade Organization, established in 1995 following negotiations among over 100 countries, became the principal target of these anxieties. The WTO was not strictly a new organization; its successor, the inelegantly named GATT, had existed in Geneva for decades.[44] However, the WTO gained prominence as the number of trade rules proliferated. It became a principal forum for negotiating further liberalization. And it had an unprecedented ability, through its Dispute Settlement Mechanism, to resolve disagreements about compliance with trade rules.

The WTO quickly became a lightning rod for opponents of liberalization. The process of negotiating trade agreements under the WTO constituted a "subversion of the democratic process," Ralph Nader complained in 1996; important decisions on trade policy were now made by "a group of unelected bureaucrats sitting behind closed doors in Geneva."[45] Within a few years this view was widely held and forcefully articulated by critics of liberalization. In November 1999, an attempt by government leaders meeting in Seattle, WA, to begin a new round of WTO negotiations was thwarted by massive street protests. Many nongovernmental organizations sympathetic to the protestors said that the WTO's problems lay in its failure to make the process of negotiation more transparent. "The WTO operates in a secretive, exclusionary manner," said one manifesto. "People must have the right to self-determination and the right to know and decide on international commercial commitments. Among other things, this requires that decision-making processes be democratic, transparent and inclusive."[46] After Seattle, the influential nongovernmental organization Oxfam asserted that the WTO confronted "a crisis of legitimacy" produced by "shadowy processes [that] are more medieval than millennial."[47]

That the WTO should be criticized for indifference to openness was, in a sense, deeply ironic. At its first meeting of ministers in Singapore in 1996, the WTO had affirmed that one of its main aims was to achieve "the maximum possible level of transparency" so far as national trade practices were concerned.[48] Much of the organization's work consisted of developing procedures to achieve this goal. One of these procedures is the Trade Policy Review Mechanism, which requires a regular review of each country's trade policy by WTO staff and other country representatives. The WTO says that the TPRM promotes "greater transparency" in national policies;[49] other observers have called it "an instrument of enforcement" intended to promote compliance with the "normative framework" promoted by the WTO.[50] TPRM reviews often provide other governments and foreign investors with evidence about a country's commitment to liberalization.[51]

With the same goal in mind, the WTO also honed policies that established a right to documents held by its member states. The oldest of the WTO agreements, the 1947 General Agreement on Tariffs and Trade, requires governments to publish laws, regulations, judicial decisions, administrative rulings, and intergovernmental agreements that affect international trade.[52] (There are limitations: A government may withhold information if it would impede law enforcement, prejudice legitimate commercial interests, or otherwise harm the public interest.) The similarity to the U.S. Administrative Procedures Act of 1946, which imposed comparable disclosure requirements on the American bureaucracy and was a forerunner to the U.S. Freedom of Information Act, is not coincidental.[53]

Just as the U.S. Administrative Procedures Act evolved, so too did the disclosure rules contained in WTO agreements. The 1994 General Agreement on Trade in Services (GATS) added an obligation for countries to establish "enquiry points" to respond to requests from other governments for "specific information" about policies affecting trade in services.[54] Several other WTO agreements now include the same requirement. Some agreements go even further, acknowledging that foreign businesses have their own right to information, which can be exercised without government assistance. Under the Agreement on Government Procurement, for example, countries must "promptly provide" foreign companies with an explanation of their procurement practices and reasons for unfavorable decisions.[55] Similarly, the 1997 Agreement on Basic Telecommunication Services states that foreign companies have a right to information about unfavorable licensing decisions.[56] The Agreement on Technical Barriers to Trade even includes rules about the price that may be charged for information requested by foreign companies, and the language in which it must be provided.[57]

All of this was aimed at promoting transparency, but only as a way of advancing the project of liberalization. It did nothing to improve the transparency of the WTO itself, and this was the real point of contention for electorates in many countries – particularly so in the United States, the European Union, Japan, and Canada, the four members of the WTO with the largest shares of world trade, often known as the Quad countries.[58] As Quad voters grew restless, their governments advocated steps to open up the WTO's own decision-making processes, but these efforts were compromised by decision rules that gave weaker states the capacity to block reform.

The push for reform of the WTO had many dimensions, one of which was more liberal access to documents circulated within the organization. At its establishment, the WTO had a strict policy: Any document circulated among WTO members was to be treated as "restricted" and not distributed publicly. In 1996, the WTO's General Council appeared to reverse this policy entirely by establishing a new rule that WTO documents should generally be "derestricted" and allowed to circulate publicly.[59] A few months later, it established a website to allow public access to its library of derestricted documents. This seemed a remarkable turnabout for a body that consisted of over 100 ambassadors who were required to reach consensus before a decision could be made.

In fact, the turnabout was not so dramatic after all. The new policy proved to have substantial limitations. It applied only to documents circulated among member states; it did not apply to draft documents prepared by the WTO's 500-person secretariat, or any of the secretariat's other internal papers. (In other words, the WTO secretariat had maintained the confidentiality that the EU Council's secretariat had fought unsuccessfully to preserve at roughly the same time.) Nor did it apply to informally circulated government documents, which are known in WTO jargon as "nonpapers." By 1996, the practice of relying on nonpapers in key negotiations was common.

The WTO's "derestriction policy" was not in any way comparable to a national disclosure law, which would have established a right to such documents, defined the limits to those rights, and described a procedure for deciding whether the documents should be released. On the contrary it was a "publication scheme,"[60] a negotiated plan for release of specified "official" documents. And even for these documents there were substantial limitations. Most documents were only to be considered for derestriction – that is, public release – six months after they had been circulated to member states. Material that was essential to follow the work of the WTO (timetables for committee meetings, agendas, and background notes) would not be publicly available until well after meetings had been held. Minutes were also withheld for six months.[61] Nor was the "derestriction" of a WTO document automatic, even after six months. The policy stipulated only that these documents would be *considered* for derestriction by the WTO's General Council; because decision making in the council is based on consensus, derestriction could be blocked if only one government objected. In 1999, for example, Mexico blocked the derestriction of background papers relating to liberalization of agricultural trade, despite arguments by the WTO secretariat and many other countries that derestriction would enhance transparency.[62]

Attempts to liberalize the WTO's policy were frustrated by the need for consensus. In 1997, a major Quad-funded nongovernmental organization suggested that the WTO should adopt a policy comparable to that contained in national disclosure laws, in which any document would be accessible unless nondisclosure could be shown to be essential to protect specified interests.[63] The Quad countries themselves made more modest proposals aimed at liberalizing the policy on derestriction of official WTO documents.[64] But these proposals failed to win support.[65] Quad countries protested that a compromise reform finally adopted by the General Council in 2002 had "considerably watered down" their proposals: Governments still retained the power to block access to their own submissions, as well as the power to block access to other documents for up to three months.[66] "If Members sought perfection on every point," the council's chairman warned, "consultation would likely continue for another four years."[67]

Countries that opposed more liberal disclosure rules may have done so only to preserve a negotiating point known to be valued by the Quad countries. However, there were other fears too, such as the concern that emphasis on "external" transparency (as it is known within the WTO) would undermine the ability of weaker national delegations to stay abreast of debates within the organization. Even in 1996, countries such as Mexico complained about the proliferation of nonpapers.[68] "Radical derestriction," as the Bulgarian delegation called it, might simply mean that the nonpaper system would flourish, producing little actual improvement in external transparency, and in fact corroding the official record.[69] Allied to this was a concern that external transparency would increase the advantage of the Quad's better-funded interest groups.

Quad efforts to improve transparency of the WTO's Dispute Settlement Mechanism (DSM) faired worse. The DSM was an innovation established at the same time as the WTO itself – a system for independent adjudication of disputes between countries about compliance with WTO rules. The DSM is a hybrid of organizational forms. Although it functions like a court, its procedures are also imbued with the ethos of diplomatic confidentiality. The expert panels appointed to resolve disputes meet in closed session. Only governments have the right to appear before a panel or have their submissions considered by it. All submissions are confidential, and so are the interim panel reports that are distributed for comment by interested governments. Comparable rules are followed by the Appellate Body, which may be asked to take up complaints about a panel report.[19]

These rules quickly became the object of protest by American nongovernmental organizations. In 1998, environmental groups complained about their inability to observe or submit briefs to a panel appointed to consider challenges to an American law mandating the use of turtle-exclusion devices by foreign shrimp fishers. (The United States government attempted to circumvent the ban on NGO briefs by including them in its own submission, a move that was unsuccessfully resisted by the four developing countries – Thailand, Pakistan,

Malaysia, and India – that initiated the case.[70]) American steel producers threatened by a European challenge to American antidumping laws also called for reform of the DSM.[71] By the end of the 1990s, the Clinton administration had declared DSM transparency to be a "priority issue" for the United States.[72] The administration said that its proposals – open hearings, a right for nongovernmental organizations to make submissions to the panel, and rapid release of draft decisions – were "critical...in ensuring the long-term credibility of the multilateral system."[73] The Bush administration took the same position, pressed by Republican legislators who argued that such reforms were essential to "defuse public mistrust" of the WTO.[74]

Developing countries strongly resisted the American proposals. In 1998 Mexico expressed the view of several governments that premature disclosure of draft panel reports encouraged "external pressures of a non-legal kind...[from] certain vested interests" in developed countries.[75] In 2002 it was reported that a group of developing countries had protested that American proposals would result in "trials by media" that could cause "miscarriages of justice."[76] Southeast Asian diplomats told journalists that calls to open up the DSM were a preoccupation of "a few western countries," and otherwise opposed by the entire membership of the WTO.[77]

The dimensions of the controversy were illustrated in 2000, when the WTO's Appellate Body, hearing a dispute over a French ban on asbestos products, decided that it had the discretion to accept briefs from nongovernmental groups.[78] In a special session of the General Council, Egypt complained that "the likely beneficiaries of such a decision were those individuals and NGOs who had the capacity in terms of resources and time...operating mainly in the developed world." India agreed that the decision would "have the implication of putting the developing countries at an even greater disadvantage in view of the relative unpreparedness of their NGOs," while Brazil worried that "the dispute settlement mechanism could soon be contaminated by political issues that did not belong to the WTO."[79] The Appellate Body finessed the dispute by rejecting every application to submit a brief that it received from a nongovernmental organization.[80]

There was a "conceptual divide" on transparency, an Indian commentator said in 2000,[81] and as a result attempts to forge consensus on DSM reform proved fruitless. In 1994, WTO members had agreed to complete a review of the DSM policy by 1988, but this deadline passed without action. The deadline was reset to 1999, and was missed; to 2003, and was missed; to 2004, and was missed yet again. In June 2004 the lead negotiator on DSM reform wisely decided against setting a new deadline.[82]

Laying siege to the Crystal Palace

The politics of disclosure differed substantially in the case of the World Bank. In the European Union, powerful states hostile to transparency had been compelled to bend to smaller states with the momentary ability to block the project of European integration. In the WTO, powerful states supportive of transparency had been stymied by the consensus rule. In the case of the World Bank, by contrast, motive and power coincided: American legislators faced domestic pressure to improve transparency and had the means to force compliance by the Bank. Even under these favorable circumstances, however, movement toward transparency again encountered firm limits.

The World Bank actually has several components. Two of the most important are the International Bank for Reconstruction and Development (IBRD) and the International Development Association (IDA). The IBRD was established in 1944 to support postwar reconstruction in Europe, but now provides loans to developing countries for major development projects. The IDA was established in 1960 to provide interest-free loans and grants to the poorest countries. Together, the IBRD and the IDA make the World Bank the most important public development finance agency for developing countries.[83]

By the early 1980s, the World Bank was beginning to suffer its own crisis of legitimacy – certainly among environmental and social activists, and particularly in the United States. At issue was the Bank's support of projects undertaken by developing countries, the effects of which on the environment and disenfranchised peoples could be catastrophic. A coalition of U.S.-based activists – led by groups such as the Environmental Policy Institute, the Natural Resources Defense Council, and the National Wildlife Federation[84] – decided to draw attention to the worst cases of World Bank-funded mismanagement. One of these was the Polonoroeste project, a massive Brazilian program for settlement of Amazon frontier that resulted in reckless deforestation and the deaths of thousands of indigenous people.

Another was the Akosombo Dam in Ghana – one of dozens of "big dams" built with World Bank support whose impact on the environment and nearby communities had spawned a transnational antidam movement.[85] The aim of the U.S. activists, one of its leaders later said, was to "lay siege to the Crystal Palace" – by which he meant the obsession with technocratic planning epitomized by the World Bank.[86]

The activists proved to be skilled in seizing opportunities presented by the United States' fractured legislative process. Between 1983 and 1987, activists persuaded American legislators to organize over twenty hearings in which witnesses testified to the damage done by World Bank-funded projects.[87] They also built an unusual coalition of liberal Democrats concerned with environmental and social causes and conservative Republicans concerned with the accountability of multilateral institutions. This coalition echoed the activists' concerns ("Congress," Larry Summers later said, "is the megaphone of the NGOs"[88]), but also – through its influence over legislation that regulated the executive branch's involvement with the World Bank – had the capacity to compel a Bank response.

Throughout the late 1980s, Congress experimented with legislative reforms intended to put pressure on the World Bank. One technique consisted of statutory directions to the director who represented the U.S. Treasury Secretary on the Bank's executive board. A 1986 congressional directive advised the American director to encourage borrower countries to "fully inform" affected communities about new projects.[89] Congressional advice quickly became more pointed. In 1989, Representative Nancy Pelosi – a liberal Democrat from San Francisco – obtained an amendment to U.S. law that instructed the American director to abstain from any vote on a project that would have a significant environmental impact unless an Environmental Impact Assessment had been made public at least four months before the vote.[90] The Pelosi Amendment (as it became known) was important because decision rules within the World Bank gave substantial power to the American director. The voting power of each national director is weighted according to the amount of financial support given to the Bank: The United States, contributing roughly 15 percent of IBRD and IDA resources, also controlled one-seventh of the Executive Board vote. (Pelosi, as a member of Congress, could also call on the General Accounting Office to act as a monitor of Bank compliance with the Amendment, as it did in a 1998 study that found shortfalls in World Bank practice regarding disclosure of environmental impact statements.[91])

Members of Congress were also prepared to use a more powerful tool for influencing disclosure policy: control over the United States' financial contributions to the Bank. In 1985, Republican Senator Robert Kasten bluntly warned World Bank President A. W. Clausen that its inattention to NGO complaints put congressional support for the Bank's financing at risk.[92] The threat was repeated in a Senate report in 1989.[93] In 1990, and again in 1992, Congress temporarily withheld funding for Bank activities because of dissatisfaction with its response to congressional requirements, including directions on access to information about World Bank-funded projects.[94]

The IDA, whose finances were "replenished" through appropriations from member countries every three years, was particularly susceptible to congressional influence. Historically, about one-fifth of IDA funding has been provided by the United States. During review of a replenishment request in 1993, Democratic Senator Patrick Leahy warned World Bank President Lewis Preston of Congress's "waning tolerance for a public institution supported with public funds that denies the public access to relevant information."[95] Leahy, discouraged by a recent report that found "fundamental failures" in the Bank's handling of the Sardar Sarovar Dam in India, also pressed the Bank to establish an independent body to investigate complaints about Bank mismanagement. When the Bank balked at taking stronger action, Democratic Senator Barney Frank threatened to delay approval of the IDA replenishment.[96]

The threat impelled the World Bank to establish an independent inspection panel and adopt its first Information Disclosure Policy, released in March 1994. It also began distributing some documents through its website and through newly established "public information centers" in its offices in major Quad capitals.[97] Congressional pressure did not ease. The Bank made more commitments on disclosure in anticipation of Congress's consideration of another replenishment round in 1999,[98] and a revised policy was released in September 2001. The next replenishment prompted promises of further action,[99] but no revision of the policy has been undertaken since 2001.

The 2001 Disclosure Policy establishes a "presumption in favor of disclosure" of World Bank documents.[100] In fact, the reality is quite the opposite. Bank policy, like the WTO policy, is a publication scheme that proceeds on the assumption that documents are not accessible unless they are explicitly listed in the policy.[101] It excludes, for example, most internal documents relating to the management of the World Bank and internal papers relating to the formulation of Bank policy – subjects that would often be the subject of information requests under national disclosure laws. There are some particularly critical omissions. Draft versions of key documents that outline the terms of the Bank's financial assistance – that is, the versions that have not yet been approved by the Executive Board – are not accessible. While the approved versions of these documents may be released, it may be too late for nongovernmental organizations to influence their terms.[102] Nor were minutes of the board's meetings made available under the 2001 policy, a practice that allowed the Executive Board to make decisions in "near total secrecy."[103] (In March 2005, the Bank revised its position to allow the release of some basic information about board meetings.[104]) While preparing the policy, the Executive Board had apparently debated the wisdom of releasing more information about its work, according to the *Financial Times*, which saw leaked minutes of the board's debate over the policy; the discussion revealed a split between industrialized countries who supported NGO demands for openness and emerging market countries who feared that transparency would "invite external actors to become involved in issues discussed by the board."[105]

The policy is essentially a compact: the product of two decades of difficult negotiations between the World Bank, borrower countries, the U.S. Congress, and nongovernmental organizations. It gives evidence of the realities that have shaped the negotiations. For example, the disclosure requirements that relate to Bank lending to its poorest clients through the IDA under the 2001 policy were more demanding than the requirements attached to IBRD lending[106] – a product of the fact that IDA financing is more open to congressional influence through the replenishment procedure. The ability of middle-income countries – those borrowing from the IBRD – to choose against disclosure of key lending documents was a key limitation of the 2001 policy. The difficulty was illustrated in 2002, when the Uruguayan government exercised its prerogative to block the release of a letter to the Bank that outlined the steps the country was prepared to take as conditions for receiving a $252 million loan. The letter – which summarized Uruguay's commitments to cut public sector salaries, pensions, and unemployment benefits – was later leaked, stirring controversy in Uruguay. The Bank Executive Board had been told that the Uruguayan government had undertaken extensive consultations with nongovernmental organizations about its plans; critics complained that the government's assurances were "completely untrue."[107]

In early 2005, the World Bank amended its policy in an effort to remedy the inconsistency in disclosure rules for poor and middle-income countries. Under the revised policy, there is a presumption that key lending documents eventually will be released for all borrowers. However, consistency has been purchased at the price of rigor: All countries have now regained the ultimate discretion to block release of key documents. Furthermore, they may choose to put sensitive material in separate memoranda not affected by disclosure rules.[108] In principle the policy of separating highly sensitive material is unobjectionable, if the test of sensitivity is fairly applied. But there is evidence that World Bank officials stretch the interpretation of disclosure requirements – a not surprising result – and there is no effective recourse (such as an ombudsman) for individuals who suspect that information is being improperly withheld.[109]

Paradoxically, the World Bank now promotes more rigorous disclosure standards for the countries to which it lends. The Bank's recent emphasis on the need to foster "good governance" as a prerequisite to social and economic development has included a call for improved transparency on the part of borrowing governments; it calls "information access" one of the key elements of its "empowerment framework" for the public in borrowing countries.[110] Its research arm promotes the adoption of disclosure laws that conform to "international standards," recognizing a right to government information and establishing a procedure for independent review of decisions to refuse access to information.[111] In 2004, the adoption of a national disclosure law was made a condition for loans granted by the Bank to two countries – Honduras and Nicaragua.[112]

A transparency revolution?

The story of openness at the World Bank's sister institution, the International Monetary Fund, seems at first glance to follow a similar path. Also established in 1944, the IMF originally aimed to coordinate the currency exchange rate policies of its member states and provide financial aid to countries dealing with balance-of-payments problems. Throughout its first four decades, says a former IMF official,

> Institutional transparency was not high on the agenda of the IMF. The IMF generally followed the practices of member countries, particularly their central banks and ministries of finance, which valued the confidentiality of their relationship with the IMF. The IMF saw itself as a technical institution, accountable to its member governments and with little need to explain itself to the broader public.[113]

In the 1980s, however, the role of the IMF began to change, and so did the public perception of its legitimacy. In 1982, the IMF responded to Mexico's debt crisis by providing assistance that was conditioned on Mexico's pursuit of significant fiscal and economic reforms. It followed by negotiating similar "structural adjustment" agreements with other Latin American countries, and later with Russia and the former Soviet Bloc states. By the end of the 1990s, the IMF was involved in structural adjustment programs in seventy countries.[114] In many countries, critics complained about the harshness of the reforms required by the IMF; moreover, they complained about the secrecy with which their own governments had negotiated agreements with the Fund.[115] Dissatisfaction mounted as the IMF responded to a series of financial crises throughout the 1990s – in Mexico again in 1994, in East Asia in 1997, and in Russia in 1998. Ten thousand protestors blocked the streets of Washington during an IMF and World Bank-hosted meeting of finance ministers in April 2000; another 5,000 protested during the institutions' annual meeting in Prague in September 2000.

Popular protests, particularly in developing countries, were one thing; dissent among policy makers within lending countries was another. The public relations office of the IMF tabulated the number of times in which it was described as "secretive" in major press outlets: The count had been insignificant before 1997, but rocketed upward afterward.[116] The Fund (as the *Wall Street Journal* editorialized in the first months of the East Asian crisis) was "one of the most secretive institutions this side of the average missile base.... What they do, or learn, or exactly what guides their decisions, is largely kept secret. For the most part, the IMF has moved for decades in an off-the-record mist of internal deliberations and closeted discussions."[117] Joseph Stiglitz, the former chief economist of the World Bank, said that secrecy was the root cause of the bad advice that the IMF had given to governments in crisis. If the Fund's decision makers had opened themselves to outside scrutiny, Stiglitz argued, "their folly might have become much clearer, much earlier."[118]

Many members of the U.S. Congress, already uneasy in their support of organizations such as the IMF, echoed these complaints. "The issue of transparency really goes to the heart of the legitimacy of the IMF...and arguably, in the long term, its survival," an advisor to the Senate Banking Committee said. "If it is not seen that the institution as a whole has some measure of accountability and transparency, then it is very hard to justify the extraordinary influence that it exercises and to hold it accountable in some way."[119] Congress had twice given a statutory direction to the American representative on the IMF Board to pursue the question of transparency,[120] with little effect. But in January 1998, Congress's capacity to influence IMF policy improved substantially when the Clinton administration approached it with a request for an $18 billion contribution to support the IMF's efforts at crisis management. Congress was hostile to the proposal; three years earlier, it had rebuffed the administration's request for assistance in dealing with the Mexican crisis.

In April 1998, Representative Jim Saxton, the Republican chair of Congress's Joint Economic Committee, responded to the administration's request by proposing the IMF Transparency and Efficiency Act, which would deny support to the IMF until it agreed to institutional reforms that included the publication of board minutes and key lending documents.[121] (Saxton also commissioned a General Accounting Office study that concluded that it was impossible, given publicly available information, to make a timely assessment of the Fund's financial position.[122]) Some of the disclosure requirements of Saxton's bill were included in the appropriations bill that eventually provided the requested $18 billion in October 1998.[123]

In Fall 1998, the IMF's managing director, Michel Camdessus, gave a speech that warned about the institutional difficulties in achieving greater openness. "The pace of change is largely in the hands of the IMF's members," Camdessus cautioned. "Calls for more IMF transparency are, in many respects, calls on the member countries. . . . Once consensus is established, we will be enthusiastic to proceed with the necessary adaptation of procedures and policies."[124] But the IMF wasted little time when the appropriations bill put $18 billion at risk: ten days after the bill's passage, Deputy Treasury Secretary Larry Summers reported to Congress that representatives of the IMF's major donor countries had agreed to adopt a more expansive disclosure policy.[125] (The IMF's commitment, Saxton claimed, "would not exist if Congress had not made an IMF reform effort over the last twelve months."[126])

The IMF announced substantial revisions to its disclosure rules in April 1999,[127] and made incremental changes to its policy in subsequent years.[128] But as the funding crisis passed, the IMF's old diffidence about radical reforms resurfaced. "We have to strike a balance between openness and the members' desire for candid and confidential advice," Camdessus' successor, Horst Köhler, told the National Press Club in 2000. "Civil society has serious questions, and I take these seriously. But we should also be firm. We have a membership – governments – that is accountable. We cannot have responsibility 'transferred' from these institutions to nongovernmental organizations."[129]

The IMF had been put under unprecedented pressure to be less secretive, a senior IMF official recalled in 2003. "To respond to those demands, the IMF started to publish documents that had been kept outside the public eye. We used to publish virtually nothing, now we publish everything."[130] This was tantamount to saying, as the World Bank had said, that there was a presumption of disclosure for documents. However, this was far from true. While the IMF had taken important steps to improve openness, it had not recognized a general right to information; instead, it had negotiated a publication scheme for a limited number of listed documents. There was no process for requesting access to administrative or other internal papers of the IMF. The list of records covered by the IMF's publication scheme also omits critical "official" documents, such as the Board's minutes (still accessible only after a ten-year waiting period) and drafts of lending documents sent to the Board for approval. The scheme presumes that countries will agree to the publication of the final versions of these documents, but it does not require publication; and in many instances governments, particularly those of developing countries, have not agreed.[131] Governments may also negotiate about the wording of publicly disclosed agreements and ask for politically sensitive material to be contained in inaccessible "side letters" to the Fund. (In 2003, Argentinian activists filed a legal complaint in national courts alleging that a side letter to a recent IMF agreement contained a concession on the raising of utility prices.[132] The IMF refused to confirm or deny the existence of the letter.[133]) IMF staff are told to avoid language "that would exacerbate domestic political challenges to implementing reforms."[134]

The Fund's new disclosure rules represented a significant and important change in practice. Yet IMF spokesmen represented its new attitude on transparency in more dramatic terms. The Fund had undergone a "transparency revolution," its chief economist, Stanley Fischer, said in 2001.[135] Another IMF official agreed: The commitment to transparency constituted an "understated revolution, ... a sea change" in the way the Fund does business.[136]

This was not simply hyperbole: Rather, it was a testament to the plasticity of the concept of transparency itself. The revolutionary aspect of changes in transparency at the Fund referred mainly to the extension of its own effort to monitor the behavior of its member states. This was motivated by a widespread perception that the financial crises of the 1990s had been caused by ignorance about the state of financial sectors in the crisis countries, and that governments in those countries had been (in the words of a senior IMF official) "economical with the truth" in reporting their financial positions.[137]

The result was an effort to improve the IMF's capacity to collect information about financial and regulatory conditions in member states. In 1977, the IMF began a routine of completing regular reviews of the domestic policies of each member state that might affect exchange rates. Authorized by Article IV of the IMF's Articles of Agreement, the scope of these "surveillance" exercises (the IMF's own phrase) broadened substantially in the 1990s, to include more detailed scrutiny of each country's financial sector and institutional arrangements that might make a country vulnerable to crisis.[138] In 1999, the IMF added another routine, producing "financial system stability assessments" for member states that include reports on the extent to which countries conform to internationally recognized standards in the management of fiscal and monetary policy, banking and securities regulation, and corporate governance.[139] In 1999 an IMF review group called this "a potentially major expansion" of its surveillance functions.[140]

These measures were all aimed at improving transparency, but not of the IMF itself. Rather, they were intended to address the threat of economic instability posed by liberalized capital flows. The IMF had no interest in new restrictions on capital flows; on the contrary, it regarded capital flow liberalization as one of its main objectives, a point it reaffirmed at the height of the Asian financial crisis.[141] But investors who were ignorant of the true conditions of the economies in which they were investing were prone to dangerous herd behavior. More extensive surveillance by the IMF would alert policy makers to conditions that might trigger investor panic, and at the same time give investors the information to make more rational and less fickle decisions.[142] IMF officials themselves characterized their new initiatives as a form of informational regulation – "a new kind of *réglementation* . . . [that will] reduce the risk of abrupt changes in market sentiment through greater transparency."[143]

The effectiveness of these surveillance efforts is heightened if the products of surveillance are accessible, so that lenders and investors can make decisions that reflect risk more accurately. This has produced added pressure from advanced economies, as well as the IMF itself, for publication of key surveillance documents. In practice, however, developing countries have often refused to consent to disclosure.[144] A 2003 report by the IMF's evaluation office observed that three countries caught in recent financial crises – Indonesia, South Korea, and Brazil – had refused to publish the IMF's most important surveillance document; the office observed that the IMF's influence would have been strengthened if the document had been published, to "promote better risk assessment by private investors and lenders."[145] Efforts to persuade less advanced economies about the merits of disclosure have been accompanied by warnings that the market may punish states that do not cooperate.[146]

Common language, separate purposes

The contest over transparency in these four institutions – the EU, WTO, World Bank, and IMF – gives a sense of the difficulty that will confront advocates of openness as the power of the traditionally structured state is diffused, either domestically to private or quasi-private actors, or to supranational or international organizations. The multiplication of centers of authority means that one large battle over openness is replaced by many smaller battles.

In the international arena, the situation is even more complex than suggested here. There are many other international organizations that wield influence but are not bound by disclosure policies comparable to those imposed on national governments – ranging from the obvious cases (such as the United Nations and its agencies) to a host of little known organizations (such as the Codex Alimentarius or the Bank of International Settlements) that play critical roles in encouraging convergence in national regulatory practices.[147] Progress in advancing disclosure rules in this sphere will be uneven, contingent upon the structure of decision rules in each body, the predispositions of influential states, and the extent to which an organization finds itself embroiled in controversy. Experience shows us that the norm of diplomatic confidentiality will prove durable – even when organizations become the object of extraordinary public protests.

The contest over openness in the international financial institutions – that is, organizations like the WTO, World Bank, and IMF – also reminds us about the dangers of accepting what might be called the naïve view of transparency, in which openness is regarded as a single commodity, and an unalloyed good. Transparency can be employed as a tool by different players for dramatically different purposes. In fact, the fight over transparency in the WTO and IMF might be said to present a clash between two doctrines of transparency. One – the neoliberal doctrine – deploys transparency as a tool for advancing the project of global economic liberalization. The neoliberal doctrine is firmly embedded in WTO trade agreements and IMF's surveillance policies. Most immediately, it serves the states and corporations in a position to exploit the opportunities presented by such liberalization.[148] Opposed to this is a rights-based doctrine of transparency, which pursues disclosure as a tool for protecting the political and economic rights of citizens affected by the process of liberalization, and which is manifested in policies intended to lay open the decision-making processes of the organizations themselves so that their decisions can be more easily influenced.

There is a second sense in which the naïve view of transparency is rebutted. As developing countries have pointed out, stakeholders in the first world – nongovernmental organizations as well as business stakeholders – are in a much better position to exploit the opportunities for influence that are created by improving transparency in international organizations. Transparency is not a neutral concept, leaders of some weaker states argue. Rather, it shapes the balance of forces that influence policy, and it may do this in ways that are unfavorable to the interests of their citizens. Indeed, one can imagine the frustration of a policy maker in a weaker state – subjected on the one hand to a system of surveillance promoted by dominant states to encourage economic liberalization, and subjected on the other hand to a rights-based rhetoric of transparency (most forcefully articulated by interest groups of the same dominant states) that complicates their ability to negotiate effectively and to implement policies at home.

Assertion is not proof, however, and it is equally possible to imagine reasons why this account may be mistaken or misguided. It may underestimate the extent to which the community of nongovernmental organizations has internationalized and the manner in which groups rooted in the advanced economies act as proxies for citizens in other countries. Or it may simply be an excuse for policy makers in developing countries who have never accepted the principle of democratic accountability. Furthermore, it neglects the possibility that the best way to remedy imbalances in influence may be to find ways of enfranchising the citizens of weaker states, rather than denying information to the citizens of stronger states.

III TECHNOLOGY

9

LIQUID PAPER

During a recent visit to Britain's National Archives, I spent time reading files produced by the Foreign Office in the early 1950s. The subject – negotiation with Americans about the balance to be struck between security needs and civil liberties while making decisions on security clearances – was fascinating. Equally fascinating, from the point of view of a researcher who learned his craft in the computer age, was the form of the documents themselves. There were relatively few, and generally concise. They took a limited number of forms – a letter, a memorandum, a short report, the minutes of a meeting. Obviously all were on paper. Some were typescript, but many were written in ink, in clear longhand script. Related documents were held together in a folder that provided, on its cover, a longhand summary of the material within. Each folder was bound with a red ribbon – the proverbial bureaucratic red tape.

Government documents had been produced and stored in much the same fashion for perhaps the preceding two centuries. The technology of production and reproduction had advanced – with the advent of the fountain pen, the typewriter, and the mimeograph duplicator – but the basic form of a government file would have been familiar to a public servant transported forward from the Foreign Office of the early 1850s.[1] In 1850, and still in 1950, technological constraints on the production and distribution of documents compelled officials to be deliberate in the composition of new records, and limited the growth of the total stock of official records. A document could more easily be inferred to be important, to say something authoritatively, because it was not easy to produce.

To a large degree this conception of "the official file" still permeates popular consciousness. The narrative about bureaucratic misconduct that is constantly replayed in news and fiction still hinges on the damning, but hidden, government file – a manila folder containing the "smoking gun" memo, with the words TOP SECRET heavily inked at its head. Many FOI laws are written with the expectation that they will reveal these official files; in fact, the laws are drafted on the assumption that this conception of "the official file" is an accurate one. The archetypal FOI request is one that seeks the disclosure of a bounded number of tangible records that are presumed to say something definitive about government policy.

The time when this conception of the official file was defensible in the advanced democracies is now long past. Over the last three decades, advances in information and communication technologies have caused profound changes in the character of information held within government agencies. In many instances, electronic media have replaced paper as the preferred method of storing information. The number of transactions that are documented in digital form has exploded, and the number of forms in which digitized information may be encapsulated – word processing documents, spreadsheets, presentation files, e-mails, structured databases, audio or video recordings, and so on – has grown. The cost of revising records has plummeted, causing a rise in the number of versions that may exist for any one record. The stockpile of government information has been liquified – broken down into a vast pool of elements whose significance, taken independently, is not easily grasped.

The metamorphosis of official information is already changing the battle over governmental openness. The struggle for access to "structured data" – the digitized information held in massive governmental databases – has been underway for decades, while the fight over access to the much larger pool of digitized "unstructured data" held by government agencies is still in its very early stages. In either case, the digitization of government information could have the unintended consequence of producing dramatic increases in transparency. But this outcome is not a given; on the contrary, there are strong bureaucratic and political forces that may prevent it. Nor is it clear that we should want such an outcome – particularly if the information at stake is personal data, or if disclosure has the effect of crippling government's ability to act effectively.

Structured data

The revolution in information and communication technologies has wrought two broad changes in the pool of information held by government agencies. The first is the growth of large electronic databanks that contain details about routine government activity, and about the businesses and individuals with whom government agencies interact. Large databases are not themselves novel: Early government projects such as the post-Civil War pension or the national census in the United States required the mass aggregation of information about citizens. However, this data existed in unwieldy paper form; the process of digitization, which gained momentum in the 1960s, dramatically reduced the cost of duplicating and manipulating such information. The application of technology to work processes also meant that agencies began to collect large amounts of information about their internal operations in new digitized databases.[2] Because the information contained in these databases is highly standardized – containing similar details for each person or company, for example – it is sometimes known as "structured data."

The emergence of large digitized databases in the years following the Second World War roughly coincided (in the United States) with the strengthening of laws that established a right to information held by government agencies. It was inevitable that the two trends would eventually collide. In the last two decades, many groups outside of government have become adept at exploiting the opportunities posed by the accumulation of digitized structured data within public agencies.

Journalists, for example, have become increasingly skilled at using bulk electronic data to scrutinize government operations. In fact, this has become a well-defined field of journalistic practice, known as computer-assisted reporting or CAR. Some major media outlets, such as the *New York Times*, have CAR editors, and since 1989 the field has had its own support organization, the National Institute for Computer-Assisted Reporting, that acts as a clearinghouse for key government databases.[3]

In 2000, the *Times* used data from the Fatality Analysis Reporting System – a database maintained by the U.S. Department of Transportation – to demonstrate that fatal crashes involving Ford Explorer sport utility vehicles were three times as likely to be related to tire failures as fatal crashes involving other brands. The *Times'* stories substantiated concerns about the reliability of Firestone tires that were routinely installed on new Explorers. Despite growing controversy over Firestone's tires, budget-constrained federal regulators had not detected the pattern in their own database.[4]

A later *New York Times* analysis of data collected by the federal Occupational Safety and Health Administration revealed a longstanding failure to seek criminal prosecution of employers whose willful violation of safety rules had caused worker deaths. In an echo of the Ford case, the agency had never studied its own data on deaths caused by deliberate noncompliance with regulations.[5] In 2004, the *Times* used data collected by federal railroad regulators to demonstrate inadequacies in procedures intended to reduce the number of deaths caused by collisions with trains at grade crossings. Its investigation led to the resignation of a top regulator and legislative proposals for tougher oversight of the railroad industry.[6]

Other journalists have exploited the potential of computer-assisted reporting as well. The *Newark Star-Ledger*, using information collected by the federal Food and Drug Administration, found that recalls of faulty medical implants were on the increase, a trend that it linked to weaker procedures for reviewing new implants.[7] In *Mother Jones* magazine, reporter Ken Silverstein matched data from three U.S. agencies – the General Services Administration, the Environmental Protection Agency, and the Occupational Safety and Health Administration – and found major contractors who continued to work for government while flouting its environmental and workplace safety rules.[8]

Academic research centers and public interest groups have also tapped government databases. Since 1989, the Transactional Records Access Clearinghouse (TRAC) at Syracuse University in New York State has used the Freedom of Information Act to obtain internal data on the activities of federal law enforcement agencies.[9] A 2003 TRAC study suggested that the federal government's efforts to prosecute cases of alleged terrorist activity had yielded few significant convictions,[10] while another of its studies found a marked decline in audits of corporate taxpayers and prosecutions for violation of federal tax law.[11] Another organization, the Center for Public Integrity, combined federal contracting data with data on political contributions to demonstrate that contracts for post-war reconstruction in

Iraq went to firms that gave heavily to the election campaigns of President George W. Bush.[12] In 2004, the center used data from the Internal Revenue Service to show that political nonprofit organizations had abused federal rules in ways that understated their level of political activity, quickly prompting a promise of more vigorous enforcement of reporting rules by the IRS.[13]

Environmental advocacy groups seized on the possibilities posed by the Toxics Release Inventory (TRI), a database established by the U.S. Environmental Protection Agency under the 1986 Emergency Planning and Community Right-to-Know Act (EPCRA). EPCRA required companies to report regularly to EPA about their use of listed toxic chemicals, and contained the unusual stipulation that these reports should be combined in a database "accessible by computer telecommunication" to the public. Environmental groups quickly used early rounds of TRI data to shame heavy polluters, often with a remarkable impact on industry behavior.[14]

The internet – a largely unknown technology at the time that EPCRA was drafted – gave advocacy groups the ability to go further, creating their own websites that allowed the public to search TRI data for information about polluters in their own community.[15] By the end of the 1990's, the Clinton administration was promoting TRI as an archetype of a powerful new approach to regulation, in which nongovernmental organizations collaborated with government to achieve regulatory objectives without resorting to conventional and heavy-handed enforcement measures.[16]

The advances that journalists and nongovernmental organizations have made in exploiting stockpiles of structured data within government agencies have been significant, but should not be overestimated. One major difficulty has been the lack of resources for pursuing this sort of work: Extracting and analyzing data can be a time-consuming and technically demanding task. (And if this is true with regard to the community of media and nongovernmental organizations that surrounds the U.S. federal government, it is doubly true with regard to the community that surrounds U.S. state and local governments, or even the national governments of other advanced democracies.) The need for a heavy investment of resources has been aggravated by the strong and continued opposition of government agencies, and private industry as well, to the release of structured data.

For three decades, many federal officials resisted the idea that there could be any right under the Freedom of Information Act to information contained in government databases. As a technical matter, many databases were not designed with the possibility of public access in mind; they were built for internal use and lacked features that would allow data to be easily exported for use by nongovernmental organizations. In these cases, new computer programs had to be written to make possible the extraction of data. This meant added work for agency staff, and even more difficulties for smaller agencies who lacked the staff with the ability to do the programming.

In a 1989 survey undertaken by the U.S. Department of Justice, over fifty federal agencies took the position that they had no obligation under FOIA to do special programming to extract information from their databases – and if information was extracted, they had no obligation to provide the information in easily managed electronic form rather than in less useful print formats. Any other position, departments warned, would "seriously disrupt their operations" and possibly make the entire FOIA program untenable.[17] Added to this was bureaucratic frustration with the uses to which information was put once released from government databases. Many officials complained that FOIA would be corrupted into a tool for businesses' exploitation of commercially valuable government data.[18] Others protested that nongovernmental organizations often used internal agency data to present a misleading and unflattering view of their operations.

The result of this bureaucratic resistance were cases such as *Public Citizen v. OSHA*, which grew out of an attempt in 1985 by Public Citizen to gain bulk data on enforcement actions by the federal Occupational Safety and Health Administration. OSHA refused the request for information, arguing that it had no obligation to do the programming needed to extract the data. In a contemporaneous case, *Dismukes v. Department of the Interior*, federal officials insisted on providing oil and gas leasing data on microfiche, even though the data was also available in electronic form. A federal court upheld the department's position.[19] Several other courts were equally hostile to FOIA requests for bulk data.[20] Finally Congress stepped in, by amending the Freedom of Information Act in 1996 to make clear that departments had an obligation to extract bulk data from their databases and – reversing the *Dismukes* decision – an obligation to provide data in easily manipulable digital formats.[21]

The 1996 changes – known as the Electronic Freedom of Information Act Amendments, or EFOIA – improved matters, but official balking at requests for electronic data also continued. In 1998, the Department of Housing and Urban Development refused a request for access to a database on money it owed to mortgagees, arguing that the request would be "extremely burdensome"; the refusal was eventually overturned by a federal court two years later.[22] In the same year, defense officials argued that the work of extracting data from a database on malpractice claims against military medical staff, requested by the *Dayton Daily News*, would be too onerous; a federal court disagreed, and the *Daily News* later won a Pulitzer Prize for its reporting on the subject.[23]

Despite EFOIA, Syracuse University's Transactional Records Access Clearinghouse also dealt with recurrent efforts by the Department of Justice to withhold information from its database on federal criminal investigations and prosecutions. The department was stung by the reports of the clearinghouse, which seemed to reveal weaknesses in federal efforts to enforce antiterrorism laws; it responded by attempting to argue that release of the data jeopardized public security.[24] In 2004 TRAC complained that the Internal Revenue Service had also stopped complying with court orders that required the release of bulk data on its enforcement of tax laws. The Center for Public Integrity encountered a novel claim while attempting to extract information from the federal government's database of foreign government lobbyists: The Department of Justice claimed that the database had become so fragile that an attempt to process the request risked a program crash and "major loss of data."[25] The case is not unusual; it is one of several instances in which rapid technological change has made databases practically inaccessible.[26]

Governments have also had more material incentives to resist the release of structured data under FOI law. Throughout the eighties and nineties, budget-constrained government agencies attempted to find ways of realizing the commercial value of the information locked in their databases – either by selling the information directly, or by enlisting businesses to refine and market their databases. ("The concept of government information as a *corporate resource*," one commentator worried in 1994, "appears to be overriding the concept of public *rights* to that information."[27]) However, commercial value can only be extracted if agencies are able to block the disclosure of information at no cost through FOI laws; as a result, many governments have attempted to interpret or amend their laws so that access can be denied if it would compromise their commercial interests. A New Jersey law proposed in 2004 included a criminal penalty for individuals who obtained commercially valuable information under the state's open government law if they violated an agreement not to put the information to commercial use.[28]

Of course, information sold by government is still publicly available, in principle, but often at a price that creates a barrier to access for many citizens. In a portentous 1994 case, the government of the Canadian province of British Columbia refused to give data to an environmental advocacy group, arguing that the data was already available for purchase at a price of $30,000. The group could not pay, and the government refused to bend, saying that exceptions would "eliminate this revenue source for the government." The agency's position was upheld on appeal; similar cases soon arose in other parts of Canada.[29]

When the information contained in government databases relates to the private sector, access to information may also be compromised because of industry pressure on government agencies. In 2004, the U.S. government was sued by major tire manufacturers in an effort to block the disclosure of data on fatal accidents that could be related to tire failures, which it began collecting after the Firestone controversy.[30] The ongoing fight over disclosure of information through the U.S. government's Toxic Release Inventory program provides another vivid illustration of industry pressure. As Mary Graham has noted, disclosure provisions in the 1986 law that authorized the TRI were restricted in three ways to overcome industry resistance to the plan: by excluding important categories of businesses, such as power plants and mining operations; by limiting the number of chemicals covered by the scheme; and – critically – by requiring that firms report only their estimate of the amount of chemicals released into the environment, rather than the amount actually used at a facility.[31]

Attempts by the Clinton administration to overcome these restrictions met strong industry resistance, which intensified as nongovernmental groups became more efficient in disseminating TRI data. (One trade journal reported "spasms" among chemical manufacturers when one environmental group launched a website that improved access to TRI data, combined with its own analysis of the results.[32])

When the Environmental Protection Agency announced its intention to broaden the list of TRI chemicals in 1994, the chemical industry responded with litigation that delayed implementation for three years.[33] In 1996, the EPA announced its intention to expand TRI to measure the use, rather than the release, of chemicals; but industry lobbyists successfully blocked the needed legislative amendments and by the end of the decade the Clinton administration had given up on its efforts.[34]

The private sector scored other successes in the effort to prevent the release of environmental information. In 1997, the EPA announced a new project, the Sector Facility Indexing Project, that would consolidate data on environmental performance and compliance for factories in five major industries, and provide an overall ranking of factories based on the environmental threat they posed.[35] The affected industries lobbied Congress and sought an injunction to block the project, which they argued would unfairly stigmatize their facilities. The EPA quickly abandoned the proposed project.[36]

The EPA encountered similar problems when, in 1996, it announced its intention to publish the "risk management plans" of over 60,000 businesses on its website beginning in 1999. Required under the Clean Air Act of 1990, the plans were intended to show how businesses would respond to catastrophic chemical accidents within their facilities. The business community fought against disclosure, arguing that internet-accessible data could be misused by terrorists. In 1998, the EPA retreated, promising that details about these "worst-case scenarios" would be removed before the plans were posted on the web. The following year, Congress went further, denying any right of access to the "worst-case scenario" data under the Freedom of Information Act – a step that prevented nongovernmental organizations from using the FOIA to access the data and construct a web-accessible database.[37]

An end to "practical obscurity"

The work of journalists and advocacy groups, while significant, pales in comparison to the efforts undertaken by businesses – known as data aggregators or commercial data brokers – to exploit new stockpiles of digitized data collected by government agencies. Much of this is personal information, and the success these businesses have had in compiling previously disparate collections of data has raised troubling questions about the erosion of privacy.

The amount of personal data that can be gleaned from government documents is surprisingly large. This includes data gleaned from so-called "vital records" on births, deaths, marriages, and divorces; information on voter registration, sometimes including party affiliation; property tax assessment information, including details on the features of a home; information on vehicle registrations, driver's licenses, accident reports, and traffic citations; information from business registrations and professional or trade license applications; details on workers' compensation claims; for public sector workers, details on employment; and police booking and arrest records. Much more personal data can be extracted out of court records – from documents produced in civil litigation, family court proceedings, bankruptcy applications, and criminal cases.[38]

In principle, much of this data has been publicly accessible for many years. However, the ability to collect and use this information has been constrained because traditionally it has been recorded on paper and stored by a large number of state and local governments. As U.S. Supreme Court Justice John Paul Stevens observed in an important 1989 decision, *Department of Justice v. Reporters Committee For Freedom of the Press*, this data existed in a state of "practical obscurity."[39] Digitization has now removed barriers to harvesting vast amounts of personal information from public records across the United States.

The data aggregation industry is increasingly dominated by a small number of businesses.[40] One of the most prominent is Choice-Point, which – like its major competitors – combines publicly accessible information with spending-habit data and other details collected within the private sector. Established in 1997, ChoicePoint has grown rapidly. In 2003 alone, it reported that it had acquired nine other firms that specialized in collecting public records and commercial information.[41] ChoicePoint, *Government Executive* reported in 2003, "owns an astounding 19 billion records, about 65 times as many pieces of information as there are people in the United States. As a result, ChoicePoint knows more about most people than the federal government does."[42]

In fact, the federal government has not been blind to this reality. ChoicePoint and other data brokers have aggressively marketed their data aggregation capabilities to federal agencies, and many – including the Federal Bureau of Investigation and Central Intelligence Agency – have contracted for their services. (In promotional material, ChoicePoint boasted to federal officials about the "one-stop mind-boggling power" of its databases.[43] A ChoicePoint executive explained to one journalist that the company acts "as an intelligence agency, gathering data, applying analytics" to generate "actionable intelligence" for its clients.[44]) Documents released to the Electronic Privacy Information Center under the Freedom of Information Act suggest that one federal agency – the United States Marshal Service – conducted between 14,000 and 40,000 searches on ChoicePoint databases each month between 1999 and 2001.[45]

The growth of these privately held databases has alarmed privacy advocates. As Daniel Solove observes, the principle of public access to government records was intended to "empower individuals to monitor their government," but the practices of commercial data brokers now threaten to turn this principle on its head. By harvesting and aggregating vast amounts of personal information, data brokers have the ability to create "digital biographies" that are often used for investigative purposes by businesses, employers, private detectives, and other individuals.[46] These massive private databanks can also be used for illicit purposes. In early 2005, ChoicePoint acknowledged that it had unwittingly sold the personal information of tens of thousands of Americans, much of it collected from government agencies, to identity thieves posing as small businessmen.[47]

The threat to personal privacy may be aggravated when government agencies begin to rely on commercial data brokers for citizen profiles. As critics have pointed out, federal privacy law would likely bar federal law enforcement agencies from creating databases analogous to the ones constructed by data brokers, and the agencies' reliance on brokers' services looks very much like a way of circumventing those privacy rules.[48] The data ChoicePoint sells to federal agencies is indexed by Social Security Number.[49] Although Americans have often balked at the idea of establishing a universal identifier (and even though there are good technical reasons why the SSN is a poor choice for an identifier),[50] government agencies effectively use the SSN for this purpose when they rely on ChoicePoint's services.

There is growing evidence that the American public is becoming sensitive to the privacy intrusions that can result from the disclosure of personal information given to the government. One warning sign was the evidence of public resistance to the 2000 national census – even though there are strong statutory protections against the disclosure of census data. Despite a legal obligation to cooperate and a $167 million advertising campaign to encourage participation, many Americans refused to answer census questions: The response rate for the census' long-form questionnaire was significantly lower that it had been ten years earlier. Census director Kenneth Prewitt attributed the decline to Americans' "heightened concern about privacy."[51] The majority of Americans who thought the census questions were too intrusive found support from Republican presidential candidate George W. Bush, who told journalists he could "understand why people don't want to give over that information to the government."[52]

In 1994, concern about the abuse of publicly accessible personal data led Congress to legislative action. The Driver's Privacy Protection Act prohibits state governments from disclosing personal information contained in their driver's license and motor vehicle registration records. (The law was strengthened in 1999.) The law was passed in response to controversy over the widespread practice among state motor vehicle departments of selling personal data to data brokers – the Justice Department claimed that New York State earned $17 million in one year by selling driver records[53] – and cases in which serious crimes had been facilitated by the disclosure of motor vehicle records. The constitutionality of the law was challenged but ultimately upheld by the U.S. Supreme Court in 2000.[54] Enforcement of the DPPA has not been easy: In Florida, for example, government officials and data brokers have been the object of at least four class action lawsuits for violations of the law.[55]

Nevertheless, DPPA may be a bellwether of a trend toward broader controls on access to government-collected personal data. Many states have recently adopted restrictions on the disclosure of Social Security Numbers, a piece of information that is highly valued by identity thieves.[56] Several states have also adopted statutory restrictions that prohibit the release of data for commercial purposes.[57] There is an analogy here to the restrictions imposed on various kinds of "homeland security information" in the months following the September 2001 terror attacks. In both cases, technology had lowered the cost of accessing and distributing information, effectively liberating data that had once existed in "practical obscurity." But this transformation brought new sensitivity to potential abuses, and subsequently new controls on access. In both cases there has been a philosophical – and often controversial – shift away from the long-standing proposition that governments have no right to consider the motives of an individual or organization when making judgments about the release of information.

The national debate over access to digitized court records turns on the question of whether – and how far – access controls should be imposed. There is a settled tradition in the United States of making court records publicly accessible – on paper, and at the courthouse. As records themselves are put in electronic form, there is no technical barrier to making them accessible on the web – and some courts have already taken that step, allowing anyone with an internet connection to browse through documents submitted by litigants or prosecutors, or issued by the courts themselves.

Privacy advocates protest that these new systems – offering instant access to social security numbers, addresses, phone numbers, credit card numbers, bank account numbers, and tax information – constitute "a treasure trove for identity thieves."[58] And perhaps worse: Information might be used for stalking, harassment, or blackmail. Finally there is the prospect of simple embarrassment, as financial, family, or medical details are revealed on the web.[59] These new information systems, says attorney George Carpinello, "turn court records into a massive data bank, opening all the information filed in every action instantaneously to the world. . . . The public will have ready access to an array of potentially private and embarrassing information regarding anyone who was a party or who was even mentioned in papers filed in any action in any court."[60]

Many governments have now recoiled from the idea of allowing universal access to digitized court files, although it remains unclear how far the retreat is likely to go. In 2002, a committee of federal judges recommended a relatively liberal approach on access to digitized court records – although it still recommended the deletion of several "personal data identifiers" and a delay on online access to criminal court records to allow further study.[61] In the same year, however, a proposed set of guidelines on access for state courts took a more severe view. It drew a sharp distinction between "courthouse access" and "remote access," recommending that remote access should be limited to basic information on proceedings and not to the full range of case documents.[62]

There is also confusion in actual practice in different states. In Maryland, for example, a committee appointed by the state judiciary in 2000 proposed sharp restrictions on access to digitized court records; after an outcry from journalists and businesses, a second committee was formed that in 2004 recommended more liberal rules on access. In Florida, by contrast, courts followed a policy of broad access until the state Supreme Court ordered a moratorium so that a study of privacy issues could be completed.[63] There is confusion, too, in the question of whether to allow businesses to purchase court records in bulk form. The 2002 guidelines for state governments suggested that there should be no bar on bulk access to data that is already accessible at the courthouse.[64] A 2003 survey, however, found several state courts refusing to release bulk data on privacy grounds.[65]

Monitoring the "paperless office"

The battle over access to structured data is accompanied by a second and growing conflict over access to the "unstructured data" in digital form that is held by government agencies. "Unstructured data" is not a familiar term: Loosely, it means the miscellany of documents within bureaucracies – e-mails, letters, memoranda, reports, spreadsheets, presentation files, and so on – that are not contained in large databases of standardized records. As Max Weber noted long ago – in somewhat different language – this mass of unstructured data constitutes the working heart of any government agency.[66] Most of the information kept by a government organization is likely held in unstructured form: In a widely cited 2000 study, the consulting firm Merrill Lynch estimated that more than 85 percent of all information in American business organizations exists as unstructured data.[67]

The definition of unstructured data gives us a sense of one of the two impacts new information technologies have had on the inventory of documents held by government agencies. The stockpile of government documents is now more *diverse* than ever before. Agencies continue to produce memoranda, reports, and paper correspondence that are comparable to those produced by agencies fifty years ago. But there are also many new species of document that are the result of technological advance – such as e-mail messages (which have supplanted communications once undertaken in nondocumentary form by means of phone or in-person conversation), electronic spreadsheets, presentation files, web pages, and desktop databases. Technology has also led to a dramatic increase in the *volume* of documents that are added to an agency's inventory every year. Archivists responsible for the preservation of significant records in the U.S. government say that they have been overwhelmed by a "tidal wave of electronic records."[68] The flow of e-mail messages alone is daunting: A 2002 study reported that the 14,000 employees of the U.S. Department of Energy dealt with one million e-mail messages a day;[69] in the same year archivists estimated that all U.S. federal employees handled thirty-seven billion messages annually.[70] (The Canadian government's chief information officer estimated that in 2002 its 150,000 public servants exchanged roughly six million e-mail messages every working day.[71]) The increase in volume is not only tied to documents in electronic form. "Hard-copy" documents have also grown in number. Office consumption of paper has increased steadily over the past decade, confounding experts who anticipated the advent of the "paperless office."[72] In 2004, the federal government was estimated to have used about 109,000 tons of paper, 12,000 tons more than in 1996.[73]

In fact, technology plays an unappreciated role in exaggerating our perceptions of government secretiveness. It is common for advocates of openness in the United States to point out the dramatic increase in the number of documents that have been classified for national security reasons over the last decade. In August 2004, for example, Senators Trent Lott and Ron Wyden complained that the number of classification decisions taken by federal officials had more than doubled over ten years, with more than 14.2 million documents being classified in 2003.[74] The complaint is based on statistics produced by the federal Information Security Oversight Office, which requires that federal agencies report every year on the number of "original" and "derivative" classification decisions their officials have made.

The distinction between the two types of decision is important. An original classification decision is made when a federal official determines that information that has not previously been classified requires special protection. A derivative classification decision is made when a document incorporates information from another document that is already classified, or when it is of a standardized type that an agency classification guide says must be classified.[75] The number of original classification decisions has changed significantly – but not radically – over the past decade, declining from 246,000 in 1993 to a low of 137,000 in 1998, and then rising again to 234,000 in 2003.[76] (In other words, the number of original classification decisions was actually lower in 2003 than in 1993.)

By contrast, the number of derivative classification decisions has grown markedly over the last decade, from 6.4 million in 1993 to 14 million in 2003. Nor was there a marked dip in the number of derivative decisions in the years of the Clinton presidency, as there was for original decisions. The result is that the ratio of derivative to original decisions has jumped as well, from roughly 20:1 in the early Clinton years to over 60:1 in the early Bush years. One of the forces driving this trend, says the ISOO, is information technology that enables the rapid and almost costless duplication of documents, and which has replaced millions of secure telephone conversations with e-mail messages that are electronically tabulated and counted as classified documents.[77] "Information technology," the ISOO concluded in 2005, "has exponentially increased the Government's ability to produce information of all sorts, both classified and unclassified."[78]

The transformation of the stock of unstructured data – both its expansion and diversification in form – has in some ways improved governmental transparency. For example, it is frequently argued that open government laws have a chilling effect on record keeping within government agencies: Officials, knowing that their documents might be publicly disclosed, are said to be more reticent about committing their views to paper. (The extent to which officials become more circumspect is open to question; one recent Canadian government study that examined documents produced before and after the adoption of Canada's Access To Information Act had found no evidence that the law had any influence on record keeping by government officials.[79]) But technology has had a countervailing effect, by causing millions of undocumented conversations to be transformed into documents – all at risk for public disclosure.

Americans had an early illustration of this countervailing effect in 1987, with the release of the report of the Tower Commission on the Iran–Contra scandal. The scandal erupted in November 1986 with revelations that President Ronald Reagan's National Security Council had sold weapons to the government of Iran (which it had publicly alleged was a sponsor of international terrorism), and then diverted the profit from those sales to rebels fighting to overthrow Nicaragua, thereby violating a ban on aid imposed by the U.S. Congress. Investigators quickly demanded access to NSC documents – and NSC staff, including its Chief, John Poindexter, responded by destroying the incriminating records.[80]

The NSC was eventually trapped by its enthusiasm for new technology. Only a year before – and well before other parts of the White House staff – the NSC had adopted a new e-mail system, which Poindexter and his staff used extensively. When the Iran–Contra investigations began, Poindexter and his subordinate Oliver North attempted to delete thousands of compromising e-mail messages – but they could not destroy the system's back-up tapes. The Tower Commission's report on the scandal, published in February 1987, relied heavily on the e-mail messages, introducing them to readers as "conversations by computer . . . [that] provide a first-hand, contemporaneous account of events."[81] The e-mail traffic, said one of the Commission's three members, former Senator Edmund Muskie, provided a "mother lode" of incriminating evidence.[82]

President Reagan and his successors tried unsuccessfully to block the disclosure of other compromising White House e-mail. The Reagan White House intended to destroy the backup tapes of all of its e-mail traffic on the evening before President George H. W. Bush's inauguration, but was blocked by last-minute litigation. The George H. W. Bush administration continued to fight for the right to destroy the tapes, and President Bush himself attempted to negotiate an agreement with the U.S. National Archives that would allow him to treat backup tapes as his own property. Later, the Clinton administration supported the Bush agreement, arguing that it did not want critics "pawing over its computer memos." The prolonged litigation resulted in a defeat for all three Presidents. E-mail would be treated under the same preservation and disclosure rules that applied to traditional paper records.[83]

A former colleague of Poindexter's argued that the risk of disclosure would "corrupt" e-mail conversations,[84] but this fear has proved to be overstated. E-mail has become too deeply entrenched in contemporary work life for self-censorship to be an effective strategy: Writing elliptically takes time, and undermines the effort to get work done.

Busy officials, struggling to manage an always expanding in-box, find it easier and faster to write candidly.

This means that e-mail continues to provide "mother lodes" of revealing information about the internal life of large bureaucracies. The Columbia Accident Investigation Board relied on e-mail to show how NASA staff had downplayed safety concerns before the January 2003 shuttle disaster.[85] The 2003 report of the Joint Congressional Inquiry into the 9/11 attacks, and the 2004 report of the 9/11 Commission, used e-mail to illustrate how bureaucratic and legal difficulties compromised the effort to deal with terrorist threats.[86] Similarly, the Senate Intelligence Committee in its 2004 report relied on e-mail to document internal dissent about the reliability of evidence about the threat posed by weapons of mass destruction in Iraq.[87] And in November 2004, Senator John McCain released e-mail traffic in which Air Force Secretary James Roche had privately campaigned against European defense contractors ("the fools in Paris and Berlin," as he called them) while publicly promising a fair competition to supply new refuelling tankers.[88]

In the United Kingdom, e-mail was a critical part of the evidence to the Hutton Inquiry during its probe of the British government's conduct before the Iraq war and after the suicide of WMD expert David Kelly.[89] (In one compromising pre-war e-mail, Prime Minister Tony Blair's chief of staff conceded there was "no imminent threat" posed by Iraq.[90]) Earlier, a senior Blair government official was pressured to resign following the disclosure of an e-mail in which she had urged public servants to regard the 9/11 attacks as an opportunity to disclose her department's "unfavorable" news items. "It can be tempting to regard email as ephemeral," said the *Financial Times* during these controversies,

> ...yet many have come to realise that emails provide a record more permanent and indestructible than many older forms of communication.... Paper documents can be burnt and conversations held in circumstances that make eavesdropping very difficult. But, once sent, an email leaves traces that may return to haunt the writer, long after the event.[91]

Paradoxically, however, the usefulness of e-mail as a tool for monitoring the internal life of bureaucracies can be undermined by its ubiquity. When the National Security Archive, a Washington-based nongovernmental organization, succeeded in its litigation to block the destruction of White House e-mail, it was like the proverbial dog chasing a fire truck: What would it do once it had caught it? The Reagan White House had accumulated seven million e-mail messages by the end of the presidency, even though working e-mail systems had been adopted little more than two years before. "The main problem was *too much* email," said the Archive's director, Tom Blanton; the job of reviewing each message to determine whether it could be released would have been massive. Blanton's organization negotiated a compromise, in which it obtained a "core sample" of e-mail from the Reagan years.[92]

Blanton's predicament is probably not unique. As technological change causes the inventory of government documents to expand, the parts of that inventory that relate to any specific topic must expand as well. So, too, must the task of searching for, and reviewing, documents that are requested under an FOI law or by any other inquiry. It is no longer a matter of retrieving neatly organized manila folders and reviewing the memoranda within them. Documents are now in multiple formats; they may be more widely scattered within an organization; and they are likely more numerous than ever before. For older digitized documents, there is also the added complication that the format in which they were stored may have become obsolete.

This means more work for officials who are charged with responding to document requests. In Montana, media requests for the e-mail of Governor Judy Martz over one month in 2002 drove state officials to use a disaster-recovery system to reconstruct the governor's e-mail account, and then to review the content of over 3000 messages, at a cost of $28,000.[93] In Canada, one Canadian government department reported that it had received – on a single day in 2002 – over 100 requests under its FOI law for "all records in the email system" of different employees. The same individual has since filed over one thousand similar requests; the department said in 2004 that it had established a special team of employees working full-time to retrieve information in response to the queries.[94]

Such complexity may mean that individuals who request documents will be more likely to face higher fees for processing requests, and therefore be more likely to abandon or narrow those requests. If they choose to continue, individuals who receive documents may face an added problem of interpretation. Traditional paper files had the virtue of boundedness and authoritativeness. The labor involved in producing documents meant that those that were produced were more likely to distill some important point; and because documents were limited in number, each could more easily be put forth as an definitive expression of a bureau's or official's point of view. Obviously the view of bureaucratic life that was available through paper files was partial and biased; technological limitations meant that the full back-and-forth within organizations was not recorded. On the other hand, the task of sorting through the documentary record was simpler, as was the job of holding officials accountable for the content of any one document. Because the document was difficult to produce, the statement within it was presumed to be important; because the stock of documents was limited, an official's capacity to dismiss it as one part of a long chain of communications, or to rebut it with another contradictory document, was also constrained.

In the digital world, we may have more facts about the internal life of organizations, but the burden of sense making – of deciding what all the back-and-forth *means* – is also increased, and put on the shoulders of individuals and organizations outside of government. Some outside observers may have the capacity to sift through a large pool of digitized and paper documents, but many do not. Furthermore, the capacity to use any single document as a "smoking gun"[95] – authoritative evidence of governmental predispositions – is also weakened. How much can one e-mail mean, in a sea of millions? How much weight can be put on the wording in one draft of a memorandum or report, if there are a dozen other variations of the same file?

Metadata: a new surveillance tool?

The growth of digitized information is creating comparable problems for officials working within government agencies. Specialists responsible for managing government documents have spent the last decade struggling to find new techniques for preserving this deepening pool of information. They have been compromised by the unwillingness of many governments, facing overall spending constraints, to allow substantial new investment in records management. The risk posed by inadequate record keeping is now being aggravated by a looming wave of retirements: As older workers leave, so too will the personal knowledge that helped to overcome inadequacies in document management. The risk of so-called "knowledge bleed" is substantial. Within the U.S. civil service, over half of the total number of program managers are expected to be eligible for retirement by 2006.[96]

To improve their capacity to organize and access inventories of internal documents, many public organizations have begun to implement Electronic Document and Records Management Systems (EDRMS). An EDRM system is designed to give structure to unstructured data. At the core of any EDRM system is a database that is intended to house any form of unstructured data that is important to an agency – any draft report, memorandum, presentation file, spreadsheet, or e-mail message. When a new document is added to the database, basic information about the document – for example, its title, subject, author, and date of creation – is also added. This basic information is known as metadata, and is roughly equivalent to the data recorded for each book in a library catalog. An EDRM system fulfills two roles. It allows better day-to-day management of documents for the ongoing business of the agency (a function known to specialists as "document management"), and it ensures that the archival tasks of preserving important documents and pruning transitory documents are handled properly (a function known as "records management.")

EDRM systems are being adopted widely in the advanced democracies. The Canadian government, repeatedly ranked by the consulting firm Accenture as the world leader in "eGovernment maturity,"[97] has deployed EDRM systems in over thirty departments and agencies. The British government aimed to establish EDRM systems in major government departments by 2004.[98] The United States has been slower in implementing EDRM systems, although standards have been adopted and implementation was made a priority within the Bush administration's management reform program.[99] The European Union has also developed standards to guide the development of electronic records management systems by its member states.[100]

Some observers have already suggested that EDRM systems can help to improve transparency in government by making it easier for agencies to find and retrieve documents that relate to a request for information. The Information Commissioner of the Canadian province of Ontario says that EDRM systems could reduce wide-spread problems of delay in responding to information requests.[101] Canada's federal government also says that EDRM systems will help it to be "truly open and transparent" by providing better tools for locating documents citizens are entitled to receive under its FOI law.[102]

In fact, EDRM systems could provide a level of transparency in government operations that might startle the agencies that are now deploying the systems. Because EDRM systems encourage the production of standardized metadata about documents, and consolidate that metadata in a central database, they will improve the capacity of workers within agencies to search the stockpile of agency documents. What may not be appreciated is that individuals *outside* the agency may also be able to access metadata in bulk form, just as they have done with older government databases.

The revolutionary potential that this may create is best illustrated by a historical example. One of the long-standing frustrations of openness advocates has been their inability to know whether there are documents held within a government agency that might be relevant to their interests – or to know where those documents might be. Those advocates point to a practice of the Swedish government that seems to remedy this problem. Under Swedish law, all public authorities must maintain a publicly accessible register of all official documents in their possession, including documents that might themselves be inaccessible: "It is therefore possible to keep the contents of a document secret, but rarely its existence."[103] The practice of maintaining public registers is often cited as evidence of Sweden's deep commitment to transparency. There is, however, a critical limitation. The class of "official documents" is defined to exclude many internal working documents – draft reports, memoranda, and e-mails – that are often sought through requests under FOI laws in other countries.[104]

By using FOI laws to extract EDRM metadata in bulk electronic format, and using that data to create their own web-accessible databases, nongovernmental organizations might go as far as Sweden – and further. An EDRM-derived database could include *every* significant document generated within a government agency – including e-mail traffic, internal memoranda, and draft reports. The documents themselves may not be accessible under FOI law, but the fact of their existence would be publicly known. Outside actors could gain an unprecedented view of the flow of information within the arteries of the organization. Even rudimentary information about the volume and subject of newly generated documents might reveal secrets about agency priorities.

This is not a hypothetical possibility. In 2004, I asked the Treasury Board Secretariat of the Canadian government – the agency responsible for oversight of management and expenditure within the federal government (roughly comparable to the U.S. Office of Management and Budget) – for a download of metadata out of its EDRMS for documents entered into the database in July of that year. TBS employs an internally developed database, the Records/Document/Information Management System (RDIMS), which has become the EDRM standard for Canadian government departments. TBS is a small agency, with only about 400 employees. Nevertheless, the volume of document production is substantial, with over 4,000 documents being added to the RDIMS database in July 2004 alone. (The variety of documents is also broad, comprising eight types of file in twelve proprietary formats.)

The metadata allows a detailed analysis of emerging priorities within TBS. For example, it is possible to look only at briefings logged into the RDIMS and determine what subjects appeared most frequently. Topping the list was a TBS review of "federal institutional governance," a subject on which 15 briefings had been prepared that month. The briefings related to a review the Canadian government promised would be undertaken by a committee of ministers in response to scandals over waste and mismanagement. RDIMS data shows that all documents on this subject were produced by a select team of analysts operating within the office of TBS's Associate Secretary.

An analysis of e-mail logged into RDIMS for the same month suggests another pressing topic in TBS: a study of government spending on biotechnology programs being undertaken by the same team of analysts. A closer look at documents entered into the RDIMS database by TBS staff who have been publicly identified (in the government's telephone directory) as members of this high-profile review team tends to confirm this view. A large majority of their "operational" documents – a catch-all for internal working papers – relate to the studies on "institutional governance" and biotechnology programs. Insight can also be gleaned from data about the subjects that do not appear in RDIMS. The team's entries into the database suggest that many areas that had been publicly identified as government priorities were not occupying its attention that month.[105]

EDRMS metadata does not simply allow outside observers to track trends within government agencies. It also allows individuals to pinpoint exactly the government documents that they want to request. This helps to resolve two basic problems that confront users of disclosure laws in many countries: a lack of knowledge about precisely what documents a government agency might have in its possession; and a suspicion (sometimes well founded) that officials will contort vaguely worded requests to exclude sensitive material. Requesters often attempt to deal with these problems by making very general requests, like this one sent by a nongovernmental organization to Canada's Department of Fisheries and Oceans in 2004:

> All briefing notes, handwritten notes, meeting minutes, correspondence and email, or any other communications or documents whatsoever sent to or received from the Department of Foreign Affairs and International Trade since June 28, 2000 on topics related to Alaskan transboundary issues.[106]

This is (figuratively, and perhaps literally) a fishing expedition – the sort of request that often exasperates government officials. Obviously EDRM metadata cannot help with handwritten notes. But with other kinds of data, it can provide nongovernmental organizations with a precise inventory of relevant documents – as well as the unique identifier that can be used to request each document. (See the following compilation, "Browsing an ERDM Library.")

As more EDRM systems come online, government agencies will begin to grapple with the unexpected potential for heightened transparency through the release of bulk metadata. Officials are not likely to view the results with equanimity, because the capacity to have any conversation in confidence could be seriously eroded. The fact that exploratory conversations on particular subjects have begun would be quickly revealed, and outside actors would be able to make rapid and precise requests for the documents generated during that conversation. Officials will be put on the defensive much more quickly.

Browsing an EDRM Library

By studying EDRM metadata, it is possible for nongovernmental organizations to track the production of documents within a government agency. In this case, I sorted metadata for the month of July 2004 from the EDRM system of Treasury Board Secretariat, a central agency in the Canadian government. The following shows a partial list of documents in the system that related to the subject "Social Insurance Number [SIN] and Data Matching." The trustee is the TBS employee responsible for the document. In this example, all documents were generated by employees of TBS's Chief Information Officer (CIO) Branch. The documents reveal a bureaucratic effort to revise government policy on the use of Social Insurance Numbers as a tool for combining personal information in different government databases. The subject of database integration had aroused intense public controversy four years earlier. Groups wishing to probe further could make a precise request for these documents by specifying the EDRM library number on the left.

Number	Title	Trustee	Application	Date
236106	Presentation for the CIO on the Status of the SIN & Data Matching Review.	Murray, Terry	POWERPOINT	07/05/04
237077	Agenda for July 14 Meeting of the Interdepartmental Committee on SIN and Data Matching.	Taillefer, Charles	MS WORD	07/09/04
238454	Notes for discussion with Office of the Privacy Commissioner regarding new uses of SIN by several institutions	Taillefer, Charles	MS WORD	07/16/04
238733	Presentation for the Rescheduled Meeting of the Committee on SIN and Data Matching.	Murray, Terry	POWERPOINT	07/19/04
237924	Presentation on the SIN & Data Matching Review for the Interdepartmental Privacy and Service Transformation Committee.	Murray, Terry	MS WORD	07/14/04
238894	SIN and Data Matching: Questions and Answers.	Taillefer, Charles	MS WORD	07/20/04
239651	SIN and Data Matching: Revised Policy.	Murray, Terry	MS WORD	07/26/04

This will exacerbate the anxiety that has already provoked governments to tighten their control over the outflow of government information. (See Chapters 3 and 4.) Elected officials and career bureaucrats will argue that this degree of transparency goes too far, and that the right to confidentiality for internal deliberations should include a right to keep secret the *topic* of conversation as much as the *content* of conversation. However, it is not clear how the bulk release of metadata can be avoided under many FOI laws. Under U.S. law, agencies might argue that metadata can be withheld because it is (in the words of the federal FOI law) related to relatively unimportant "internal practices" of an agency[107] – but this is unlikely to be a tenable defense, because it will be widely recognized that the information is being withheld precisely because it is critically important. Other laws are crafted to deal with the content of specific documents; it would likely require a significant and controversial interpretation of existing law to allow the withholding of bulk data on the grounds that it reveals compromising information about the *pattern* of conversation within an agency.

There is an alternative response: Officials may begin to evade the system by generating documents that are not logged within their EDRM system. This might easily be done if officials are not pressed to comply with ERDMS requirements. Indeed, our small sample of data from TBS suggests that compliance with its EDRMS requirements could be spotty. Technological enthusiasts working for the government's Chief Information Officer appear much more likely to enter documents into RDIMS than employees in other TBS branches. Routines for recording significant e-mail messages also seem erratic across TBS's branches, with a low proportion of total traffic being entered into the system.

There is already a notorious precedent for the tactic of evasion. In his early years as director of the FBI, Herbert Hoover revolutionized its capabilities by introducing an advanced method of documents management – the Central Records System, which provided a standardized method of classifying information about FBI investigations and simplified the task of searching for and retrieving information by FBI employees. In retrospect we can see this as a precursor of EDRMS. However, Hoover soon realized that there were records he did not want logged in the widely accessible Central Records System, and within a few years he began to develop separate and secret record-keeping procedures. Memoranda on sensitive (and often illegal) activities were captioned "Do Not File" to ensure that they would not be entered into the Central Records System. The separate procedures helped to thwart oversight. As Senator Richard Schweiker observed during 1975 hearings on FBI misconduct, the system allowed the bureau to say that its central records system revealed no evidence of illegal conduct.[108]

Whether a comparable strategy of evasion could work in a contemporary bureaucracy is unclear. It is difficult for large organizations to get work done while relying on informal and covert procedures. The willingness of employees to quietly accept practices that clearly contravene formal policy has also declined. This implies that the more probable response to the threat posed by EDRM systems is likely to be a reinterpretation or amendment of existing law.

Reacting to digitization

The digitization of government-held information appears, at first glance, to provide extraordinary opportunities for improving transparency. It seems to provide new tools for monitoring the work of government itself – either by accessing bulk data about routine government transactions or by profiling the pool of unstructured data held within government agencies. It also seems to provide new opportunities for monitoring business, by allowing access to data that government itself collects from the private sector. Finally, and most problematically, digitization creates new opportunities for monitoring citizen behavior, by allowing businesses and other actors – including, in sometimes circuitous ways, government agencies – easier access to the mass of personal information that is aggregated within public bureaucracies.

The extent to which these opportunities will remain available is unknown and is, in fact, likely to be one of the major points of contention in coming years. As the power of these new monitoring techniques becomes apparent, we can expect the actors that are subject to monitoring (businesses, citizens, governments) to react by seeking to restrict the inflow of information to government databases, or the outflow of that information from public agencies. In fact, we can already see these battles over the inflow and outflow of digitized data intensifying.

In some respects, reaction against the impact of digitization is not only predictable but justified. Closer monitoring of governmental or business practices is one thing; tighter surveillance of individual behavior is another. Indeed, it would be ironic if transparency laws that are justified in the name of human rights had the effect, in practice, of compromising civil liberties. And it is far from clear that a radically heightened capacity for monitoring *governmental* activity is necessarily in the public interest. Although the prospect is now entirely hypothetical, we could envisage a moment when businesses, exploiting the opportunities posed by access to ERDMS metadata, are capable of closely tracking the work of government agencies, intervening to nip unfavorable policies before they are even partly formed. Public agencies, subject to a degree of openness that is far greater than that imposed on the businesses and other organizations with which public officials must work, might be incapacitated by transparency.

The result of these struggles may be the imposition of new legal restrictions on access to digitized data, including rules that restrict access to certain kinds of individuals or impose conditions on the use of information. For many, the idea of differentiating access rights in this way is anathema: It seems to undermine the long-standing principle that rights of access should be equal and universal – a notion sometimes caught in the phrase "public is public." However, the reality has never been so simple. The act of inspecting records at the town office or courthouse imposed its own costs: the knowledge needed to determine the location of the records; the time needed to visit the office; the nerve often needed to request even information that is, as a settled matter of law, publicly accessible. These practical barriers assured a rough form of access control, discouraging access by individuals who were not from the community, familiar with the law and processes of government, and known by local officials. Technological change may be causing us to articulate access restrictions that were already embedded in informal practice.

While new technologies destroy these old practical barriers to access, new practical barriers could also be created. The growing pool of digitized information will be accessible only to nongovernmental organizations that have the technical expertise to understand how information is structured within government agencies and understand as well the agencies' capacity to extract that information from their databases in usable form. Manipulating that data, or extracting meaning from a large mass of data, will also impose substantial burdens on nongovernmental organizations. It is one thing to thumb through a few thousand pages of memoranda; it is another to manipulate tens of thousands of digitized records, each containing dozens of fields of data, released in tab-delimited ASCII format; and another to make sense of the several hundred thousand lines of ERDMS metadata that might be generated in a few months by a reasonably sized agency.

These new barriers to access can be substantial. Technical and financial constraints already limit the capacity of American journalists to undertake computer-assisted reporting projects. The cost to the nongovernmental organization Environmental Defense of its establishing a website to exploit the mass of Toxic Release Inventory data collected by the EPA was initially $1.5 million; the work got done with the support of private philanthropies.[109] These are the constraints imposed in the United States, which is affluent and advantaged by a thriving media and nongovernmental sector. As a matter of practice, the impediments to access to digitized government information in other countries could be much more substantial. This has two implications. The first is that the opportunities for heightened transparency could be undercut, not only by the reaction of other stakeholders, but by the practical difficulties associated with extracting and manipulating digitized data. The second is that problems in *equity* of access to government information might be even more severe than they are today.

IV CONCLUSION

10

THE END OF THE STORY?

Many students of contemporary journalism argue that news production consists largely of the reproduction of stock stories – the retelling of archetypal narratives already familiar to both journalists and their audiences. The facts may change from year to year; the plot does not. Relying on an archetypal story line, journalists achieve certain efficiencies. They know what facts are needed to make the story work, and they do not need to explain to readers or viewers what the story is "about." The story helps to organize reality. Moreover, the story line imposes a moral order: When we begin to tell a story, or read a story, we are led to a certain view of how it ought to end.[1]

This sounds very abstract. But at least one of these archetypal narratives will be instantly familiar. Imagine the following story line: Powerful officials abuse their authority and injure innocent people. They attempt to hide their abuses. Tenacious outsiders struggle to reveal the facts, but are thwarted by official indifference and outright obstruction. Ultimately, however, the truth comes out. The citizenry is outraged, and officials are brought to account. Reforms are introduced to prevent future abuses. The story comes to a satisfying conclusion.

It is not difficult to find this story line at work in the American media. A famous example is the Watergate scandal, in which two determined reporters for the *Washington Post*, Bob Woodward and Carl Bernstein, exposed the role of the Nixon White House in orchestrating a break-in at the Democratic Party national headquarters and "dirty tricks" during the 1972 presidential campaign. Here politics merged with popular culture. The film version of the scandal,

All the President's Men, was pitched by Warner Brothers Studio as "The most devastating detective story of the century!"[2] The dénouement was equal in scale to the conflict that preceded it: Not only did the President resign, but Congress adopted a series of legislative checks it hoped would prevent comparable scandals in the future (see Chapter 3).

Even in 1972, this story line was not new. On the contrary, it was an old mainstay of progressive reformers. Seventy years earlier, in 1902, Ida Tarbell tallied the misdeeds of the Standard Oil trust in a series of articles for *McClure's* Magazine, fueling a controversy that led eventually to the breakup of the trust. Another journalist, Upton Sinclair, exposed horrific conditions in the meat-packing industry in his 1906 book *The Jungle*, provoking Congress to pass new laws regulating the industry. A third muckraker, Lincoln Steffens, detailed the corruption of major American cities, prompting prosecutions and the turn-out of legislators who had tolerated graft. The sequence was always the same: abuse, exposé, outrage, reform.

Revelation of misconduct was the crucial second step. "Sunlight is said to be the best of disinfectants," said Supreme Court Justice Louis Brandeis in *Harper's Weekly* in 1913, "electric light the most efficient policeman."[3] This faith in the catalytic power of disclosure bolstered reformers in subsequent years: If only the facts were made public (many thought), justice would follow.

In the spring of 2004 the controversy over abuse of detainees held by U.S. forces in Iraq and at Guantanamo Bay seemed to be evolving to fit this old story line. A recalcitrant executive branch appeared determined to hide the facts from the American public. (According to polls taken in early 2004, many Americans believed that the Bush administration was "mainly trying to cover up" reports of prisoner abuse.[4]) Nevertheless the facts came out. Documents and photographs were leaked; investigations were undertaken; entire books were written. It was clear that senior administration officials had attempted to contort traditional understandings of national and international law to justify more aggressive methods of interrogation. Poorly trained and inadequately supervised troops were seen to have engaged in horrific abuses. Many of the military's detainees were acknowledged to have little or no intelligence value; they were minor players caught by events.

Despite the administration's secretiveness, these facts appeared to take hold in the popular consciousness. According to polls, a majority of Americans believed that their government was using torture in its campaign against terrorism "as a matter of policy"; a larger majority believed that their government was using "physical abuse that falls short of torture."[5] (A post-election poll showed that two-thirds of the American public believed that torture of prisoners by Americans had taken place in Iraq and Afghanistan over the preceding two years; 40 percent believed that torture was *still* happening, in spite of the Abu Ghraib controversy.[6]) Most Americans said that Justice Department memos interpreting the legal constraints on torture contributed to the Abu Ghraib abuses,[7] and over one-third believed that leaders in Washington were involved in a "decision" to abuse and torture the Abu Ghraib detainees.[8] Moreover, Americans said that this sort of behavior violated norms of acceptable conduct; a substantial majority said that torture was *never* acceptable. A majority was even prepared to say that "physical abuse that falls short of torture" was never acceptable.[9]

By the early fall of 2004 the abuse story appeared to be nearing its natural conclusion. All that was needed was a fitting conclusion – the rendering of justice. Officials had to be held accountable for the outrage. There was already dissatisfaction among editorialists over the reluctance of government-appointed inquiries to acknowledge the culpability of senior officials. On the other hand, there was a hope that the story might be closed in another way: in the forthcoming presidential election. "The electorate would make its own judgment," wrote Craig R. Whitney, an assistant managing editor of the *New York Times*, in October 2004, "on what responsibility should be borne by those who made the political and policy decisions that led, indirectly or not, to the aberrations at Abu Ghraib."[10]

As it turned out, hope that the electorate would make such a judgment proved to be wildly misplaced. Polls showed that treatment of detainees was a nonissue in the 2004 presidential campaign.[11] Even more telling were the three presidential debates, and one vice presidential debate, held a month before Election Day. Each debate lasted ninety minutes; in sum, then, there were six hours of argument on the major issues confronting the United States. The transcripts of the four debates contain over 60,000 words, roughly three-quarters of the length of this book. But here are words that do not appear at all:

> Guantanamo
> Abu Ghraib
> detention
> detainee
> prisoner

"Torture" appears once – when President Bush, justifying his rush to war, reminds us that Saddam Hussein "tortured his own people." "Abuse" appears once as well – when Vice President Cheney tells us that "lawsuit abuse is a serious problem in this country."[12]

On November 2, 2004, President Bush was re-elected, this time with a clear majority of the popular vote. Weeks after the election, John Yoo – the former deputy assistant attorney general who drafted memoranda on the legality of interrogation methods – told *The New Yorker*: "The issue is dying out. The public has had its referendum."[13]

Yoo's comment inflamed liberal opinion. Editors of the *New York Times* called the statement "outrageous."[14] In the *New York Review of Books*, Anthony Lewis challenged Yoo's assumption that "an election in which the torture issue was not discussed has legitimized President Bush's right to order its use."[15] Admittedly, the lawfulness of the government's interrogation techniques – or the question of whether the human rights of detainees had been respected – could not be settled by majority vote. On the other hand, it was a *Times* editor, Charles Whitney, who earlier suggested that the election would provide a moment of reckoning on prisoner abuse. Moreover, the difficulty was not simply that voters had weighed the arguments and voted to endorse (or at least tolerate) the Bush administration's policy. As Lewis said, *the torture issue was not discussed.*

Perhaps the frustration of liberal critics grew out of a failure of narrative. The story line had proceeded along its normal course and then unwound. There was no satisfying dénouement. "The worst aspect of the Abu Ghraib scandal is this," the *Washington Post* editorialized a month after the election. "The system survived its public exposure."[16] Senior officials had not been held responsible. On the contrary, some – such as White House counsel Alberto Gonzales, appointed as Attorney General – had been rewarded. ("Is no one accountable?" asked the *Times'* Bob Herbert, similarly frustrated.[17]) Journalist Mark Danner put the issue directly:

At least since Watergate, Americans have come to take for granted a certain story line of scandal, in which revelation is followed by investigation, adjudication and expiation. Together, Congress and the courts investigate high-level wrongdoing and place it in a carefully constructed narrative, in which crimes are charted, malfeasance is explicated and punishment is apportioned as the final step in the journey back to order, justice and propriety.

When Alberto Gonzales takes his seat before the Senate Judiciary Committee today for hearings to confirm whether he will become attorney general of the United States, Americans will bid farewell to that comforting story line. . . . Though the revelations of Abu Ghraib transfixed Americans for a time, in the matter of torture not much changed. . . . The system of torture has, after all, survived its disclosure. We have entered a new era; the traditional story line in which scandal leads to investigation and investigation leads to punishment has been supplanted by something else. Wrongdoing is still exposed; we gaze at the photographs and read the documents, and then we listen to the president's spokesman "reiterate," as he did last week, "the president's determination that the United States never engage in torture." And there the story ends. [18]

Had the story line actually lost its power? Some explanations could be brought forward to rebut Danner's case. Perhaps, as some observers suggested, voters did not adequately appreciate facts critical to the story – such as the innocence of many abused detainees, or the complicity of senior civilian officials in approving tactics that voters were prepared to condemn.[19] From this point of view, the story failed due to its incompleteness: All of its essential elements were not in place. Or perhaps this was an illustration of a divergence in values between a liberal elite and a more conservative electorate. When talking to pollsters, voters may have exaggerated their actual opposition to abuse or torture. (There is a plausible argument that hypocrisy on torture is the best policy.[20]) The fact that voters did not react to *this* story might not have meant that they had become immune to *any* story built on the traditional elements of abuse, exposé, outrage, and reform.

On the other hand, perhaps Danner is right, and the story line *has* lost its power. The root problem might not be an ideological divergence between voters and elites, but a growing sense of disconnection between voters of all political stripes and the institutions of government. Evidence of public detachment from the political process is substantial. According to National Election Study data, only one out of six Americans believes that government pays "a good deal" of attention to what people think when it decides what to do – half the proportion of forty years ago.[21] In a national poll conducted by the Maxwell School of Syracuse University shortly before the 2004 election, over half of respondents said that "government is generally too complicated for most people to understand." A similar proportion of respondents said they did not trust government officials.[22]

For citizens who hold such views, the business of government may have degenerated into what Douglas Kellner has called a "politics of spectacle" – something that may be watched, and even viewed with disgust, but nonetheless regarded as a series of events with which the individual citizen is not directly involved.[23] Lacking a sense of involvement, citizens may also lack a sense of shared responsibility for correcting misconduct in the political sphere. The feeling of complicity that spurs citizens into action may be absent. "We are all torturers now," Mark Danner wrote in January 2005[24] – but this may be exactly where Danner gets it wrong. The disconnected citizen may not feel responsibility for what he sees going on inside the circus ring. And this may lead to the discomfiting prospect of a world in which transparency is achieved but the prospect of reform remains distant nonetheless.

Public disaffection with the political process is a complex phenomenon that is driven by many factors – including the reality that political influence *is* unfairly distributed and elected officials often *have* abused power. However, we must also consider the troubling possibility that the rhetoric of antisecrecy campaigners may feed this sense of disconnection. I do not mean "rhetoric" in its pejorative sense. Rather, I mean a kind of public argumentation that emphasizes the persistence and growth of government secrecy, and that attributes secretiveness to the base motives of political leaders – that is, that characterizes secrecy as the product of selfish officials determined to hide compromising facts. The rhetoric of secrecy has intensified over the last two decades, for reasons I have already explained in some depth. One is that the antisecrecy movement is larger than ever before. Another is that there is a more extensive set of disclosure laws that routinely generate conflicts that give prominence to governmental obduracy over the release of information. And there is no doubt that the problem of excessive secrecy has worsened recently. Official resistance to transparency requirements has stiffened, and the structure of government has changed – through privatization, the elaboration of security networks, the rise of supranational bodies – in ways that undercut disclosure requirements.

The intensified rhetoric of secrecy has had an impact on American public opinion. The conviction that there is too much governmental secrecy is now firmly entrenched. In a 2005 survey, a large majority of Americans said that they were "somewhat" or "very" concerned about government secrecy. Such secrecy, said the poll's respondents, threatened to "undermine the functioning of good government."[25]

But what do Americans do with this professed concern over governmental secrecy? We might expect that it would serve as a spur to political action. However, as another *New York Times* editorialist observed on the eve of the 2004 vote, the "ominous" trend toward increased secrecy garnered "only a trivial level of attention" during the presidential campaign.[26]

Unfortunately, we can also imagine an alternative and bleaker scenario, in which complaints about secrecy are deployed by citizens to rationalize their disengagement from the political process, or their tolerance of noxious policies. How, after all, can citizens be expected to participate actively in politics, if critical information is being withheld from them? How can they share responsibility for the actions of their leaders if they have incomplete knowledge of those actions? The beliefs that government leaders cannot be trusted, that there is too much government secrecy, that government is too complicated to be readily understood – all of these may combine to form a powerful *ethic of detachment*, which leads to (and justifies) a failure to engage actively in political affairs or to insist vigorously on the accountability of political leaders. Worse still, the ethic of detachment may hold sway even when enough critical facts about specific problems *are* in the public domain. We may complain about excessive secrecy, and others may accept the reasonableness of our complaints about secrecy, even when – with regard to specific issues – there actually is enough information at hand to form an opinion about the justness of a political leader's conduct. We may watch all of the political spectacle, and still use the rhetoric of secrecy to justify our decision to do nothing more than watch.

Abu Ghraib, and the broader question of the treatment of detainees, became one of the main fronts in the campaign against secrecy during the first term of the George W. Bush administration. But much of the truth eventually came out – if not enough to firmly fix accountability, then certainly enough for a duty of further inquiry to be activated. In the longer run, the significance of Abu Ghraib may also lie in the extent to which we overestimated the catalytic effect of exposure. We can condemn the executive branch for its obstinacy and the Congress and the media for their timidity; but having done this we can still also challenge the quiescence of the American public.

The struggle to advance transparency is important, and it is far from over. In some respects it is more complicated than ever before. But transparency by itself is not enough. The United States has perhaps the most comprehensive set of transparency rules in the world, a vigorous and free media, and an educated and enfranchised population. But even in conditions such as these, we cannot assume that the revelation of injustice will lead automatically to a remedy for injustice. Do we have a right to information? Certainly. But we also have a responsibility to act on it.

NOTES

1. The glass case

1. "Today we are all in a glass house, because today everything is seen, everything is read and everything is heard."
2. This account of the Kelwara meeting draws on my own notes as well as: Richard Calland, *Transparency in the Profit-Making World: The Case for the Right to Know* (Cape Town: Open Democracy Advice Centre, 2004), Rama Lakshmi, "Opening Files, Indians Find Scams," *Washington Post*, March 9, 2004, A17.
3. A Hero Honda is a popular Indian motorcycle maker; Maruti, a car manufacturer.
4. Roy, a remarkable and highly regarded activist, described her philosophy in a recent lecture: Aruna Roy, *Dan Sanders Peace and Justice Lecture* (Mumbai, India: 2004). See also Aruna Roy and Nikhil Dey, *Fighting for the Right to Know in India* (Devdungri, Rajasthan: Mazdoor Kisan Shakti Sangathan, 2003). The MKSS's campaign also led to the adoption of disclosure rules in Rajasthan's Panchayat Raj Act.
5. Assam, Delhi, Goa, Jammu and Kashmir, Karnataka, Madhya Pradesh, Maharashtra, Rajasthan, and Tamil Nadu. India's central government adopted a similar law in 2002, but by 2004 it had not yet gone into force. Activists pressed the Congress government elected in May 2004 to pass a strengthened version of the law. A revised Right to Information Act was adopted by the Indian Parliament in May 2005, scheduled to go into effect in September 2005.
6. More information about Parivartan can be found on its website, http://www.parivartan.com
7. Chetan Chauhan, "Act Prises Open Official Registers for Public," *Hindustan Times*, October 9, 2004. Satark Nagrik Sangathan's website is http://www.snsindia.org.
8. *India Today*, "57 Ways to Make India a Better Place," August 23, 2004, 22.
9. *Indian Express*, "You Have the Right To Know How She Misuses Her Car," February 26, 2004.

10. Ampa Santimetaneedol and Sirikul Bunnag, "Sumalee Limpa-Ovart: Teaching Schools a Lesson," *Bangkok Post*, March 1, 1999; Julian Gearing, "The Whistleblowers," *Asiaweek.com*, March 31, 2000; *Asiaweek*, "Making Thai History," May 4, 2000; Nakorn Serirak, "Right To Know Has Its Headaches," *Bangkok Post*, December 12, 2001.

11. Lawrence Repeta, *Local Government Disclosure Systems in Japan* (Seattle, WA: National Bureau of Asian Research, 1999). A discussion of the early history of the Japanese movement is also provided in Lawrence Repeta, *The Birth of the Freedom of Information Act in Japan: Kanagawa 1982*, Working Paper 03–01 (Boston, MA: MIT Japan Program, 2003).

12. David Boling, "Access to Government-Held Information in Japan," *Stanford Journal of International Law* 34, no. 1 (1998): 1–38, 4.

13. Lawrence Repeta and David Schultz, *Japanese Government Information: New Rules for Access* (Washington, DC: freedominfo.org, July 5, 2002 [Accessed November 10, 2004]), available from http://www.freedominfo.org/analysis/japan1/.

14. *The Daily Yomiuri*, "Slush Fund Partly Revealed," November 19, 2003.

15. *Asahi News Service*, "Ministry To Come Clean on Hepatitis," February 21, 2004.

16. The Ugandan Parliament approved the Access to Information Bill in April 2005.

17. Article 41(1), Constitution of the Republic of Uganda, 1995.

18. The Monitor, "Court Orders Gov't To Produce Bujagali Power Agreement," *Africa News*, July 13, 2002.

19. International Rivers Network, "World Bank Dam in Uganda Overpriced by $280 Million," *AllAfrica News Service*, November 22, 2002.

20. The project had also been dogged with allegations of corruption, and a World Bank Inspection Panel criticized the procedures by which the Bank agreed to provide support for the project, as well as the terms of the agreement. The government's first response to the High Court's ruling had been to reverse itself and claim that no agreement existed; however, this claim was undermined when Greenwatch provided the court with a leaked copy of the document.

21. Vicente Fox, *Fox Contigo: Transcript* (Mexico: Presidencia de la Republica, October 18, 2003 [Accessed February 28, 2005]), available from http:origin.presidencia.gob.mx/?P=16&Orden=Leer&Tipo=DI&Art=6609.

22. The National Society Party (PSN) led by Gustavo Riojas Santana, which received over $30 million in funding over the preceding four years, was fined $13 million in May 2003 and another $5 million in December 2003. The party no longer exists.

23. FOIA Advocates Network, *Mexico: Court Rules in Favour of Access to Political Party Data* (Yerevan, Armenia: FOI Advocates Network, July 15, 2004 [Accessed November 15, 2004]), available from http://www.foiadvocates.net/news/150704.htm.

24. Ginger Thompson, "Mexico Opens Files Related to '71 Killings," *New York Times*, February 13, 2005, 8.

25. freedominfo.org, *Freedom of Information Makes News around the World, 2004* (Washington, DC: freedominfo.org, September 28, 2004 [Accessed November 20, 2004]), available from http://freedominfo.org/survey/rtk2004.htm.

26. Department for Constitutional Affairs, *News Release: Falconer Hails New Freedom of Information Era* (London: Department of Constitutional Affairs, 2005).

27. David Hencke and Rob Evans, "Royal Farms Get £1m from Taxpayers," *The Guardian*, March 23, 2005, 1.

28. Matthew Tempest, "Treasury Papers Reveal Cost of Black Wednesday," *Guardian Unlimited*, February 9, 2005, Web: http://politics.guardian.co.uk/foi/story/0,9061,1409254,1409200.html.

29. Rob Evans and David Leigh, "Papers Show Government Authorised Arms Bribes," *The Guardian*, February 18, 2005, 10.

30. *People's Daily Online*, "Transparency Widespread, China Opening Wider," June 28, 2003.

31. *The Economist*, "The Right To Know," October 25, 2003. See also Jamie Horsley, *Shanghai Advances the Cause of Open Government Information in China* (Washington, DC: freedominfo.org, April 20, 2004 [Accessed November 15, 2004]), available from http://www.freedominfo.org/news/shanghai/.

32. Murray Tanner, "China Rethinks Unrest," *Washington Quarterly* 27, no. 3 (2004): 137–156, 138.

33. Jamie Horsley, "Guangzhou's Pioneering Foray into Open Government," *China Business Review* 30, no. 4 (2003): 40–43.

34. Horsley, *Shanghai Advances the Cause of Open Government Information in China*; Alexis Grant, "Freeman, Open-Government Guru, Taking His Trade, Expertise to China," *Gannett News Service*, August 9, 2003.

35. Fang Yu, "Shanghai Citizens for the First Time Sue the Government for Non-Disclosure of Public Information," *Economic Observer*, July 5, 2004.

36. *China Daily*, "Shanghai Government Information Is Now Open to the Public," November 1, 2004, Web: http://www.chinadaily.com.cn/english/doc/2004-20112001/content_387559.htm.

37. This description of developments in pre-revolutionary France relies on Robin J. Ives, "Political Publicity and Political Economy in Eighteenth-Century France," *French History* 17, no. 1 (2003): 1–18.

38. Jean Bodin, *Six Books of the Commonwealth*, trans. M. J. Tooley (Oxford: Basil Blackwell, 1955), Book III. Secrets should not be revealed, Tacitus wrote, because "the condition of holding empire is that an account cannot be balanced unless it be rendered to one person." Cornelius Tacitus and Michael Grant, *The Annals of Imperial Rome*, Rev. ed. (Harmondsworth, England: Penguin Books, 1973), Book I.

39. Robert Filmer, *Patriarcha, or the Natural Power of Kings* (1680).

40. Elaine Scarry, "Resolving to Resist," *Boston Review* 29, no. 1 (2003).

41. Max Weber, *Essays in Sociology*, trans. and ed. H. H. Gerth and C. Wright Mills (New York: Oxford University Press, 1946), 233–234.

42. Arthur M. Schlesinger, Jr., *The Age of Roosevelt: The Politics of Upheaval* (Boston: Houghton Mifflin, 1957), 284; Morton Horwitz, *The Transformation of American Law, 1870–1960* (New York: Oxford University Press, 1992), 219–220.

43. Richard Polenberg, *Reorganizing Roosevelt's Government* (Cambridge, MA: Harvard University Press, 1966); William Edward Leuchtenburg, *Franklin D. Roosevelt and the New Deal, 1932–1940*, 1st ed. (New York: Harper & Row, 1963), 279.

44. *Federal Trade Commission v. Ruberoid Co.*, 343 U.S. 470 (1952).

45. Gordon Hewart, *The New Despotism* (London: Benn, 1929).

46. On the politics surrounding the adoption of the APA, see Horwitz, *The Transformation of American Law, 1870–1960*, 230–233; David H. Rosenbloom, *Building a Legislative-Centered Public Administration* (Tuscaloosa, AL: University of Alabama Press, 2000), 2–22. A contemporary review of the law is provided by Foster Sherwood, "The Federal Administrative Procedure Act," *American Political Science Review* 41, no. 2 (1947): 271–281.

47. United States Department of Justice, *Attorney General's Manual on the Administrative Procedure Act* (Washington, DC: United States Department of Justice, 1947), 25.

48. Harold L. Cross, *The People's Right To Know* (New York: Columbia University Press, 1953). A history of the early FOI movement is provided by George Kennedy, "Advocates of Openness: The Freedom of Information Movement" (PhD dissertation, University of Missouri, 1978).

49. For a description of one of the early press battles over Cold War secrecy, see Kathleen Endres, "National Security Benchmark: Truman, Executive Order 10290, and the Press," *Journalism Quarterly* 67, no. 4 (1990): 1071–1077.

50. Sam Archibald, "The Early Years of the Freedom of Information Movement, 1955 to 1974," *PS: Political Science and Politics* 26, no. 4 (1993): 726–731. Archibald was Staff Director of the Special Subcommittee on Government Information from 1955 to 1966. The Committee was chaired by Representative John Moss, a California Democrat who was the leading proponent of a new FOIA.

51. David Vogel, "The Public-Interest Movement and the American Reform Tradition," *Political Science Quarterly* 95, no. 4 (1981): 607–627.

52. Horwitz, *The Transformation of American Law, 1870–1960*, 232.

53. Ralph Nader, "Freedom from Information," *Harvard Civil Rights-Civil Liberties Law Review* 5, no. 1 (1970): 1–15; Justin Martin, *Nader: Crusader, Spoiler, Icon* (Cambridge, MA: Perseus, 2002), 167–170.

54. Based on data provided in David Banisar, *Freedom of Information and Access to Government Records around the World* (Washington, DC: freedominfo.org, May, 2004 [Accessed May 31, 2004]), available from http://www.freedominfo.org/survey.htm.

55. Anthony Giddens, *The Third Way and Its Critics* (Cambridge, UK: Polity Press, 2000), 61–62.

56. Sol Picciotto, "Liberalization and Globalization: The Forum and the Hearth in the Era of Cosmopolitan Post-Industrial Capitalism," *Law and Contemporary Problems* 63, no. 4 (2000): 157–178.

57. Thomas Blanton, "The World's Right To Know," *Foreign Policy*, July/August, 2002, 50–58.

58. Alan Murray, "Who Wins in the New Economy?" *Wall Street Journal*, June 27, 2000, B1.

59. Government of Canada, *Speech from the Throne to Open the Second Session of the Thirty-Sixth Parliament of Canada* (Ottawa: Privy Council Office, 1999).

60. G8, *Okinawa Charter on Global Information Society* (Okinawa, Japan: 2000).

61. Peter Lyman and Hal Varian, *How Much Information? 2003* (Berkeley, CA: University of California at Berkeley, 2003).

62. Walter Rugaber, "Consumers Press Drive To Tap Big Reservoir of Federal Data," *New York Times*, September 2, 1969, 24.

63. David Shenk, *Data Smog* (New York: HarperCollins, 1997), 31; David Shenk, *The End of Patience* (Bloomington: Indiana University Press, 1999), 29–30.

64. Hugh Heclo, "Downteching: The Coming Heresy," *The Observer: Columbia University Journal for General Studies* 6, no. 7 (1994): 7. See also Eli M. Noam, *Visions of the Media Age: Taming the Information Monster*, paper presented at the Third Annual Colloquium, Alfred Herrhausen Society for International Dialogue (New York: Columbia Business School, 1995); Todd Gitlin, *Media Unlimited* (New York: Metropolitan Books, 2001).

65. Blanton, "The World's Right To Know."

66. Charles Anderson, *Pragmatic Liberalism* (Chicago: University of Chicago Press, 1990).

2. Secrecy and security

1. On the Stasi archives generally, see Jens Gieseke, *The GDR State Security: Shield and Sword of the Party* (Berlin: Federal Comissioner for the Records of the State Security Service, 2002); Anna Funder, *Stasiland* (London: Granta Books, 2003), 56. A concise history of the final days of the German Democratic Republic is provided by William F. Buckley, *The Fall of the Berlin Wall* (Hoboken, NJ: John Wiley & Sons, 2004). I visited the Stasi File Authority in May 2004, and am grateful to Mr. Bert Rosenthal and his colleagues for their assistance.

2. The process of reconstituting the torn documents was halted in October 2004 because of its growing cost.

3. Denis Staunton, "Old Stasi Files Still Hold the Power to Destroy," *The Observer*, March 27, 1994, 21.

4. Luke Harding, "Court Orders Release of Stasi Files on Kohl's Political Life," *The Guardian*, June 24, 2004, 14.

5. Pilar Wolfsteller, "Profile: Joachim Gauck," *German Life*, March, 1996, 12.

6. The 1994 law provided victims of the former secret police with access to their files, but did not allow disclosure of the identity of informants. The 2003 law provided a limited right of access to information about informants as well. I am grateful to Ivan Szekely for an explanation of Hungarian legal developments. This paragraph also draws on an excellent summary of access legislation: Banisar, *Freedom of Information and Access to Government Records around the World*.

7. In addition to Banisar, see Mirel Bran, "Romania: Dossier 666," *Le Monde*, October 8, 2002. Slovakia's Institute for National Memory began to make secret police files available in late 2004, and in 2005 Romania's Securitate began transferring its archives to an independent body, the National College for the Study of the Securitate Archives, as a first step toward public disclosure of archival records.

8. Neil Kritz, ed., *Transitional Justice: How Emerging Democracies Reckon with Former Regimes*, 3 vols. (Washington, DC: United States Institute of Peace Press, 1995), Vol. III, 736.

9. Christopher M. Andrew and Vasili Mitrokhin, *The Sword and the Shield*, 1st ed. (New York: Basic Books, 1999).

10. These arguments are laid out more generally by Ruti G. Teitel, *Transitional Justice* (Oxford; New York: Oxford University Press, 2000), 69–117.

11. National Commission on the Disappearance of Persons, *Nunca Más* (Buenos Aires: National Commission on the Disappearance of Persons, 1984).

12. The Brazilian title was *Brasil: Nunca Mais*. The translated version of the report was published as Archdiocese of São Paulo, *Torture in Brazil: A Report* (New York: Vintage Books, 1986).

13. National Commission on Truth and Reconciliation (Rettig Commission). See Priscilla Hayner, "Fifteen Truth Commissions," *Human Rights Quarterly* 16, no. 4 (1994): 597–655.

14. John Dinges, *The Condor Years* (New York: New Press, 2004), 233–241.

15. Larry Rohter, "A Torture Report Compels Chile to Reassess Its Past," *New York Times*, November 28, 2004, 14.

16. Other countries that established post-transition commissions included Bolivia, El Salvador, Guatemala, and Paraguay. See Hayner, "Fifteen Truth Commissions."

17. Kate Doyle, "Forgetting Is Not Justice: Mexico Bares Its Secret Past," *World Policy Journal* 20, no. 2 (2003): 61–72, 71.

18. Truth commissions have also been established in Chad, Sierra Leone, and Rwanda.

19. Truth and Reconciliation Commission, *Final Report* (Pretoria, South Africa: Truth and Reconciliation Commission, 1998), Vol. 1, Ch. 8, Benita de Giorgi, "The Open Democracy Bill," *Politeia* 18, no. 2 (1999): http://www.unisa.ac.za/dept/press/politeia/182/con18299.html.

20. See Volume 1, Chapter 8 of Truth and Reconciliation Commission, *Final Report*. The destruction of records in the last years of apartheid is also

discussed in Verne Harris, "'They Should Have Destroyed More': The Destruction of Public Records by the South African State in the Final Years of Apartheid," in *Archives and the Public Good*, ed. Richard J. Cox and David A. Wallace (Westport, CT: Quorum Books, 2002).

21. Advisory Committee on Human Radiation Experiments, *Final Report* (Washington, DC: Advisory Committee on Human Radiation Experiments, 1995).

22. A scholarly analysis of the released records is contained in Richard Breitman et al., *U.S. Intelligence and the Nazis* (Washington, DC: National Archives and Records Administration, 2004).

23. The review began under an executive order issued by the Clinton administration but was later bolstered by a statutory direction. See Peter Kornbluh, *The Pinochet File* (New York: New Press, 2003), 469–481; Dinges, *The Condor Years*, 38–40.

24. The power of the doctrine of national security in Latin America is discussed in Lawrence Weschler, *A Miracle, a Universe: Settling Accounts with Torturers* (New York: Pantheon Books, 1990).

25. Hayner, "Fifteen Truth Commissions." In 2005, a working group established by the Office of the United Nations High Commissioner for Human Rights continued to work on a "normative instrument" that would acknowledge a "right to know the truth about the circumstances of an enforced disappearance and the fate of the disappeared person."

26. Teitel, *Transitional Justice*, 100–102.

27. Martha Farmelo, *The Freedom of Information Campaign in Argentina* (Washington, DC: freedominfo.org, October, 2003 [Accessed October 31, 2004]), available from http://www.freedominfo.org/case/argentina.htm. President Néstor Kirchner signed an executive decree containing rules on access to public information in December 2003.

28. Larry Rohter, "Hidden Files Force Brazil To Face Its Past," *New York Times*, January 31, 2005, 6.

29. On the state of openness in Chile generally, see Felipe Gonzalez, "Access to Information and National Security in Chile," in *National Security and Open Government*, ed. Alasdair Roberts (Syracuse, NY: Campbell Public Affairs Institute, Syracuse University, 2003).

30. Elizabeth Cavero, "Falta Firmeza En Ley De Acceso a La Información," *La Republica*, June 29, 2002.

31. Carlos Osorio and Kathleen Costar, *Ecuador Enacts Transparency and Access to Information Law* (Washington, DC: freedominfo.org, May 20, 2004 [Accessed July 3, 2004]), available from http://www.freedominfo. org/news/ecuador/20040520.htm. The law allows decisions on the classification of information to be extended indefinitely.

32. SITA, "NBU Says Revision to Classified Information Law Is Necessary," *SITA Slovak News Agency*, July 31, 2002.

33. Judgment of the Constitutional Court of the Republic of Latvia in Case 2002–20–0103, April 23, 2003.

34. Siddarth Varadarajan, "Secret Society," *The Times of India*, March 27, 2004.

35. Verne Harris, "NIA: A Friendlier Big Brother?" *Natal Witness*, March 15, 2004.
36. United Kingdom, *Your Right To Know: The Government's Proposals for a Freedom of Information Act*, Cm 3818 (London: Stationery Office, 1997), para. 2.3. The excluded organizations include the country's domestic security service, MI5; its overseas intelligence service, MI6; its signals intelligence agency, GCHQ; and its special military forces, the SAS and the SBS.
37. Freedom of Information Act 2000, sections 23 and 24.
38. Australian Law Reform Commission, *Protecting Classified and Security Sensitive Information*, Discussion Paper 67 (Canberra: Australian Law Reform Commission, 2004), 61–63.
39. For example, Belgium and Spain.
40. United States Department of Justice, *Freedom of Information Act Guide* (Washington, DC: U.S. Department of Justice, Office of Information and Privacy, 2004).
41. Information Security Oversight Office, *Report to the President 2004* (Washington, DC: Information Security Oversight Office, 2005).
42. The Central Intelligence Agency, National Reconnaissance Office, National Imagery and Mapping Agency, and National Security Agency. A fifth organization – the Defense Intelligence Agency – attempted unsuccessfully to obtain a similar exemption in 2000. It made the same proposal again in 2005.
43. See, for example, Teitel, *Transitional Justice*.
44. Jon Elster, *Closing the Books: Transitional Justice in Historical Perspective* (New York: Cambridge University Press, 2004), 117.
45. See generally: Alasdair Roberts, "The Informational Commons at Risk," in *The Market or the Public Domain*, ed. Daniel Drache (London: Routledge, 2001).
46. Daniel Moynihan, *Secrecy: The American Experience* (New Haven, CT: Yale University Press, 1998), 214.
47. Journalist Seymour Hersh claimed in 2004 that the federal government operated a highly secretive "special access program" to seize suspected terrorists; this was disputed by government officials, but there was little doubt that in at least one case American agents had covertly seized terror suspects in Sweden: Seymour Hersh, *Chain of Command: The Road from 9/11 to Abu Ghraib* (New York: HarperCollins, 2004).
48. John Podesta, "Need To Know: Governing in Secret," in *The War on Our Freedoms*, ed. Richard C. Leone and Greg Anrig, Jr. (New York: Public Affairs, 2003), 223.
49. Although FERC took steps to restrict access soon after September 11, 2001, its new policy on access was not formalized until February 2003: Final Rule on Critical Energy Infrastructure Information, *Federal Register* 68(41): 9857–9873 (February 21, 2003).
50. The rules were authorized by the Homeland Security Act of 2002, section 214(a)(1)(A). An analysis of the CIA's weaknesses is provided by Rena

Steinzor, "Democracies Die Behind Closed Doors: The Homeland Security Act and Corporate Accountability," *Kansas Journal of Law & Public Policy* 12, no. 2 (2003): 641–670.

51. Brent Walth, "Security at PDX Spotty over Time," *Sunday Oregonian*, September 23, 2001, A1; Patrick O'Donnell, Elizabeth Marchak, and Dave Davis, "Airport Security Lapsed in 1990s, FAA Records Show," *Cleveland Plain Dealer*, September 23, 2001, B1.

52. Blake Morrison, "Weapons Slip Past Airport Security," *USA Today*, March 25, 2002, 1A.

53. Mitchel Sollenberger, *Sensitive Security Information and Transportation Security: Issues and Congressional Options*, RL32425 (Washington, DC: Congressional Research Service, 2004).

54. *Coastal Delivery Corp. v. United States Customs Service*, 272 F. Supp. 2d 958.

55. Nuclear Regulatory Commission, *News Release: NRC Modifies Availability of Security Information for All Nuclear Plants* (Washington, DC: Nuclear Regulatory Commission, 2004).

56. Henry Kissinger, quoted in Robert Kagan, *Of Paradise and Power: America and Europe in the New World Order* (New York: Knopf, 2003).

57. John Lewis Gaddis and Paul Kennedy, "Kill the Empire! (or Not)," *New York Times*, July 25, 2004, 23.

58. Matthew Brzezinski, *Fortress America* (New York: Bantam Books, 2004), 17.

59. Glen McGregor, "Who's Winning the Larger War?" *The Ottawa Citizen*, August 11, 2002, C6.

60. John C. Baker et al., *Mapping the Risks: Assessing the Homeland Security Implications of Publicly Available Geospatial Information* (Santa Monica, CA: RAND, 2004), 4.

61. Joseph Jacobson, *Safeguarding National Security through Public Release of Environmental Information*, Master of Laws Thesis (Washington, DC: George Washington University Law School, 2002), 81–87.

62. Baker et al., *Mapping the Risks*, xxvi and 122–123.

63. *Living Rivers v. United States Bureau of Reclamation* 272 F. Supp. 2d 1313 (C.D.U.T. 2003).

64. *Living Rivers Currents*, "Dam Risks: Interior Denies Public Right to Know," May 10, 2002.

65. *NOW with Bill Moyers*, "Transcript: Right To Know under Assault," (2003); Joseph Davis, "Terrorism Fears Thwart Journalists' Reporting," *Nieman Reports*, Summer, 2004, 18–19, 19.

66. Sean Reilly, "New Policy Keeps Records from the Public," *Mobile Register*, October 28, 2003.

67. FERC reversed itself slightly in September 2004: Kristen McNamara, "FERC, Seeking to Thwart Terror, Extends Reach to Media," *Dow Jones Newswires*, September 17, 2004.

68. FERC, *Notice Soliciting Public Comments Re Critical Energy Infrastructure Information under RM02-4 Et Al.*, Docket No. RM02-4-002, et al. (Washington, DC: Federal Energy Regulatory Commission, 2004).

69. Steinzor, "Democracies Die Behind Closed Doors,," 664. See also Kristen Uhl, "The Freedom of Information Act Post-9/11," *American University Law Review* 53, no. 1 (2003): 261–311, 295–297. The rules also provide businesses with civil immunity for problems revealed to government officials.
70. *Atlanta Journal-Constitution*, "Elements of Concern," August 26, 2004, 18A.
71. Bennett Ramberg, "Safety or Secrecy?" *New York Times*, May 20, 2003, A27.
72. Jonathan Riskind, "Reaction Harsh to Government's Nuclear Secrecy," *Columbus Dispatch*, August 6, 2004, 1A.
73. Keay Davidson, "Security Faulted at Nuclear Reactors," *San Francisco Chronicle*, September 15, 2004, A10.
74. National Academy of Sciences, *Safety and Security of Commercial Spent Nuclear Fuel Storage* (Washington, DC: National Academy of Sciences, Board on Radioactive Waste Management, 2005).
75. National Commission On Terrorist Attacks Upon the United States, *Final Report* (New York: W.W. Norton and Company, 2004), 355–356.
76. Ibid., 264–265 and 277.
77. Ibid., 416–417.
78. Bruce Berkowitz, "Secrecy and National Security," *Hoover Digest* 2004, no. 3 (2004).
79. Roberta Wohlstetter, *Pearl Harbor: Warning and Decision* (Stanford, CA: Stanford University Press, 1962).
80. National Commission On Terrorist Attacks Upon the United States, *Final Report*, 265.
81. Kamil Skawinski, "IT and SETI: The Role of Computer Technology in the Search for Extraterrestrial Intelligence," *California Computer News* (2002): http://www.ccnmag.com/index.php?sec=mag&id=156.150.
82. Hersh, *Chain of Command*, 104–107.
83. Transcript, *The O'Reilly Factor*, February 15, 2002.
84. Kristen Breitweiser, *Statement before the Joint Committees on Intelligence* (Washington, DC: September 11 Advocates, 2002).
85. Joint Inquiry, *Report of the Joint Inquiry into Intelligence Community Activities before and after the Terrorist Attacks of September 11, 2001*, S. Rept. 107–351 and H. Rept. 107–792 (Washington, DC: Government Printing Office, 2003), 124.
86. In an ABC News/Washington Post poll conducted in April 2003, 70 percent of respondents thought "the war in Iraq was worth fighting, all in all."
87. Steven Kull, Clay Ramsay, and Evan Lewis, "Misperceptions, the Media, and the Iraq War," *Political Science Quarterly* 118, no. 4 (2004): 569–598; Linda Feldmann, "The Impact of Bush Linking 9/11 and Iraq," *Christian Science Monitor*, March 14, 2003.
88. CBS News Poll, March 6, 2003.
89. Senate Intelligence Committee, *Report on the U.S. Intelligence Community's Prewar Intelligence Assessments on Iraq* (Washington, DC: United States Senate Select Committee on Intelligence, 2004), 347–349.

90. Douglas Jehl, "A New CIA Report Casts Doubt on a Key Terrorist's Tie to Iraq," *New York Times*, October 6, 2004, 13.

91. Douglas Jehl, "U.S. Report Finds Iraqis Eliminated Illicit Arms in 90's," *New York Times*, October 7, 2004, 1. A preliminary report of the Group released a year earlier suggested a similar conclusion; in January 2004, the Group's first head, David Kay, said that he did not believe such weapons existed at the time of the war: Andrew Buncombe, "Saddam's WMD Never Existed, Says Chief American Arms Inspector," *The Independent*, January 24, 2004.

92. Dan Balz and Robin Wright, "Kerry Urges Bush to Admit Mistakes," *Washington Post*, October 6, 2004, A12.

93. Douglas Jehl, "US Intelligence Shows Pessimism on Iraq's Future," *New York Times*, September 16, 2004, 1.

94. John Prados, *Hoodwinked* (New York: The New Press, 2004), 33 and 113.

95. Joseph Cirincione, Jessica Mathews, and George Perkovich, *WMD in Iraq: Evidence and Implications* (Washington, DC: Carnegie Endowment for International Peace, 2004), 16–17.

96. Irving Lester Janis, *Groupthink: Psychological Studies of Policy Decisions and Fiascoes*, 2nd ed. (Boston: Houghton Mifflin, 1983).

97. Senate Intelligence Committee, *Report on the U.S. Intelligence Community's Prewar Intelligence Assessments on Iraq*, 18–22.

98. Gregory Moorehead, Richard Ference, and Chris Neck, "Group Decision Fiascoes Continue: Space Shuttle Challenger and a Revised Groupthink Framework," *Human Relations* 44, no. 6 (1991): 539–550, 541 and 549.

99. Commission on Intelligence Capabilities of the United States Regarding Weapons of Mass Destruction, *Report to the President* (Washington, DC: 2005), 104.

100. Douglas Jehl, "CIA Review Criticizes Prewar Iraq Analysis," *New York Times*, September 22, 2004, 21.

101. The committee has been criticized for its overemphasis on this view, which has the effect of reducing the culpability of more senior officials for the decision to invade Iraq. Commentators have noted that in some cases the internal debate over evidence was vigorous: David Barstow, William Broad, and Jeff Gerth, "How White House Embraced Suspect Arms Intelligence," *New York Times*, October 3, 2004, 1.

102. Foreign Affairs Committee, *The Decision To Go to War in Iraq. Ninth Report of Session 2002–2003*, HC 8134 (London: House of Commons Foreign Affairs Committee, 2003).

103. Paul Waugh, "Iraq Crisis: Number 10 Admits It Used Thesis by Student," *The Independent*, February 8, 2003, 4.

104. Tony Blair, *The Opportunity Society; Speech to the Labour Party Annual Conference* (London: Labour Party, 2004).

105. Jehl, "US Intelligence Shows Pessimism on Iraq's Future."

106. Office of the Secretary of Defense, *Transcript of Secretary Rumsfeld Media Availability with Afghan President Karzai* (Washington, DC: Office of the Secretary of Defense, 2003).

107. Council on Foreign Relations, *Iraq: The Day After* (New York: Council on Foreign Relations, 2003).

108. Peter Slevin, "U.S. Military Lays Out Postwar Iraq Plan," *Washington Post*, February 12, 2003, A21.

109. James Fallows, "Blind into Baghdad," *The Atlantic Monthly*, January–February, 2004, 53–74.

110. James C. Thomson, Jr., "How Could Vietnam Happen?" *The Atlantic*, April, 1968, 47–53.

111. Article 21 of the Universal Declaration of Human Rights, like several other declarations, says that individuals have the right to take part in the government of their country, and that government should exercise its authority on the basis of the will of the people.

112. Eric Alterman, *Who Speaks for America? Why Democracy Matters in Foreign Policy* (Ithaca, NY: Cornell University Press, 1998).

113. According to a Washington Post poll completed in October 2001, 64 percent of Americans trusted government to do what is right most or all of the time – a level of support not seen in comparable polls since the mid 1960s and a dramatic contrast to the 20 percent levels of trust found in the mid 1990s. The poll also showed that large majorities would support measures that restricted civil liberties. Dana Milbank and Richard Morin, "Public Is Unyielding in War against Terror," *Washington Post*, September 29, 2001, A1. In the NPR/Kaiser/Kennedy School National Survey on Civil Liberties conducted in November 2001, 51 percent of respondents agreed that it would be necessary for the "average person to give up some rights and liberties" to curb terrorism: http://www.npr.org/programs/specials/poll/civil_liberties/

114. Daniel Ellsberg, *Secrets* (New York: Penguin Group, 2002), 46.

3. Regime change

1. Donald Rumsfeld, *Remarks to the Newspaper Association of America/American Society of Newspaper Editors* (Washington, DC: United States Department of Defense, 2004).

2. "It should not be a surprise today that there's still remnants of that regime that would like to take it back. They had a very good thing. They could go around killing tens of thousands of people and piling them in mass graves. They could torture people and have rape rooms and the world would turn their head from that and let it happen. But they can't do that anymore": Donald Rumsfeld, *Transcript of Interview with Nick Childs, BBC* (Washington, DC: Department of Defense, 2004).

3. Maj. Gen. Antonio Taguba, *Article 15–6 Investigation of the 800th Military Police Brigade* (Washington, DC: United States Central Command, 2004).

4. The Freedom of Information Act prevents access to properly classified material. Whether the Taguba report was properly classified was open to question: Federal policy says that information may not be classified "in order to . . . conceal violations of law, inefficiency, or administrative error." Steven Aftergood, "Torture and Secrecy," *In These Times*,

June 2, 2004, Web edition: http://www.inthesetimes.com/site/main/article/torture_and_secrecy/.

5. Gary Younge and Julian Borger, "CBS Delayed Report on Iraqi Prison Abuse after Military Chiefs Plea," *The Guardian*, May 4, 2004.

6. Bradley Graham and Charles Babington, "Probes of Detainee Deaths Reported," *Washington Post*, May 5, 2004, A1.

7. "Chris Matthews, *Transcript of "Hardball with Chris Matthews"* (New York: MSNBC TV, 2004).

8. Lawrence Di Rita, *Media Availability with the Principal Deputy Assistant Secretary of Defense* (Washington, DC: United States Department of Defense, 2004).

9. Vivienne Walt, "Military Personnel: Don't Read This!" *Time*, May 8, 2004.

10. Seymour Hersh, "Torture at Abu Ghraib," *The New Yorker*, May 10, 2004, 42–47.

11. Dana Milbank, "U.S. Tries to Calm Furor Caused by Photos," *Washington Post*, May 1, 2004, A1.

12. Douglas Jehl and Eric Schmitt, "Army Discloses Criminal Inquiry on Prison Abuse," *New York Times*, May 5, 2004, A1.

13. Donald Rumsfeld, *Defense Department Operational Update Briefing* (Washington, DC: Department of Defense, 2004).

14. *Washington Post*, "Transcript of Rumsfeld Testimony before Senate Armed Services Committee," May 7, 2004, Web edition, *Washington Post*, "Rumsfeld Testifies before House Armed Services Committee," May 7, 2004, Web edition.

15. Mark Tapscott, "Too Many Secrets," *Washington Post*, November 20, 2002, A25.

16. *EPA v. Mink*, 410 U.S. 73 (1973), interpreting Exemption 1 of the 1966 FOIA.

17. Exemption 7 of the 1966 FOIA was interpreted to provide protection for "investigatory files compiled for law enforcement purposes" regardless of whether any further law enforcement proceeding was likely or would be harmed by disclosure: Harry Hammitt, David Sobel, and Mark Zaid, *Litigation under the Federal Open Government Laws* (Washington, DC: EPIC Publications, 2002).

18. Veto Message from the President on the Freedom of Information Act, *Congressional Records*, November 18, 1974, page 36243.

19. According to CIA memoranda posted by thememoryhole.org.

20. Antonin Scalia, "The Freedom of Information Act Has No Clothes," *Regulation* 6, no. 2 (1982): 14–20, 15–16.

21. Arthur Schlesinger, Jr., *The Imperial Presidency* (Boston: Houghton Mifflin, 1973).

22. Michel Crozier, Samuel P. Huntington, and Joji Watanuki, *The Crisis of Democracy* (New York: New York University Press, 1975). The following paragraphs draw principally on Huntington's analysis of the United States, presented in pages 59–118 of the report.

23. Ibid., 175.

24. Baumgartner and Jones show that the number of issues on the government agenda – which they define as the number of discrete topics that were the subject of hearings by Congress in a particular year – expanded substantially between 1975 and the late 1980s: Frank R. Baumgartner and Bryan D. Jones, *Policy Dynamics* (Chicago: University of Chicago Press, 2002).

25. Frank R. Baumgartner and Beth L. Leech, *Basic Interests* (Princeton, NJ: Princeton University Press, 1998), Table 6-1.

26. Beth L. Leech et al., "Drawing Lobbyists to Washington: Government Attention and Interest-Group Mobilization," *Political Research Quarterly* (Forthcoming).

27. Jonathan Rauch, *Demosclerosis* (New York: Times Books, 1994).

28. Project for Excellence in Journalism, *The State of the News Media 2004* (Washington, DC: Project for Excellence in Journalism, 2004), Overview.

29. Ibid.

30. Bill Kovach and Tom Rosenstiel, *Warp Speed: America in the Age of Mixed Media* (New York: Century Foundation Press, 1999).

31. Ari Fleischer, *Taking Heat: The President, the Press, and My Years in the White House* (New York: William Morrow, 2005), ix and 8.

32. Susan Pharr, Robert Putnam, and Russell Dalton, "A Quarter-Century of Declining Confidence," *Journal of Democracy* 11, no. 2 (2000): 5–25, 9–10. The authors observe that confidence in representative institutions in most Trilateral countries had declined since the original report, "and in that sense most of these democracies are troubled." See also Joseph Nye, Jr., Philip Zelikow, and David King, eds., *Why People Don't Trust Government* (Cambridge, MA: Harvard University Press, 1997). To some degree, these conclusions reflect trends up to the early 1990s, when trust in government sank to an historic low. Trust rebounded in the late 1990s, although not to the levels of the early 1960s.

33. Julian E. Zelizer, *On Capitol Hill* (Cambridge, UK: Cambridge University Press, 2004), 10–13.

34. Crozier, Huntington, and Watanuki, *The Crisis of Democracy*.

35. "Prior to 1974, Presidents exercised complete control over their presidential papers": Morton Rosenberg, *Statement before the House Subcommittee on Efficiency, Financial Management and Intergovernmental Relations Concerning HR 4187, the Presidential Records Act Amendments of 2002* (Washington, DC: Congressional Research Service, 2002).

36. Barry Snyder, *Testimony before the House Subcommittee on Government Efficiency and Financial Management on the 25th Anniversary of the Inspector General Act* (Washington, DC: Executive Council on Integrity and Efficiency, 2003).

37. "A key purpose of the 1980 Act was to strengthen GAO's ability to access records in the face of opposition by agencies including the White House." Letter from Comptroller General David Walker to Vice President Richard Cheney, August 17, 2001.

38. Jonathan Swift, *Gulliver's Travels* (1726), Part I.

39. Rumsfeld's testimony was later published by the Heartland Institute, a Chicago-based libertarian thinktank: Donald Rumsfeld, *Thoughts from the Business World on Downsizing Government* (Chicago: The Heartland Institute, 1995).

40. Donald Rumsfeld, *Speech at National Defense University on "21st Century Transformation" of U.S. Armed Forces* (Washington, DC: Office of the Secretary of Defense, 2002).

41. Donald Rumsfeld, *Testimony to the Senate Armed Services Committees on the 2003 Defense Budget Request* (Washington, DC: Office of the Secretary of Defense, 2002).

42. Jim Lobe, "The Strong Must Rule the Weak, Said Neo-Cons' Muse," *Inter Press Service*, May 7, 2003.

43. In 2003 Professor Carnes Lord, a student of Strauss who had served as an assistant to the Vice President for national security affairs in the administration of George H. W. Bush, presented a diagnosis of the predicament of modern leadership that followed similar lines. Lord was particularly critical of the power of the media and the corrosive effect of media intrusions on the deliberative processes of government: Carnes Lord, *The Modern Prince* (New Haven: Yale University Press, 2003), 1–10 and 187.

44. In a March 27, 2001 speech to the National Association for Business Economics. The speech was referred to by Senator Robert Byrd in an exchange with O'Neill during a February 7, 2002 hearing of the Senate Budget Committee.

45. In the same exchange with O'Neill. I am grateful to Professor Donald Moynihan for pointing out this reference, as well as the reference in the 2003 budget documents: Donald P. Moynihan, "Homeland Security and the U.S. Public Management Policy Agenda," *Governance* 18, no. 2 (2005): 171–196.

46. Office of Management and Budget, *Budget of the U.S. Government, Fiscal Year 2003* (Washington, DC: Office of Management and Budget, 2002). The image reproduced in the Budget is taken from a trade card produced for the U.S. subsidiary of Coats Thread Company, a Scottish firm, in the late nineteenth century. However, the Coats Company had used the same image in its earlier British advertising.

47. Quoted in John Dean, *Worse than Watergate* (New York: Little, Brown and Co., 2004), 3. Klayman made the comment in an August 2002 speech.

48. FACA applies to an advisory committee that is not composed exclusively of government officials. If the NEPDG's report were taken at face value, then FACA would not apply. However, the District of Columbia Court of Appeals held in 1993 that a nongovernmental individual might be regarded as a "de facto" member of an advisory committee, thus triggering FACA requirements. *(Ass'n of Am. Physicians & Surgeons, Inc. v. Clinton*, 997 F.2d 898, 902–03 (D.C. Cir. 1993.) Sierra Club and Judicial Watch sought to argue that energy executives were de facto members of the NEPDG. In May 2005, the U.S. Court of Appeals for the District of Columbia Circuit took a narrow view of the "de facto member" principle and refused to allow

the groups to seek further evidence that would allow them to substantiate their case.

49. In the General Accounting Office Act of 1980.
50. ABC's *This Week*, January 27, 2002.
51. Richard Cheney, *Letter Regarding Actions of the Comptroller General* (Washington, DC: Office of the Vice President, 2001), 6.
52. United States Supreme Court, *Cheney v. U.S. District Court for the District of Columbia*, Brief for the Petitioners: 15.
53. Press Conference by the President, March 13, 2002. http://www.fas.org/sgp/news/2002/03/gwb031302.html.
54. John F. Stacks, "Hard Times for Hard News," *World Policy Journal* 20, no. 4 (2004): 12–21, 20.
55. Executive Order 13233, November 1, 2001.
56. The order also appeared to allow former Vice Presidents an independent capacity to block release of documents: Rosenberg, *Statement before the House Subcommittee on Efficiency, Financial Management and Intergovernmental Relations Concerning Hr 4187, the Presidential Records Act Amendments of 2002*. A coalition of advocacy groups led by the Public Citizen Litigation Group challenged the order, but the United States District Court for the District of Columbia concluded in March 2004 that their complaint was premature, as harm had not yet been established. *American Historical Association, et al., v. National Archives and Records Administration, et al.*, Civil Action No. 01-2447, Memorandum Opinion, March 28, 2004.
57. Janet Reno, "Statement of the Attorney General Regarding Implementation of FOIA," in *Litigation under the Federal Open Government Laws*, ed. Allan Adler (Washington, DC: American Civil Liberties Union, 1993), John Ashcroft, *Memorandum on Freedom of Information Act* (Washington, DC: Department of Justice, 2001).
58. Andrew H. Card, Jr., *Memorandum on Action to Safeguard Information Regarding Weapons of Mass Destruction and Other Sensitive Documents Related to Homeland Security* (Washington, DC: Executive Office of the President, 2002).
59. According to the advocacy group OMBWatch: http://www.ombwatch.org/article/articleview/1145/1/18/.
60. Homeland Security Act, PL 107–296, section 214. The law also created a criminal penalty for unauthorized disclosure of critical infrastructure information – a level of protection not granted to classified information.
61. National Defense Authorization Act for Fiscal Year 2004, PL 108–136, section 922.
62. Executive Order 13292, March 25, 2003, amending Executive Order 12958, regarding Classified National Security Information. Sections 1.1(a)(4), 1.1(c) and 1.4(e)–(g).
63. Agencies that received new classification authority included the Department of Health and Human Services, the Department of Agriculture, and the Environmental Protection Agency, as well as the Department of Homeland Security after its establishment in January 2003.

64. J. William Leonard, *Remarks to the National Classification Management Society's Annual Training Seminar* (Washington, DC: Information Security Oversight Office, 2004).

65. Information Security Oversight Office, *Notes on Revisions to Executive Order 12958 on Classified National Security Information* (Washington, DC: Information Security Oversight Office, 2003). See section 1.7(c) of the revised Executive Order 12958.

66. Rep. Henry Waxman and Rep. John Tierney, *Letter to the Hon. Donald Rumsfeld Regarding Classification of a Report by the Office of Operational Test and Evaluation* (Washington, DC: House of Representatives, 2004).

67. Eric Lichtblau, "Material Given to Congress in 2004 Is Now Classified," *New York Times*, May 20, 2004, 18.

68. "It is wrong. It is against the law. It costs the lives of Americans." Donald Rumsfeld, *Memorandum on the Impact of Leaking Classified Information* (Washington, DC: Office of the Secretary of Defense, 2002).

69. United States Department of Justice, *Task Force Report on Unauthorized Disclosure of Classified Information* (Washington, DC: Department of Justice, 2002).

70. David Cole, *Enemy Aliens: Double Standards and Constitutional Freedoms in the War on Terrorism* (New York: The New Press, 2003), 25.

71. The Department successfully fought a legal challenge to its denial brought by a coalition of nineteen advocacy groups. The United States District Court for the District of Columbia overruled the Justice Department and ordered release of the requested information, but this decision was reversed on appeal. See *Center for National Security Studies v. U.S. Department of Justice*, D.C.C.A., June 17, 2003. In January 2003, the United States Supreme Court refused to hear a further appeal. The Justice Department also barred state and local governments from releasing information about detainees held under contract in their facilities.

72. Cole, *Enemy Aliens*, 26–28.

73. Mark Mazetti et al., "Inside the Iraq Prison Scandal," *U.S. News and World Report*, May 24, 2004, 18–22. In early 2004, there were about twenty facilities in Afghanistan alone.

74. Reed Brody, "What About the Other Secret U.S. Prisons?" *International Herald Tribune*, May 4, 2004, 8.

75. For a critical assessment of the Defense Department's February 2004 plan for the operation of military tribunals at Guantanamo, see Human Rights First, *Trials under Military Order: A Guide to the Final Rules for Military Commissions* (New York: Human Rights First, 2004).

76. *Rasul et al. v. Bush, President of the United States, et al*, United States Supreme Court, decided June 28, 2004.

77. John Hendren and Mark Mazzetti, "Proposal to Keep Some Prisoners 'Off the Books' Went against Promises for Yearly Case Reviews," *Los Angeles Times*, July 9, 2004.

78. Joint Inquiry, *Report of the Joint Inquiry into Intelligence Community Activities before and after the Terrorist Attacks of September 11, 2001*.

79. Michael Isikoff and Mark Hosenhall, "The Secrets of September 11," *Newsweek*, April 30, 2003.
80. David Johnston and Douglas Jehl, "Bush Refuses to Declassify Saudi Section of Report," *New York Times*, July 30, 2003, 1.
81. Senators McCain and Lieberman first introduced legislation to establish an independent commission in December 2001. The commission was established in November 2002. Generally, see Steven Strasser and Craig R. Whitney, *The 9/11 Investigations*, 1st ed., *PublicAffairs Reports* (New York: PublicAffairs, 2004).
82. Philip Shenon, "Bush, in Reversal, Supports More Time for 911 Inquiry," *New York Times*, February 5, 2004, 21.
83. T. Christian Miller, "Panel Presses Rice to Testify," *Los Angeles Times*, March 29, 2004, 1.
84. President Bush relented in February 2004.
85. Eric Lichtblau, "911 Report Cites Many Warnings About Hijackers," *New York Times*, February 10, 2005, A1.
86. Bob Woodward, *Plan of Attack* (New York: Simon and Schuster, 2004). The allegation is further discussed by Cass Sunstein in *The Secret $700 Million* April 22, 2004 [Accessed July 8, 2004]), available from http://www.salon.com/opinion/feature/2004/04/22/700million/.
87. Fallows, "Blind into Baghdad." Deputy Secretary of Defense Paul Wolfowitz publicly attacked the "outlandish" view of likely post-war obligations offered by Army Chief of Staff Eric Shinseki in February 2003. According to Fallows, Shinseki's "uncooperative attitude" made him the target of several "calculated insults" by Secretary Rumsfeld. Senior officers later said that the treatment of Shinseki exemplified the attitude toward public dissent held by the department's civilian leadership: Thomas Ricks, "Dissension Grows in Senior Ranks on War Strategy," *Washington Post*, May 9, 2004, A1.
88. Elizabeth Drew, "Bush: The Dream Campaign," *New York Review of Books*, June 10, 2004, 23–26, 24.
89. A critical assessment of the Bush administration's behavior before the war is provided by John Prados in *Hoodwinked*, 19–110.
90. Walter Pincus, "Intelligence Report for Iraq War Was 'Hastily Done'," *Washington Post*, October 24, 2003, A18.
91. Cirincione, Mathews, and Perkovich, *WMD in Iraq: Evidence and Implications*, 16–17.
92. All of the committee's rationale for conclusions regarding the discussion paper has been withheld on national security grounds. See Senate Intelligence Committee, *Report on the U.S. Intelligence Community's Prewar Intelligence Assessments on Iraq*, 295–297.
93. *New York Times*, "Lott Seeks Oversight of Classified Data," July 11, 2004.
94. Douglas Jehl and Neil Lewis, "U.S. Disputed Protected Status of Iraq Inmates," *New York Times*, May 23, 2004. In May 2004, General Janis Karpinski testified that military intelligence officers went "to great lengths to try to exclude the ICRC from access" to the interrogation wing of the

Abu Ghraib prison: Philip Shenon, "Officer Suggests Iraqi Jail Abuse Was Encouraged," *New York Times*, May 2, 2004, 1.

95. Taguba, *Article 15–6 Investigation of the 800th Military Police Brigade*, Finding 33.

96. Dana Priest and Bradley Graham, "U.S. Struggled over How Far To Push Tactics," *Washington Post*, June 24, 2004, A1.

97. Elise Ackerman, "Policy Let U.S. Hold Detainees in Secret, Military Officers Say," *Knight Ridder/Tribune News Service*, September 8, 2004.

98. Army Field Manual FM 34–52 (*Intelligence Interrogation*, Revision of May 8, 1987) states that "the use of force, mental torture, threats, insults, or exposure to unpleasant and inhumane treatment of any kind is prohibited by law and is neither authorized nor condoned by the U.S. government."

99. It was later learned that Secretary Rumsfeld had approved new rules for Guantánamo detainees on December 2, 2002. The rules were contained in a memorandum classified as SECRET/NOFORN. Revised rules were contained in an April 16, 2003, memorandum from Rumsfeld that was also classified as SECRET/NOFORN on his authority. According to the *Washington Post*, interrogation rules for Iraqi detainees that followed Rumsfeld's directions were contained in a classified memorandum signed by Lt. Gen. Ricardo Sanchez, the U.S. commander in Iraq, on September 12, 2003: Washington Post, "A Partial Disclosure," *Washington Post*, June 24, 2004, A24.

100. Washington Post, "Unanswered Questions," *Washington Post*, July 11, 2004, B6.

101. Reporters' Committee for Freedom of the Press, *Homefront Confidential, Fourth Edition* (Washington, DC: Reporters' Committee for Freedom of the Press, 2003), 1.

102. Dean, *Worse than Watergate*, 1.

103. Arthur M. Schlesinger, Jr., *War and the American Presidency*, 1st ed. (New York: W. W. Norton, 2004), 61.

104. I noted these ten major statutes earlier in this chapter. The series began with the Federal Advisory Committee Act of 1972 and ended with the General Accounting Office Act of 1980.

105. A 1978 *Washington Post* editorial praised the new law for creating an "impartial arbitrator" to oversee the executive branch. It noted that the bill had the support of "many of [the intelligence agencies'] most persistent critics": *Washington Post*, "National Security Wiretaps," September 6, 1978, A14.

106. Monica McCullough, *The "Secret" Foreign Intelligence Surveillance Court: Exaggerated Concern and Transparency Rhetoric*, Unpublished paper (Syracuse: Maxwell School, 2003), 1. A critique of weaknesses in the oversight mechanisms provided by FISA is also provided by Paul T. Jaeger, J. C. Bertot, and C. R. McClure, "The Impact of the USA Patriot Act on Collection and Analysis of Personal Information under the Foreign Intelligence Surveillance Act," *Government Information Quarterly* 20 (2003): 295–314.

107. The American Civil Liberties Union and the National Emergency Civil Liberties Committee. A group of congressmen also filed an amicus brief.

108. Eric Lichtblau, "Whistle-Blowing Said To Be Factor in FBI Firing," *New York Times*, July 29, 2004, 1. Although details of the report were leaked in July 2004, an unclassified summary of the report did not become available until January 2005.

109. National Security Archive, *The Ashcroft Memo: "Drastic Change" or "More Thunder than Lightning"?* (Washington, DC: National Security Archive, 2003).

110. Blaine Harden and Dana Milbank, "Photos of Soldiers' Coffins Revive Controversy," *Washington Post*, 2004, A10.

111. The documents, and NDRC's analysis, are located at http://www.nrdc.org/media/pressreleases/040401.asp.

112. Center for Public Integrity, *U.S. Contractors Reap the Windfalls of Post-War Reconstruction* (Washington, DC: Center for Public Integrity, 2003).

113. Electronic Privacy Information Center, *EPIC Celebrates International Right To Know Day* (Washington, DC: Electronic Privacy Information Center, 2004).

114. Dan Eggen and Susan Schmidt, "Data Shows Different Spy Game since 911," *Washington Post*, May 1, 2004, A1.

115. Dan Eggen and Susan Schmidt, "Secret Court Rebuffs Ashcroft," *Washington Post*, August 23, 2002, A1.

116. The controversy is described in *In Re: Sealed Case No's 02–001 and 02–002*, 310 F.3d 717 (FISA Court of Review, 2002).

117. For example: *Washington Post*, "Chipping Away at Liberty," November 19, 2002, A24.

118. Ellsberg began on October 1, 1969, and finished in mid-November. "The nightly routine" consisted of taking a briefcase of papers from RAND late in the evening, copying them until the next morning, sleeping until the early afternoon, then returning to work. Ellsberg, *Secrets*, 328.

119. David Sanger, "Discipline Takes a Break at the White House," *New York Times*, May 30, 2004, 1. The documents were collected as part of a Treasury Department archiving process in which the Secretary's records were routinely converted into digital form.

120. Ellsberg, *Secrets*, 295, 365, 373 and 387. The Nixon administration's request for a restraining order was subsequently extended to the *Washington Post* when it also published excerpts of the paper.

121. http://thepriceofloyalty.ronsuskind.com/thebushfiles/.

122. http://www.thememoryhole.org/war/coffin_photos/dover/.

123. Michael Weisskopf, "Reporter's Notebook," *Time*, June 3, 2002, 6.

124. Richard A. Clarke, *Against All Enemies: Inside America's War on Terror* (New York: Free Press, 2004).

125. Dana Milbank and Mike Allen, "White House Counters Ex-Aide," *Washington Post*, March 23, 2004, A1.

126. Miller, "Panel Presses Rice To Testify."

127. Alberto Gonzales, *Letter to the National Commission on Terrorist Attacks Upon the United States* (Washington, DC: Executive Office of the President, 2004).

128. Douglas Jehl, "In a Few Words, Many Clues to CIA's Working Method," *New York Times*, April 12, 2004, A12. For a contrary view of the PDB's significance, see Thomas Blanton, "Who's Afraid of the PDB?" *Slate*, March 22, 2004.

129. Edward Alden, "Bush Close to Releasing Secret Briefing," *Financial Times*, April 10, 2004, 7.

130. Dan Eggen, "911 Panel To Have Rare Glimpse of Presidential Briefings," *Washington Post*, November 16, 2003, A9.

131. Eric Lichtblau and David Sanger, "August '01 Brief Is Said To Warn of Attack Plans," *New York Times*, April 10, 2004, 1.

132. Office of the Press Secretary, *Background Briefing Via Conference Call on the President's PDB of August 6, 2001* (Washington, DC: Executive Office of the President, 2004).

133. Lydia Polgreen, "Families Savor Their Victory over Grief and a Reluctant Government," *New York Times*, July 23, 2004, 11.

134. National Commission On Terrorist Attacks Upon the United States, *Final Report*. The new revelations were summarized by Philip Shenon, Douglas Jehl, and David Johnston, "Correcting the Record on Sept. 11, in Great Detail," *New York Times*, July 25, 2004, 1.

135. Joseph Wilson, "What I Didn't Find in Africa," *New York Times*, July 6, 2003, 9.

136. James Risen and David Sanger, "CIA Chief To Face Panel on Dubious Iraq Arms Data," *New York Times*, July 16, 2003, 10.

137. See Prados, *Hoodwinked*; Cirincione, Mathews, and Perkovich, *WMD in Iraq: Evidence and Implications*.

138. http://thepriceofloyalty.ronsuskind.com/thebushfiles/archives/000067. html.

139. Steven Weisman, "Airing of Powell's Misgivings Tests Ties in the Cabinet," *New York Times*, April 19, 2004, 1.

140. The *Boston Phoenix* subsequently reported that the author was Michael Scheuer, a twenty-year veteran of the CIA who had been deeply involved in its efforts against al Qaeda. The CIA had required that Scheuer publish his book anonymously: Jason Vest, "The Secret History of Anonymous," *Boston Phoenix*, July 2–8, 2004.

141. Tommy Franks, *American Soldier* (New York: Regan Books, 2004), 362.

142. Raymond Bonner, Don Van Natta, Jr., and Amy Waldham, "Questioning Terror Suspects in a Dark and Surreal World," *New York Times*, March 9, 2003, 1.

143. Neil Lewis and Eric Schmitt, "Lawyers Decided Bans on Torture Didn't Bind Bush," *New York Times*, June 8, 2004, 1.

144. Jess Bravin, "Pentagon Report Set Framework for Use of Torture," *Wall Street Journal*, June 7, 2004, A1.

145. Lewis and Schmitt, "Lawyers Decided Bans on Torture Didn't Bind Bush"; Dana Priest and R. Jeffrey Smith, "Memo Offered Justification for Use of Torture," *Washington Post*, June 8, 2004, A1.

146. Richard Serrano, "Prison Interrogators's Gloves Came Off before Abu Ghraib," *Los Angeles Times*, June 9, 2004, 1.

147. Office of the Press Secretary, *Press Briefing by White House Counsel Judge Alberto Gonzales, DoD General Counsel William Haynes, DoD Deputy General Counsel Daniel Dell'orto and Army Deputy Chief of Staff for Intelligence General Keith Alexander* (Washington, DC: Executive Office of the President, 2004), Scott Lindlaw, "White House Plans To Release Large File of Documents on Deliberations Leading to Interrogation Tactics," *Associated Press*, June 22, 2004.

148. Osha Gray Davidson, "The Secret File of Abu Ghraib," *Rolling Stone*, August 19, 2004, 48.

149. Richard Serrano and Greg Miller, "Documents Provide More Details on Prisoner Abuse Allegations," *New York Times*, October 22, 2004, A4.

150. Steven Strasser, *The Abu Ghraib Investigations* (New York: PublicAffairs, 2004), 1–14 and 52. A second report on abuses at Abu Ghraib, prepared by Major General George Fay and Lieutenant General Anthony R. Jones, was also released in August 2004. Portions of the Fay/Jones report were classified, but leaked to the *New York Times* and the *Washington Post* within days.

151. Hersh, *Chain of Command*.

152. The phrase was used by the Schlesinger panel: Strasser, *The Abu Ghraib Investigations*, 33.

153. William Gibson, "The Road to Oceania," *The New York Times*, June 25, 2003, 25.

154. Kim Zetter, "Downloading for Democracy," *Wired News*, July 19, 2004, Web edition: http://www.wired.com/news/politics/0,1283,64237,64200.html.

155. *Washington Post*, "The CIA's Prisoners," July 15, 2004, A20.

4. Message discipline

1. Senior government officials issued a press release describing Kelly's position, and agreed that they would confirm Kelly's identity if it was guessed by a journalist. Simon Rogers, ed., *The Hutton Inquiry and Its Impact* (London: Politico's Publishing, 2004), 126–127.

2. http://www.the-hutton-inquiry.org.uk/.

3. Lord Hutton, *Report of the Inquiry to the Circumstances Surrounding the Death of Dr. David Kelly* (London: The Hutton Inquiry, 2004), 144.

4. Rogers, ed., *The Hutton Inquiry and Its Impact*, 4–8 and 10–27.

5. Peter Riddell, *Hug Them Close: Blair, Clinton, Bush and the "Special Relationship"* (London: Politico's, 2004), 215.

6. Anthony Sampson, *Who Runs This Place?* (London: John Murray, 2004), 82. For an early complaint about the Blair government's preoccupation

with "message discipline," see House of Lords *Hansard*, October 28, 1997, Column 1026.

7. Iain Byrne and Stuart Weir, "Democratic Audit: Executive Democracy in War and Peace," *Parliamentary Affairs* 57, no. 2 (2004): 453–468, 458–459, Committee on Standards in Public Life, *Ninth Report*, Cm 5775 (London: Committee on Standards in Public Life, 2003), 4.20.

8. Committee on Standards in Public Life, *Ninth Report*, 8.3, Government Communications Review Group, *An Independent Review of Government Communications* (London: Government Communications Review Group, 2004).

9. Evidence of Mr. Bob Phillis to the House of Commons Public Administration Committee, January 22, 2004.

10. Nicholas Fraser, "To BBC or Not To BBC," *Harper's Magazine*, May, 2004, 55.

11. United Kingdom, *Your Right To Know: The Government's Proposals for a Freedom of Information Act*, Preface.

12. Jack Straw, *House of Commons Debates* (London: House of Commons, 1999).

13. Lord Chancellor's Department, *Annual Report on Bringing Fully into Force Those Provisions of the Freedom of Information Act 2000 Which Are Not yet Fully in Force* (London: Lord Chancellor's Department, 2002), 19.

14. Maeve McDonagh, *Freedom of Information in Ireland: Five Years On* (Washington, DC: freedominfo.org, September 22, 2003 [Accessed October 15, 2003]), available from http://www.freedominfo.org/reports/ireland/ireland.pdf. On the controversy over the invocation of cabinet confidentiality, see Seamus Dolan, "The Penumbra of Cabinet Confidentiality and the Irish Constitution," *The Galway Student Law Review* 2 (2003): 136–151, 142–143.

15. Joe Carroll, "Spring Gets Cabinet Secrecy Poll in Hope of Changing Strict Rules," *The Irish Times*, December 5, 1994, 7.

16. Minister of Finance, *Fifth Report on Freedom of Information* (Dublin: Ministry of Finance, 2003), Table 1.3. The following cases are noted by McDonagh, *Freedom of Information in Ireland: Five Years On*.

17. FOI Civil Service Users' Network, *Review of Administrative and Procedural Arrangements Governing FOI* (Dublin: Department of Finance FOI Central Policy Unit, 1999).

18. Information Commissioner of Ireland, *Annual Report 2001* (Dublin, Ireland: Office of the Information Commissioner, 2002), 18.

19. Emily O'Reilly, *Address to the Second Annual Conference on Freedom of Information of the School of Law, Trinity College, Dublin* (Dublin, Ireland: Office of the Information Commissioner, 2003).

20. Louisa Nesbitt, "Information Laws 'Corroded Process of Government'," *Press Association News*, March 1, 2003.

21. Martin Rosenbaum, *Open to Question: Journalism and Freedom of Information* (Oxford: Reuters Foundation Fellowship Programme, 2004).

22. Dáil Debate, June 1, 2004.

23. Mark Brennock, "Journalists' Exposes the Only Competition Discouraged," *Irish Times*, July 5, 2003, 12, Karlin Lillington, "Openness and Transparency of State Only Go in One Direction," *The Irish Times*, August 22, 2003, 53. Rosenbaum, *Open to Question: Journalism and Freedom of Information*, 13.

24. Rosenbaum, *Open to Question: Journalism and Freedom of Information*, McDonagh, *Freedom of Information in Ireland*.

25. Information Commissioner of Ireland, *Review of the Operation of the Freedom of Information (Amendment) Act 2003* (Dublin: Office of the Information Commissioner, 2004), 14–19.

26. Irish Examiner, "Govt Made FOI Concept "Almost Useless": Labour," *Irish Examiner*, May 16, 2004.

27. In 1969, political scientist Denis Smith lamented that Canadian government had been transformed into a "thinly-disguised Presidential system," without the benefit of a strong legislature to balance presidential power. Denis Smith, "President and Parliament: The Transformation of Parliamentary Government in Canada," in *Apex of Power: The Prime Minister and Political Leadership in Canada*, ed. Thomas A. Hockin (Toronto: Prentice-Hall, 1977).

28. Andrew Osler, "Journalism and the FOI Laws: A Faded Promise," *Government Information in Canada* 17 (1999): http://www.usask.ca/library/gic/17/osler.html.

29. A brief chronology is provided in Annex 8 of Access to Information Review Task Force, *Access to Information: Making It Work for Canadians* (Ottawa: Treasury Board Secretariat, 2002). See also Privy Council Office, "Discussion Paper on Freedom of Information Legislation," in *The Complete Annotated Guide to Federal Access to Information*, ed. Michel Drapeau and Marc-Auréle Racicot (Toronto: Carswell, 2001), 47.

30. John Roberts, "Green Paper on Legislation on Public Access to Government Documents," in *The Complete Annotated Guide to Federal Access to Information*, ed. Michel Drapeau and Marc-Auréle Racicot (Toronto: Carswell, 2001).

31. The efforts to avoid the law were revealed following the investigation of the handling of a 1997 AIA request made by Ethyl Canada. The case is discussed in Information Commissioner of Canada, *Annual Report 2002–2003* (Ottawa: Office of the Information Commissioner, 2003), 15–16.

32. Information Commissioner of Canada, *Annual Report 1996–1997* (Ottawa: Office of the Information Commissioner, 1997), 63–72. The decision to destroy records became public knowledge following a public inquiry in 1995.

33. Canada's Federal Court later overruled the government. *Canada (Information Commissioner) v. Canada (Prime Minister)*, (1993) 1 F.C. 427.

34. John Crosbie, *No Holds Barred* (Toronto, Ontario: McClelland and Stewart, 1997), 300.

35. Liberal Party of Canada, *Creating Opportunity: The Liberal Plan for Canada* (Ottawa: Liberal Party of Canada, 1993).

36. Donald Savoie, *Governing from the Centre* (Toronto: University of Toronto Press, 1999); Jeffrey Simpson, *The Friendly Dictatorship* (Toronto: McClelland and Stewart, 2001).
37. The comment is made in an e-mail released to the author following an Access to Information Act request to Canadian Department of Citizenship and Immigration.
38. Donald Savoie, *Breaking the Bargain* (Toronto: University of Toronto Press, 2003), 164.
39. Alasdair Roberts, "New Strategies for Enforcement of the Access to Information Act," *Queen's Law Journal* 27 (2002): 647–683, 653–654.
40. Alasdair Roberts, *Statement to the MPs' Committee on Access to Information* (Syracuse, NY: Campbell Public Affairs Institute, 2001).
41. Alasdair Roberts, "Retrenchment and Freedom of Information: Recent Experience under Federal, Ontario, and British Columbia Law," *Canadian Public Administration* 42, no. 4 (1999): 422–451; Roberts, "New Strategies for Enforcement of the Access to Information Act," 654–658 and 670–671.
42. Ann Rees, "Red File Alert: Public Access at Risk," *Toronto Star*, November 1, 2003, A32. The following discussion draws on the same documents used by Rees, as well as other documents obtained by the author through other AIA requests. A more detailed discussion is provided in Alasdair Roberts, "Spin Control and Freedom of Information," *Public Administration* 83, no. 1 (2005): 1–23.
43. Gomery Commission, *Transcript of Public Hearing, October 14, 2004* (Ottawa, Canada: Commission of Inquiry into the Sponsorship Program and Advertising Activities, 2004), 3672.
44. The practice of categorizing requesters actually began so that ministries could provide a public report of the type of individuals using the disclosure law. However, some departments refined these categories, adding some – such as Parliament, Political Party, Consultant, or Lawyer – that are only used for internal purposes.
45. Whether this bar on disclosure is always respected is uncertain. In 2001 the Information Commissioner fought a legal battle that hinged on the question of how a PCO official had learned the identity of a requester. Information Commissioner of Canada, *Annual Report 2000–2001* (Ottawa, Ontario: Office of the Information Commissioner, 2001), 114. It may also be easy for an official to guess the identity of a requester once his or her occupation is disclosed: Alasdair Roberts, "Singled Out for Special Treatment," *Media Magazine* 10, no. 4 (2004): 16–17.
46. Again, this is an adaptation of a feature originally added for other reasons. See Alasdair Roberts, "Administrative Discretion and the Access to Information Act: An 'Internal Law' on Open Government?" *Canadian Public Administration* 45, no. 2 (2002): 175–194.
47. For further details on CAIRS, see Roberts, "Spin Control and Freedom of Information."
48. Frank Howard, "Information Commissioner Warns New Access Process Will Stem Leaks," *Ottawa Citizen*, July 3, 1992, A4.

49. Government Telecommunications and Informatics Services, *Coordination of Access to Information Requests CAIR System: Replacement of Current System – Business Requirements* (Ottawa, Ontario: Government Telecommunications and Informatics Service, 1999), 1.
50. Rees, "Red File Alert: Public Access at Risk."
51. Jonathan Murphy, "Your Candle's Flickering, Jean," *Globe and Mail*, May 17, 2002, A15.
52. Roberts, "Spin Control and Freedom of Information."
53. Roberts, "Administrative Discretion and the Access to Information Act: An "Internal Law" on Open Government?"
54. Roberts, "Spin Control and Freedom of Information."
55. Evidence of Mr. Charles Guité to the House of Commons Standing Committee on Public Accounts, April 22, 2004.
56. Gomery Commission, *Transcript of Public Hearing, October 14, 2004*, 3667–3674.
57. Daniel Leblanc, "Globe's Sponsorship Probe Led Ottawa to Invent Rules," *Globe and Mail*, October 15, 2004.
58. The case is discussed in more detail in Roberts, "Spin Control and Freedom of Information."
59. For example: Robert Hazell, "Freedom of Information in Australia, Canada and New Zealand," *Public Administration* 67, no. 2 (1989): 189.
60. The lack of good evidence is noted by Dave Clemens, *Requests Made under the Official Information Act 1982: A Survey at the Agency Level. Master's Thesis, Degree of Master of Library and Information Studies* (Wellington, New Zealand: School of Communications and Information Management, Victoria University of Wellington, 2001); Edward Adams and Andrew Ecclestone, *Implementation of the Freedom of Information Act 2000: Study Visit to Australia and New Zealand* (London: Department of Constitutional Affairs, 2003).
61. Brian Ellwood, *Report of the Chief Ombudsman on Leaving Office* (Wellington, New Zealand: Office of the Chief Ombudsman, 2003), 11 and 13. The Ombudsmen's Annual Reports for 2001 to 2004 showed that about 40 percent of complaints relating to requests under the Official Information Act came from journalists or parliamentarians and their staff.
62. Adams and Ecclestone, *Implementation of the Freedom of Information Act 2000: Study Visit to Australia and New Zealand*, 4. Another recent study concludes that journalists in New Zealand are more active users of their disclosure law than journalists in Australia, Canada, or the United States: Stephen Lamble, "Media Use of FOI Surveyed," *Freedom of Information Review* 109 (2004): 5–9.
63. Marie Shroff, "Behind the Official Information Act: Politics, Power and Procedure," in *The Official Information Act* (Wellington, New Zealand: Victoria University of Wellington, 1997), 20.
64. Adams and Ecclestone, *Implementation of the Freedom of Information Act 2000: Study Visit to Australia and New Zealand*, 10.
65. Nicky Hager, *A Researcher's View of New Zealand's Official Information Act: Comments to the International Symposium on Freedom of Information*

and Privacy (Auckland, New Zealand: Office of the Privacy Commissioner, 2002).

66. James Buwalda, *Report of an Investigation into the Department of Labour's Management of Information in Relation to Mr. Ahmed Zaoui* (Wellington, New Zealand: Department of Labour, 2003), 8–12.

67. Mel Smith, *Report Upon the Actions of the Department of Labor in Regard to an Official Information Act Complaint by Sarah Boyle, of the Office of the Leader of the Opposition* (Wellington, New Zealand: Office of the Ombudsman, 2004), 29 and 38.

68. The *Tampa* controversy is discussed in: David Marr and Marian Wilkinson, *Dark Victory: How a Government Lied Its Way to Political Triumph* (Crow's Nest, New South Wales: Allen & Unwin, 2003).

69. Patrick Weller, *Don't Tell the Prime Minister* (Melbourne: Scribe Publications, 2002).

70. Ibid., 51–89.

71. Martin Chulov, "How FOI Became Freedom from Information," *The Australian*, June 21, 2001, M1. See also Rick Snell, "FOI and the Delivery of Diminishing Returns, or How Spin-Doctors and Journalists Have Mistreated a Volatile Reform," *The Drawing Board: An Australian Review of Public Affairs* 2, no. 3 (2002): 187–207, 193.

72. Rick Snell, "Contentious Issues Management: The Dry Rot in FOI Practice?" *Freedom of Information Review*, no. 102 (2002): 62–65, 63.

73. Ombudsman of New South Wales, *Annual Report 2001–2002* (Sydney, Australia: Office of the Ombudsman, 2002), 73.

74. Paola Totaro, "No Such Thing as a Free Set of Documents," *Freedom of Information Review* 101 (2002): 53–54, 53.

75. Information and Privacy Commissioner of Ontario, *Annual Report 2000* (Toronto: Office of the Information and Privacy Commissioner, 2001), 4–6.

76. Ann Rees, "Public Access under Attack," *Toronto Star*, September 20, 2003, A1; Ann Rees, "Information Requests Stir Privacy Debate," *Toronto Star*, September 21, 2003, A7. In 2004 the Commissioner called on the government to reform the procedures: Information and Privacy Commission of Ontario, *Annual Report 2003* (Toronto: Information and Privacy Commissioner of Ontario, 2004), 6.

77. Roberts, "Retrenchment and Freedom of Information: Recent Experience under Federal, Ontario, and British Columbia Law," Table 5.

78. Alasdair Roberts, "Treatment of Sensitive Requests under British Columbia's Freedom of Information Law," *Freedom of Information Review* 109 (2004): 2–4.

79. Ann Rees, "Watchdog Probes Claim That Province Violated Privacy Law," *Vancouver Sun*, March 20, 2004, A1.

80. Ann Rees, *Freedom of Information under Surveillance in British Columbia* (Vancouver: Simon Fraser University, School of Communication, 2004), 17.

81. Richard Halloran, "Information Act Scored as Futile," *New York Times*, March 15, 1972, 19.

82. Otto Kahn-Freund, "On Uses and Misuses of Comparative Law," *Modern Law Review* 37 (1974): 1–27, 12–13.

83. Gunther Teubner, "Legal Irritants: Good Faith in British Law or How Unifying Law Ends up in New Divergencies," *Modern Law Review* 61, no. 1 (1998): 11–32, 12.

84. *Asahi News Service*, "More Lists: Many Agencies Are Recording Inappropriate Details," August 30, 2002, *Mainichi Daily News*, "Ministries May Face Inspection over Private Data Collection," May 29, 2002.

85. See Adams and Ecclestone, *Implementation of the Freedom of Information Act 2000: Study Visit to Australia and New Zealand*, 4. However, this proposition should be treated cautiously. It was a comment made about the Australian and New Zealand systems, for which data on patterns of use is not available. Experience in jurisdictions with better data shows that officials sometimes prefer to route simple and noncontentious requests through the formal disclosure process for a variety of reasons, including organizational simplicity and the capacity for fee collection: Roberts, "Retrenchment and Freedom of Information: Recent Experience under Federal, Ontario, and British Columbia Law."

86. OECD, *Governance in Transition: Public Management Reforms in OECD Countries* (Paris: Organization for Economic Cooperation and Development, 1995).

87. OECD, *Ministerial Symposium on the Future of Public Services* (Paris: OECD, 1996), Session 2.

88. Committee on Standards in Public Life, *Ninth Report*, 4.18.

89. Butler Committee, *Review of Intelligence on Weapons of Mass Destruction* (London: The Stationery Office, 2004), 146–148; Michael White and Patrick Wintour, "Straw Cites Leakers in Defence of Blair Style," *The Guardian*, July 16, 2004, 5.

90. Government Communications Review Group, *An Independent Review of Government Communications*.

91. Phillip Bobbitt, *The Shield of Achilles: War, Peace, and the Course of History* (New York: Anchor Books, 2002), 226.

92. In the United Kingdom, this argument has been laid out by Sampson, *Who Runs This Place?*

93. For example, by the recognition of voting rights for racial minorities, or by the reduction of the minimum voting age to 18 years.

94. Such distrust may be exacerbated by the contemporary media, but it was hardly fostered by it: Mass skepticism of central authority was noted long before the advent of contemporary communications technologies.

95. Sidney Blumenthal, *The Permanent Campaign*, Rev. ed. (New York: Simon and Schuster, 1982); Committee on Standards in Public Life, *Ninth Report*, 4.18.

96. P. Webb and T. Poguntke, eds., *The Presidentialization of Democracy* (Oxford University Press, 2004).

97. Government Communications Review Group, *An Independent Review of Government Communications*, 12.

98. Ibid., 23.

99. Peter Riddell, *Parliament under Pressure* (London: Gollancz, 1998), 99.
100. Nicholas Watt, "Openness Bill Gets Cold Reception," *The Guardian*, October 23, 1999, 10.
101. Rob Evans and David Hencke, "Blair "Big Bang" Theory to Delay Freedom Act," *The Guardian*, October 26, 2001, 15.
102. The Code of Practice on Access to Government Information was adopted in April 1994 and revised in January 1997. As a nonstatutory code, remedies for noncompliance were relatively weak.
103. This data is drawn from annual monitoring reports for the Code of Practice on Access to Government Information published on the website of the Department of Constitutional Affairs.
104. David Hencke and Rob Evans, "Blair Wins Battle to Put Open Government on Ice," *The Guardian*, October 30, 2001, 12.
105. FOI Practitioner's Group, *Minutes of Meeting on January 24, 2003* (London: Lord Chancellor's Department, 2003), 4 and 8–9. The document was provided in response to a request under the Code of Practice.
106. A March 25, 2004, memorandum for the government's Access To Information Project Board states that there should be a central "coordination unit" to provide advice on difficult requests and "co-ordinate responses to round-robin requests" Access to Information Project Board, *Memorandum for the Board on Critical Success Factors for the Implementation of the Freedom of Information Act* (London: Department of Constitutional Affairs, 2004). In April 2004, another advisory body – the Freedom of Information Practitioners' Group – was assured that "measures will be taken to ensure consistency in dealing with round-robin requests." FOI Practitioner's Group, *Minutes of Meeting of April 19, 2004* (London: Department of Constitutional Affairs, 2004), 4. These documents were released in response to a request under the Code of Practice.
107. Written Answers To Questions, *Hansard*, September 8, 2004: "I announced the establishment of the Ministerial Committee on Freedom of Information (MISC28) to Parliament on Thursday 27 May 2004." Blair refused to provide further information about its work.
108. The Mirror, "Cabinet Fear Freedom Law," *The Mirror*, July 9, 2004, 2.
109. David Hencke, "Treasury Accused as Cost of Information Soars," *The Guardian*, May 18, 2004, 1.
110. Maurice Frankel, *Comments on the Draft Final Paper of the Fees Working Group* (London: Campaign for Freedom of Information, 2004), 7.
111. Patrick Wintour, "Falconer Promises Low User Cost for Legislation That Will Bring "More Trust" in Government," *The Guardian*, October 18, 2004, 2.
112. Charles Falconer, "Farewell to the Blight of Secrecy," *The Guardian*, December 29, 2004, 18.
113. Michael White and David Hencke, "Parties Dig for Dirt as Election Looms," *The Guardian*, February 5, 2005, 1.
114. Department of Constitutional Affairs, *Access to Information Central Clearing House: Toolkit for Practitioners* (London: Department of Constitutional Affairs, 2005).

5. Soft states

1. Jacob Söderman, "The EU's Transparent Bid for Opacity," *Wall Street Journal Europe*, February 24, 2000.
2. Colin Bennett, "Understanding Ripple Effects: The Cross National Adoption of Policy Instruments for Bureaucratic Accountability," *Governance* 10, no. 3 (1997): 213–234; Colin J. Bennett, *Globalization and Access to Information Regimes* (Ottawa: Government of Canada, Access to Information Review Task Force, 2001).
3. Daniel Kaufmann, Aart Kraay, and Massimo Mastruzzi, *Governance Matters III: Governance Indicators for 1996–2002* (Washington, DC: World Bank, 2003). The authors provide data on each of the five measures for each country for 1996, 1998, 2000, and 2002. For countries adopting laws before 1996, 1996 data was used. As most of these were stable OECD democracies this seemed a reasonable decision. For later adopters, data for the nearest preceding year was used; for example, 1998 data was used for a country adopting a law in 1999.
4. This was encouraged by scholars and nongovernmental organizations within the United States; for example, see Ralph G. Elliott, "Constitutionalizing the Right of Freedom of Information: A Modest Proposal for the Nations of Central and Eastern Europe," *Connecticut Journal of International Law* 8 (1993): 327–357.
5. Gunnar Myrdal, *The Challenge of World Poverty* (New York: Pantheon Books, 1970), 208–252.
6. Council of Europe Recommendation Rec(2002)2, February 22, 2002. On the influence of the Council of Europe, see Alex Grigorescu, "European Institutions and Unsuccessful Norm Transmission: The Case of Transparency," *International Politics* 39, no. 4 (2002): 467–489.
7. Communiqué of the Commonwealth Law Ministers' Meeting, Kingstown, St. Vincent and the Grenadines, November 21, 2002.
8. Organization of American States, AG/Res. 2057, "Access to Public Information: Strengthening Democracy," June 8, 2004.
9. http://www.article19.org.
10. ARTICLE 19, *Joint Declaration by the UN Special Rapporteur on Freedom of Opinion and Expression, the Osce Representative on Freedom of the Media and the Oas Special Rapporteur on Freedom of Expression* (London: ARTICLE 19, 2004).
11. http://www.humanrightsinitiative.org
12. http://www.ihf-hr.org
13. http://www.cartercenter.org
14. http://www.justiceinitiative.org
15. Fredrik Galtung, "A Global Network to Curb Corruption: The Experience of Transparency International," in *The Third Force*, ed. Ann Florini (Washington, DC: Carnegie Endowment for International Peace, 2000).
16. Jeremy Pope, *Press Release: Greater Access to Official Information and Containing Conflicts of Interest "Key to Containing Corruption"* (Berlin: Transparency International, 1998).

17. United Nations Development Program, *Corruption and Good Governance* (New York: UNDP Management Development and Governance Division, 1997), 78.

18. *Xinhua News Agency*, "CPC Leader Calls for More Transparency in Government Work," September 26, 2003. See also Hou Qi and Wei Ziyang, "Information Must Flow Freely," *China Daily*, July 2, 2004.

19. Pakistan, *Memorandum of Economic and Financial Policies for the Remainder of Fy 2002/03* (Washington, DC: International Monetary Fund, 2002); Banisar, *Freedom of Information and Access to Government Records around the World*.

20. Mohammad Kamran, "Information Law Not Being Implemented," *Pakistan Daily Times*, November 23, 2004.

21. Kimberly Barata, Piers Cain, and Anne Thurston, "Building a Case for Evidence," *Records Management Journal* 10, no. 1 (2000).

22. Australian Law Reform Commission, *Draft Recommendations Paper on Review of Archives Act* (Canberra: Australian Law Reform Commission, 1997).

23. Kimberly Barata, Piers Cain, and Anne Thurston, *From Accounting to Accountability: Managing Accounting Records as a Strategic Resource* (London: International Records Management Trust, 1999), 68.

24. Piers Cain and Anne Thurston, *Personnel Records: A Strategic Resource for Public Sector Management* (London: University College London, 1997), 35.

25. International Records Management Trust, *Personnel and Payroll Records and Information Systems in Tanzania* (London: International Records Management Trust, 2002), 13. The Trust found similar difficulties in a study of personnel records in the Indian state of Uttar Pradesh: International Records Management Trust, *Personnel Information and Civil Service Establishment Controls in Uttar Pradesh* (London: International Records Management Trust, 2002).

26. International Records Management Trust, *Legal and Judicial Records and Information Systems in Ecuador* (London: International Records Management Trust, 2002).

27. Musila Musembi, "Fighting Poor Records Keeping in Kenya," in *Information for Accountability Workshops Sourcebook*, ed. Dawn Routledge, Kimberly Barata, and Piers Cain (London: International Records Management Trust, 2000). Manipulation of files to hide corruption is also reported in Gambia. See Barata, Cain, and Thurston, *From Accounting to Accountability: Managing Accounting Records as a Strategic Resource*, 21.

28. Attorney General of Australia, *Annual Report on the Freedom of Information Act, 2003–2004* (Canberra: Attorney General's Department, 2004).

29. Treasury Board Secretariat, *Review of the Costs Associated with Administering Access to Information and Privacy (ATIP) Legislation* (Ottawa: Treasury Board Secretariat, 2000).

30. The Australian FOI system handles a larger proportion of requests for personal information, which are processed more easily.

31. United States Department of Justice, *Summary of Annual FOIA Reports for Fiscal Year 2003*, FOIA Post 22 (Washington, DC: Department of Justice, Office of Information and Privacy, 2004).

32. Most requests to the Social Security Administration are from individuals seeking geneological information needed to trace their family trees, while most VHA requests involve medical and personnel records: Martha Mendoza, "Four Million FOIA Requests in 2004 Tops Previous High," *Associated Press*, March 18, 2005. In 2003, over 98 percent of the 1.7 million VHA requests resulted in total disclosure; the average processing cost was less than twenty dollars.

33. ARTICLE 19, *A Model Freedom of Information Law* (London: ARTICLE 19, 2001), Section 11.

34. In Chapter 4, I noted the impact of fee increases in Ireland and the Canadian province of Ontario. In Australia, a 1987 increase in FOIA fees that yielded revenues equal to 3 percent of costs also caused a 10 percent decline in requests: Tom Riley, "Freedom of Information and the Right to Know," in *Information for Accountability Workshops Sourcebook*, ed. Dawn Routledge, Kimberly Barata, and Piers Cain (London: International Records Management Trust, 2000), 39.

35. The office also had other responsibilities that were part of the government's program of constitutional modernization.

36. Minutes of the Freedom of Information Practitioners' Group, March 1, 2004. Released in response to a request under the Code of Practice on Access to Government Information.

37. The Jamaican law went into effect on a phased basis; the first phase began in January 2004.

38. Figures taken from the Government of Jamaica's *2004–2005 Budget*, April 15, 2004.

39. The report also included two countries, Armenia and Macedonia, that did not have a disclosure law in force.

40. Open Society Justice Initiative, *Access to Information Monitoring Tool: Report from a Five Country Study* (New York: Open Society Justice Initiative, 2004), 15. The study also included results from Armenia, whose law was not in force at the time of the survey; and Macedonia, which had no law at the time of the survey.

41. BBC Monitoring Service, "Moldovan Law on Information Access Seriously Violated," *BBC Monitoring Service*, September 29, 2004.

42. The observations in this paragraph draw on the U.S. State Department's Country Reports on Human Rights Practices for 2003. The reports are located at http://www.state.gov/g/drl/rls/hrrpt/2003/.

43. Nakorn Serirak, "Making Sense of the Right to Know," *Bangkok Post*, September 24, 2002.

44. The mission statements are provided by Guidestar.org, a guide to nonprofit organizations.

45. Again, the following observations draw on the U.S. State Department's Country Reports on Human Rights Practices for 2003.

46. Ken Stier, "Post-Soviet Georgia Struggles to Find Democracy," *Christian Science Monitor*, July 24, 2002, 7.
47. From the U.S. State Department's Country Report on Georgia for 2003; similar observations were made in its 2003 reports for Armenia and Albania, which have also adopted disclosure laws.
48. Data taken from the Open Society Justice Initiative's website, http://www.justiceinitiative.org/. Accessed December 14, 2004.
49. Jeremy Page, "My Friend the Dictator Wants to Chat," *The Times of London*, March 22, 2004, 13.
50. Again, in the words of the U.S. State Department. Its assessment of electoral processes in Ukraine came before the controversy over the 2004 presidential election.
51. Banisar, *Freedom of Information and Access to Government Records around the World*; Toby Mendel and Rashweat Mukundu, *The Access to Information and Protection of Privacy Act: Two Years On* (London: ARTICLE 19/MISA-Zimbabwe, 2004).
52. U.S. Department of State, *Country Reports on Human Rights Practices, 2003* (Washington, DC: Bureau of Democracy, Human Rights, and Labor, 2004).
53. Daniel Kwan, "Journalist Has Prison Term Cut by Two Years," *South China Morning Post*, March 19, 2003, 5, Perry Link, "China: Wiping out the Truth," *New York Review of Books*, February 24, 2005, 36–38.
54. Josephine Ma, "Lawyer Barred from Meeting Reporter in States Secret Case," *South China Morning Post*, September 25, 2004, 5.
55. Philip Pan, "In China, an Editor Triumphs, and Fails," *Washington Post*, August 1, 2004, A1. The editor of the *Southern Metropolitan Daily*, Cheng Yizhong, received the UNESCO/Guillermo Cano World Press Freedom Prize in 2005.
56. Philip Pan, "Chinese Pressure Dissident Physician," *Washington Post*, July 5, 2004, A1.
57. United Nations Development Programme, *Nigerian Governance and Human Rights Programme* (Lagos: United Nations Development Programme, 2003). The House bill will become law when approved by the Nigerian Senate.
58. *Vanguard*, "Hail Brave New World," September 1, 2004.

6. Opaque networks

1. The penalty was contained in section 303 of HR 4392, the Intelligence Authorization Act for Fiscal Year 2001.
2. The decision was announced by Senator Robert Graham on September 4, 2001. The main advocate of the new penalty was Senator Richard Shelby. The battle over this proposal is described by Jack Nelson, *U.S. Government Secrecy and the Current Crackdown on Leaks* (Cambridge, MA: Joan Shorenstein Center for Press, Politics and Public Policy, 2003).

3. William Safire, "The Secrecy Legacy," *New York Times*, November 2, 2000, 31.
4. *St. Louis Post-Dispatch*, "Leaky Reasoning," September 2, 2001, B2.
5. Lars-Erik Nelson, "Congress' Secrecy Bill Lowers Iron Curtain," *Daily News*, November 1, 2000, 39.
6. John Dean, "Bush's Unofficial Official Secrets Act," *FindLaw*, September 26, 2003.
7. The Commission on Government Secrecy was begun with a congressional mandate in January 1955. The Coolidge Committee was established by Secretary of Defense Charles Wilson in August 1956.
8. Reston's criticism, and other reactions to the proposals, are described in Moynihan, *Secrecy: The American Experience*, 166–168.
9. Minutes of the Ministerial Meeting of the North Atlantic Council, Paris, April 23–25, 1953.
10. I discuss this episode in more detail in Alasdair Roberts, "Entangling Alliances: Nato's Security Policy and the Entrenchment of State Secrecy," *Cornell International Law Journal* 36, no. 2 (2003): 329–360. NATO records relating to the work of the Security Committee were declassified in the 1990s.
11. An advisor to Prime Minister Attlee observed: "We want the American Atomic secrets and we won't get them unless they modify the McMahon Act. Officials have already offered the procedure now proposed [positive vetting] and nothing short of that offer – and the direct question to the candidate about Communist association is from the Americans' point of view a *sine qua non* – will secure their cooperation": Richard Aldrich, *The Hidden Hand: Britain, America and Cold War Secret Intelligence* (New York: The Overlook Press, 2002), 425.
12. The NATO standards adopted in the late 1950s were not released by NATO until 2003. The criteria were closely modeled on those contained in an executive order on security clearances approved by President Eisenhower in November 1953.
13. *Bucharest Ziua*, "NATO Used as Scarecrow to Pass Law on Secrets,"April 8, 2002, Internet edition.
14. A few months later, the Bulgarian government restored access to the secret police files: *Agence France Presse*, "Bulgaria's Secret Police Files Re-Opened," July 25, 2002.
15. *Trud*, "NATO Probes Bulgaria for Russian Spies," May 8, 2003, 13.
16. Radio Free Europe, "Powell Pledges U.S. Support for Bulgarian NATO Membership, Reform Efforts," *RFE/RL Newsline*, May 16, 2003, Part II. The proposal was later defeated by the Bulgarian Parliament Access to Information Programme, *Access to Public Information in Bulgaria 2003* (Sofia, Bulgaria: Access to Information Programme, 2004), 20.
17. The two prerequisites for the emergence of networked governance structures – autonomy and interdependence – are further described by W. Kickert, E.-H. Klijn, and J. Koppenjan, *Managing Complex Networks: Strategies for the Public Sector* (Thousand Oaks, CA: Sage Publications, 1997), 6.

18. Alasdair Roberts, "Australia's "Great Surprise" for the US: Negotiating the 2002 Security of Information Agreement," *Freedom of Information Review*, no. 106 (2003): 50–51.

19. This data was provided by the Office of the Secretary of Defense in response to a request under the Freedom of Information Act in 2002.

20. The presumption in favor of classification of foreign government information was established in Section 1.1(c) of Executive Order 13292, March 25, 2003, amending Executive Order 12958, regarding Classified National Security Information. Properly classified information is protected from disclosure under Exemption 1 of the Freedom of Information Act.

21. Agreement Between The Government of Australia And The Government Of Canada Concerning The Protection Of Defence Related Information, October 31, 1996.

22. The United Kingdom, Australia, and Canada.

23. Memorandum of Understanding Between Secretary of Defense on Behalf of the Department of Defense of the United States of America and the Secretary of State for Defense of the United Kingdom of Great Britain and Northern Ireland Concerning Ballistic Missile Defense, June 12, 2003. A copy of the agreement was obtained by the British American Security Information Council, a nongovernmental organization based in London.

24. Alasdair Roberts, "Multilateral Institutions and the Right to Information: The Case of the European Union," *European Public Law* 8, no. 2 (2002): 255–275, 264–267; Roberts, "Entangling Alliances: NATO's Security Policy and the Entrenchment of State Secrecy," 356.

25. Memo from the Security and Intelligence Secretariat of the Canadian Privy Council Office, to the head of an internal task force reviewing the Access to Information Act. May 29, 2001. This document was released in response to a request under the Canadian Access To Information Act.

26. Arar Commission, *Transcript of Public Hearing, June 21, 2004* (Ottawa: Commission of Inquiry Into The Actions Of Canadian Officials In Relation to Maher Arar, 2004), 107, 172.

27. Section 13 of the Access to Information Act. The obligation to consult has been inferred by the Federal Court of Canada.

28. Confidential memo provided by Privy Council Office to an internal task force reviewing the Access to Information Act on April 23, 2001. This document was released in response to a request under the Canadian Access To Information Act.

29. Draft summary of discussion of security, defense, and law enforcement officials regarding reform of the Access to Information Act. April 25, 2001. This document was released to the author in response to a request under the Canadian Access To Information Act.

30. Section 87 of the Anti-Terrorism Act, which created section 69.1 of the Access to Information Act.

31. Evidence of the Minister of Justice, Anne McLellan, before the House of Commons Standing Committee on Justice and Human Rights, October 18, 2001.

32. Opening Statement Of The Attorney General, Commission of Inquiry Into The Actions Of Canadian Officials In Relation to Maher Arar, Ottawa, Canada, June 18, 2004.

33. Motion On Behalf of Maher Arar For Disclosure of Documents, Commission of Inquiry Into The Actions Of Canadian Officials In Relation to Maher Arar, Ottawa, Canada, May 30, 2004.

34. Juliet O'Neill, "Canada's Dossier on Maher Arar," *Ottawa Citizen*, November 8, 2003, A1.

35. Evidence of Garry Loeppky, Deputy Commissioner of the Royal Canadian Mounted Police, before the House of Commons Standing Committee on Foreign Affairs and International Trade, October 7, 2003.

36. Opening Statement Of The Attorney General, Commission of Inquiry Into The Actions Of Canadian Officials In Relation to Maher Arar, Ottawa, Canada, June 18, 2004; Submissions of the Attorney General of Canada in Response to Mr. Arar's Motion For Disclosure, Commission of Inquiry Into The Actions Of Canadian Officials In Relation to Maher Arar, Ottawa, Canada, July 2, 2004.

37. Ruling on Confidentiality, Commission of Inquiry Into The Actions Of Canadian Officials In Relation to Maher Arar, Ottawa, Canada, July 19, 2004.

38. Commission of Inquiry Into The Actions Of Canadian Officials In Relation to Maher Arar, Press Release, December 20, 2004; Michael Den Tandt, "Expert Warns 'Culture of Secrecy' May Block Truth About Arar Case," *Toronto Globe and Mail*, May 4, 2005.

39. David Cole, "Accounting for Torture," *The Nation* 280, no. 11 (2005): 4–5.

40. Eugene Solomonov, "U.S.-Russian Mutual Legal Assistance Treaty: Is There a Way to Control Organized Crime?" *Fordham International Law Journal* 23 (1999): 165; Sean Murphy, "Note: Mutual Legal Assistance Treaties with the European Union, Germany, and Japan," *American Journal of International Law* 98 (2004): 596.

41. The United Nations Convention Against Illicit Traffic in Narcotic Drugs and Psychotropic Substances, also known as the Vienna Convention, was agreed on December 19, 1988, and came into force in 1996.

42. The Financial Action Task Force is now housed in the headquarters of the OECD in Paris.

43. Janet Reno, *Statement by the Attorney General to the Symposium of the Americas: Protecting Intellectual Property in the Digital Age* (Washington, DC: Department of Justice, 2000).

44. Rules on mutual legal assistance are also contained in the Convention Against Transnational Organized Crime adopted by the United Nations in 2000, which entered into force in 2003, and also in the 1996 Inter-American Convention on Mutual Assistance in Criminal Matters.

45. See Articles 6 and 14 of the Treaty on Mutual Legal Assistance In Criminal Matters Between France and The United States of America, signed in 1998. Similar language is used in other MLATs.

46. Amitai Etzioni, *From Empire to Community* (New York: Palgrave Macmillan, 2004), 103–109.

47. Congressional Joint Inquiry, *Findings and Conclusions of the Congressional Joint Inquiry into September 11* (Washington, DC: Government Printing Office, 2002).

48. National Commission On Terrorist Attacks Upon the United States, *Final Report*, 355–356.

49. Philip Shenon, "Local Officials Accuse FBI of Not Cooperating," *New York Times*, November 12, 2001, 6. Daniel Oates, "The FBI Can't Do It Alone," *New York Times*, November 5, 2001, 17. See also National Commission On Terrorist Attacks Upon the United States, *Final Report*, 360–361.

50. McKinsey & Company, *Improving NYPD Emergency Preparedness and Response* (New York: McKinsey & Company, 2002), 28.

51. John Miller, Michael Stone, and Chris Mitchell, *The Cell* (New York: Hyperion, 2002).

52. John Arquilla and David Ronfeldt, "Fight Networks with Networks," *RAND Review* 25, no. 3 (2001): 18–19; John Arquilla and David Ronfeldt, *Networks and Netwars: The Future of Terror, Crime and Militancy* (Santa Monica, CA: RAND, 2001).

53. National Commission On Terrorist Attacks Upon the United States, *Final Report*, 418.

54. Office of Homeland Security, *National Strategy for Homeland Security* (Washington, DC: Office of Homeland Security, 2002).

55. Michael Janofsky, "Intelligence To Be Shared, Ridge Tells Governors," *New York Times*, August 19, 2003, A19.

56. There were two noteworthy changes. The preamble to the Executive Order was modified to include defense against transnational terrorism and protection of homeland security as one of the aims of the policy. The list of categories of information that could be properly classified was also expanded to include information relating to homeland security, such as information on vulnerabilities of domestic infrastructure or activities in defense against transnational terrorism. (See section 1.4(g) of the revised order.)

57. See Federal Register 66.239 (December 12, 2001), pages 64345–64347; Federal Register 67.189 (September 30, 2002), pages 61463–61465; and Federal Register 67.90 (May 9, 2002), page 31109. The EPA briefly held similar authority in the 1980s.

58. Data on the number of clearance decisions made by early 2004 is contained in General Accounting Office, *Security Clearances: FBI Has Enhanced Its Process for State and Local Law Enforcement Officials*, GAO-04-596 (Washington, DC: General Accounting Office, 2004). The policy of providing clearances to state and local officials was endorsed in the Homeland Security Act, section 891(b)(6).

59. Information Security Oversight Office, *Classified Information Nondisclosure Agreement, Rev. 1-03*, Standard Form 312 (Washington, DC: Information Security Oversight Office, 2003). In August 2003, Homeland Security Secretary Tom Ridge confirmed that all state governors had signed nondisclosure agreements. Tom Ridge, *Speech to the National Governors'*

Association (Washington, DC: U.S. Department of Homeland Security, 2003).

60. A state official might argue that the shared information is not under the control of a state agency, and therefore not subject to state law, because of terms included in the nondisclosure argument. Alternatively, a state agency might argue that disclosure requirements contained in state law are simply trumped by the federal government's restrictions. The federal government asserts that rules governing the classification system – contained in Executive Order 12958 – are drafted on the basis of the President's constitutional authority to regulate information relating to national security. Courts are likely to accept the argument that these federal rules preempt state law, particularly if national security is said to be at risk.

61. Hearing of the National Security, Emerging Threats and International Relations Subcommittee of the House Government Reform Committee, August 24, 2004.

62. David Walker, *Statement on the 9/11 Commission Report: Reorganization, Transformation, and Information Sharing*, GAO-04-10333T (Washington, DC: Government Accountability Office, 2004), 11.

63. Robert Jordan, *Statement before the Senate Committee on the Judiciary on Information Sharing Initiatives* (Washington, DC: Federal Bureau of Investigation, 2002).

64. Office of Homeland Security, *National Strategy for Homeland Security*, 25–26, Congressional Joint Inquiry, *Findings and Conclusions of the Congressional Joint Inquiry into September 11*, 88–89 and 361.

65. Letter, Stuart A. Maislin, Los Angeles Police Department, to author, October 28, 2003. The Chicago and New York Police Departments also refused to release their MOU.

66. Sue Lindsay, "ACLU Is Suing City over Work of FBI," *Rocky Mountain News*, October 16, 2003, 24A.

67. The FBI's correspondence to the City of Springfield, and correspondence among the City, the university and the Massachusetts ACLU, were provided by the ACLU.

68. In response to a Freedom of Information Act request.

69. The deputation of state and local law enforcement personnel appears to be authorized by 21 USC 878. This provision stipulates that deputized personnel shall be deemed to be federal employees for the purposes of several provisions listed in 5 USC 3374(c)(2). One of these provisions is a criminal penalty for the unauthorized disclosure of confidential information acquired in the course of an investigation (18 USC 1905).

70. Eric Lichtblau, "FBI Scrutinizes Antiwar Rallies," *New York Times*, November 23, 2003, 1.

71. Eric Lichtblau, "FBI Goes Knocking for Political Troublemakers," *New York Times*, August 16, 2004, A1.

72. Karen Abbott, "FBI Admits Probe," *Rocky Mountain News*, July 29, 2004, 4A.

73. Kieran Nicholson, "Contempt Citations Loom Via Spy Files," *Denver Post*, May 16, 2003, B3.

74. Sarah Kershaw, "In Portland, Ore., a Bid to Pull out of Terror Task Force," *New York Times*, April 23, 2005, A8.
75. Lowell Jacoby, *Statement for the Record for the Joint 9/11 Inquiry* (Washington, DC: Defense Intelligence Agency, 2002).
76. Rolf Palmer, *Presentation on the Joint Regional Information Exchange System for the Annual Security Symposium of the National Defense Industrial Association* (Defense Intelligence Agency, 2003).
77. Department of Homeland Security, *Homeland Security Launches Expansion of Information Exchange System* (Washington, DC: Department of Homeland Security, 2004).
78. In a letter written in response to a request under the Illinois Freedom of Information Act.
79. The agreement was released in response to a request under the Texas Public Information Act.
80. Ian Hoffman, Sean Holstege, and Josh Richman, "State Monitored War Protesters," *Oakland Tribune*, May 18, 2003; Josh Richman, "Lockyer Shakes up Anti-Terror Agency," *Oakland Tribune*, May 23, 2003.
81. Strictly, there are two schemes: one for "critical infrastructure information," and the other for "critical energy infrastructure information." These policies, as well as the policy on sensitive homeland security information, are discussed in more detail in the following article: Alasdair Roberts, "ORCON Creep: Networked Governance, Information Sharing, and the Threat to Government Accountability," *Government Information Quarterly* 21, no. 3 (2004): 249–267.
82. Manuel Castells, *The Rise of the Network Society, Vol. 1: The Information Age* (Malden, MA: Blackwell Publishers, 1996), 164–172. Castells is describing the private sector, but comparable arguments have been made about the public sector.
83. Ronald Diebert and Janice Gross Stein, "Social and Electronic Networks in the War on Terror," in *Bombs and Bandwidth*, ed. Robert Latham (New York: The New Press, 2003), 159–160.
84. While conducting research in the British archives on the United Kingdom's role within NATO in its early years, I found that Foreign Office files had been carefully cleaned of any documents that had been sent by NATO a half-century earlier.
85. According to the Department of Justice's 2003 annual report on the administration of the Freedom of Information Act, the median processing time for complex requests was over 370 days.

7. The corporate veil

1. State of the Union Address, January 23, 1996.
2. Daniel Yergin and Joseph Stanislaw, *The Commanding Heights* (New York: Simon & Schuster, 1998).
3. David Osborne and Ted Gaebler, *Reinventing Government* (New York: Plume, 1992).

4. Anthony Giddens, *The Third Way and Its Critic* (Cambridge, United Kingdom: Polity Press), 55–56.
5. Alasdair Roberts, *Transborder Service Systems: Pathways for Innovation or Threats to Accountability?* (Washington, DC: IBM Center for the Business of Government, 2004).
6. P. W. Singer, "Warriors for Hire in Iraq," *Salon.com*, April 15, 2004.
7. Ian Traynor, "The Privatisation of War," *The Guardian*, December 10, 2003, 1.
8. Singer, "Warriors for Hire in Iraq."
9. Acacia Prison Services Agreement, between the State of Western Australia and Corrections Corporation of Australia Pty Ltd., 2000.
10. *AAP Newsfeed*, "WA Govt Publishes Prison Contract Details on Internet," March 23, 2000.
11. Paul Moyle, "Private Prison Research in Queensland, Australia: A Case Study of Borallon Correctional Centre, 1991," in *Private Prisons and Police: Recent Australian Trends*, ed. P. Moyle (Leichhardt, Australia: Pluto Press, 1994), 148–150; Paul Moyle, *Profiting from Punishment: Private Prisons in Australia* (Annandale, New South Wales: Pluto Australia, 2000), 81–86, 220–243.
12. Richard Harding, *Private Prisons in Australia: The Second Phase* (Canberra: Australian Institute of Criminology, 1997), 1.
13. Arie Freiberg, "Commercial Confidentiality, Criminal Justice and the Public Interest," *Current Issues in Criminal Justice* 9, no. 2 (1997): 125, 139; Arie Freiberg, "Commercial Confidentiality and Public Accountability for the Provision of Correctional Services," *Current Issues in Criminal Justice* 11, no. 2 (1999): 119–134.
14. Liz Curran, "Unlocking the Doors on Transparency and Accountability," *Current Issues in Criminal Justice* 11, no. 2 (1999): 135–152, 145.
15. *The Age*, "Private Prisons, Public Rights," May 23, 1999.
16. Finn Poschmann, *Private Means to Public Ends: The Future of Public-Private Partnerships* (Toronto: C.D. Howe Institute, 2003), 14.
17. Ibid., 22. See also Order P-1516 of the Information and Privacy Commissioner of Ontario.
18. Parts of the contract were eventually released. Dan McDougall, "Numbers Just Don't Add Up," *The Scotsman*, May 21, 2004, 2.
19. allAfrica.com, "Secret Contracts Row Puts Spotlight on Water Management," *AllAfrica News*, March 22, 2003.
20. The Irish and New Zealand laws treat contractor records as though they were held by the contracting agency, so that they are subject to disclosure requirements. A few state laws in the United States take a similar approach. However, these provisions are often interpreted narrowly by courts: Alasdair Roberts, "Structural Pluralism and the Right to Information," *University of Toronto Law Journal* 51, no. 3 (2001): 243–271, 250.
21. Maude Barlow and Tony Clarke, *Blue Gold* (Toronto: Stoddart, 2002), 92.
22. Michael Hedges, "Iraq Prison Scandal," *Houston Chronicle*, May 6, 2004, 1.

23. Strasser, *The Abu Ghraib Investigations*, 146–147.
24. Taguba, *Article 15–6 Investigation of the 800th Military Police Brigade*, 44. The Schlesinger panel report also criticized the inadequate training provided to CACI and other contractor staff: Strasser, *The Abu Ghraib Investigations*, 73.
25. *ACLU v. Department of Defense, et al.*, United States District Court, Southern District of New York, September 15, 2004.
26. Joshua Chaffin, "Contract Interrogators Hired to Avoid Supervision," *Financial Times*, May 21, 2004, 6; John Cushman, "Private Company Finds No Evidence Its Interrogators Took Part in Prison Abuse," *New York Times*, August 13, 2004, 8.
27. Fox Butterfield, "Justice Dept. Report Shows Trouble in Private U.S. Jails Preceded Job Fixing Iraq's," *New York Times*, May 21, 2004, 22.
28. Gary Salazar, "Inmate's Mom Seeks Answers," *Albuquerque Journal*, April 17, 2003, 1.
29. Julie Ann Grimm, "Parties Settle Inmate Suicide Lawsuit," *Sante Fe New Mexican*, June 12, 2004, B1.
30. In 2004, 42 percent of the state's prisoners were in private prisons: Dan Shingler, "Prisoners for Profit?" *Albuquerque Tribune*, July 26, 2004, B1.
31. In 1996, Corrections Corporation of America reached a settlement with the New Mexico Foundation for Open Government in which it agreed to release basic information about its prisoners, without conceding that it was subject to the state's public records law: *Albuquerque Journal*, "Pact Affirms Open Records," October 23, 1996, 4.
32. P. W. Singer, *Corporate Warriors, Cornell Studies in Security Affairs* (Ithaca, NY: Cornell University Press, 2003), x.
33. Ibid., 152–168.
34. Daniel Guttman, "Governance by Contract: Constitutional Visions; Time for Reflection and Choice," *Public Contract Law Journal* 33, no. 2 (2004): 321–360.
35. Robert O'Harrow, Jr., and Ellen McCarthy, "Private Sector Has Firm Role at the Pentagon," *Washington Post*, June 9, 2004, E1.
36. Government Accountability Office, *Interagency Contracting: Problems with DoD's and Interior's Orders to Support Military Operations*, GAO-05-201 (Washington, DC: Government Accountability Office, 2005), 3.
37. Eric Eckholm, "Memos Warned of Billing Fraud by Firm in Iraq," *New York Times*, October 23, 2004, 1; Joshua Chaffin, "Halliburton Workers Paint a Portrait of a Disorganized Company," *Financial Times*, June 16, 2004, 9.
38. Singer, *Corporate Warriors*, 222; Robert Capps, "Outside the Law," *Salon.com*, June 26, 2002, Web: http://www.salon.com/news/feature/2002/2006/2026/bosnia/?CP=RDF&DN=2310.
39. Shirley Downing, "Officials Still Seek Cause of Riots at Two Prisons," *The Commercial Appeal*, October 31, 1995.
40. Janice Morse, "Guards Faulted in Escapes," *The Cincinnati Enquirer*, August 5, 1998, B1.

41. E. S. Savas, *Privatization and Public-Private Partnerships* (New York: Chatham House Publishers, 2000), 259–266.

42. Andrew Parker and George Parker, "Utilities Win Fight to Curb Freedom Act Impact," *Financial Times of London*, July 22, 1998, 8.

43. Martin Mittelstaedt, "Hydro Lobbying Won Change to Law," *Toronto Globe and Mail*, January 26, 2001, A17. The restructuring plan encountered substantial problems, and in 2004 a new provincial government brought Ontario Power Generation and Hydro One, the transmission company, back under the provincial Freedom of Information law.

44. Shawn McCarthy, "Brownouts Were Deliberate, Group Says," *Toronto Star*, June 30, 1990, C1.

45. Australian Law Reform Commission, *Open Government: A Review of the Federal Freedom of Information Act 1982*, 77 (Canberra: Australian Law Reform Commission, 1995), Para. 16.17.

46. Greg Palast, Jerrold Oppenheim, and Theo MacGregor, *Democracy and Regulation* (London: Pluto Press, 2003), 185.

47. Ibid., 9–10, 21, 125, 171.

48. Ibid., 151–155; Bethany McLean and Peter Elkind, *The Smartest Guys in the Room* (New York: Portfolio, 2004).

49. Dennis Berman, "Online Laundry: Government Posts Enron's E-Mail," *Wall Street Journal*, October 6, 2003, A1.

50. Neil Gunningham and Joseph Rees, "Industry Self-Regulation: An Institutional Perspective," *Law and Policy* 19, no. 4 (1997): 363–414; A. Michael Froomkin, "Wrong Turn in Cyberspace: Using ICANN to Route around the APA and the Constitution," *Duke Law Journal* 50 (2000): 17–186; Daniel Drezner, "The Global Governance of the Internet: Bringing the State Back In," *Political Science Quarterly* 119, no. 3 (2004): 477–498.

51. Michael Walzer, "Liberalism and the Art of Separation," *Political Theory* 12, no. 3 (1984): 315–330.

52. The various approaches taken in American state law are discussed by Craig Feiser, "Protecting the Public's Right to Know: The Debate over Privatization and Access to Government Information under State Law," *Florida State University Law Review* 27 (2000): 825–864. The restricted approach taken in U.S. federal law, and possible alternative approaches, are discussed in Craig Feiser, "Privatization and the Freedom of Information Act: An Analysis of Public Access to Private Entities under Federal Law," *Federal Communications Law Journal* 52, no. 1 (1999): 21–62. Contrasting approaches taken in laws outside the United States are also discussed in Roberts, "Structural Pluralism and the Right to Information."

53. Nicole Casarez, "Furthering the Accountability Principle in Privatized Federal Corrections," *University of Michigan Journal of Law Reform* 28, no. 2 (1995): 249–303, 251.

54. A comparable question is raised by Daphne Barak-Erez, "A State Action Doctrine for an Age of Privatization," *Syracuse Law Review* 45 (1995): 1169–1192, 1188–1189.

55. See Casarez, "Furthering the Accountability Principle in Privatized Federal Corrections," 251.

56. Open Democracy Advice Centre, *The Challenge of Implementation: The State of Access to Information in South Africa* (Cape Town: Open Democracy Advice Centre, 2004).
57. Interim Constitution of the Republic of South Africa, 1993, Section 23 and Schedule 4, Principle IX.
58. COSATU, *Submission to the Constitutional Assembly on the New Constitution* (Cape Town: Congress of South African Trade Unions, 1996).
59. Calland, *Transparency in the Profit-Making World: The Case for the Right to Know*, 14–15.
60. Constitution of the Republic of South Africa, 1996, Section 32(1)(b). The Constitution referred to information held by "persons," but this includes entities with legal status as persons, such as private corporations.
61. Gideon Pimstone, "Going Quietly About Their Business: Access to Corporate Information and the Open Democracy Bill," *South African Journal of Human Rights* 15, no. 1 (1999): 2–24. The new rules are contained in the Promotion of Access to Information Act, Act No. 2 of 2000, Part 3. The name of the law tells something about its provenance: Elements of the law were modeled on the Canadian Access to Information Act.
62. Several of these cases were brought by the Open Democracy Advice Centre. See Calland, *Transparency in the Profit-Making World: The Case for the Right to Know*.
63. The phrase is Murray Hunt's: Murray Hunt, "Constitutionalism and Contractualisation of Government," in *The Province of Administrative Law*, ed. Michael Taggart (Oxford: Hart Publishing, 1997), 29.
64. Pimstone, "Going Quietly About Their Business: Access to Corporate Information and the Open Democracy Bill," 11–18.
65. The purpose of the law, Klaaren and Currie argue, "is to require private-sector transparency to prevent harm to those *fundamental* rights associated with a human rights culture." Jonathan Klaaren and Ian Currie, *The Promotion of Access to Information Act Commentary* (Cape Town: SiberInk, 2002), 67–71.
66. For example, see this influential American case: Supreme Court of California, *Tarasoff v. Regents of the University of California*, Case No. S.F. 23042, Judgment July 1, 1976. The case considered the "duty to warn" of psychotherapists.
67. The growing popularity of pollutant release registers is discussed in Czech Ministry of the Environment, *Discussion Paper for the First Meeting of the UN/Ece Task Force on Pollutant Release and Transfer Registers* (Prague: Czech Ministry of the Environment, 2000).
68. James McLellan, "Hazardous Substances and the Right To Know," *International Labour Review* 128, no. 5 (1989): 639–650. Tom Tietenberg and David Wheeler, *Empowering the Community: Information Strategies for Pollution Control* (Waterville, ME: Colby College, Department of Economics, 1998).
69. Several jurisdictions recognize a public interest defense in actions for breach of confidence. In the United Kingdom, such disclosures are also protected by the Public Interest Disclosure Act 1998.

70. United Nations Declaration of Human Rights, Art. 3.
71. See the United Nations Declaration of Human Rights, Art. 26, and the United Nations Covenant on Economic, Social and Cultural Rights, Art. 13.1.
72. Access to educational records is provided for in the Family Educational Rights and Privacy Act, 20 USC 1232(g); other disclosure requirements are created by the Student Right to Know and Campus Security Act, 20 USC 1092.
73. John Portz, "Plant Closings and Advance-Notice Laws: Putting the Pieces Together," *Economic Development Quarterly* 9, no. 4 (1995): 356–372.
74. Commission for Children and Young People Act of 1998, section 43.
75. In the United States, the relevant law is the Fair Credit Reporting Act, 15 USC 1681; in Britain, the Consumer Credit Act 1974 and the Access to Medical Reports Act 1988.
76. "Everyone is the rightful owner of their personal information, no matter where it is held, and this right is inalienable." House of Commons Standing Committee on Human Rights, *Privacy: Where Do We Draw the Line?* (Ottawa: House of Commons, 1997). See also Jessica Litman, "Information Privacy/Information Property," *Stanford Law Review* 52 (2000): 1283–1313.
77. Commonwealth Human Rights Initiative, *Open Sesame: Looking for the Right to Information in the Commonwealth* (New Delhi: Commonwealth Human Rights Initiative, 2003).
78. For an argument that the right to information *is* a fundamental human right, see Patrick Birkinshaw, "Freedom of Information and Openness as a Fundamental Human Right," in *Proceedings of the International Institute of Human Rights* (Brussels, Belgium: Bruylant, Forthcoming).
79. Associated Press, "Prison with Isle Inmates in Lockdown after Brawl," *Honolulu Star-Bulletin*, May 16, 2004.
80. And perhaps even more than this: A study of the controversial Youngstown prison found that risks of disorder and escape were tightly linked to disciplinary procedures as well as work and educational opportunities. John Clark, *Inspection and Review of the Northeast Ohio Correctional Center* (Washington, DC: Department of Justice Office of the Corrections Trustee, 1998).
81. In 1999, California adopted a law that prohibits private prisons from holding out-of-state inmates; residents of Oklahoma could choose to impose a similar ban.
82. A summary of state laws is provided by the Reporters' Committee for Freedom of the Press on its website, http://www.rcfp.org. On the interpretation of Hawaii law, see Feiser, "Protecting the Public's Right to Know: The Debate over Privatization and Access to Government Information under State Law," Note 18. Although the three states in question do not impose residency restrictions under their disclosure laws, this is not always true; for example, a New Yorker cannot make a request for information under Pennsylvanian law.

83. The distinction was first proposed by the French jurist Karel Vasak in 1979. Vasak actually described three generations of rights, but for simplicity I have omitted his third category.
84. For a discussion and rebuttal of this view, see Jack Donnelly, *International Human Rights*, 2d ed. (Boulder, CO: Westview Press, 1998), 24–26.
85. I develop this argument in more detail in Roberts, "Structural Pluralism and the Right to Information," 263 and 267–268.
86. Australian Law Reform Commission, *Open Government: A Review of the Federal Freedom of Information Act 1982*, Para. 15.15.
87. David Banisar and Simon Davies, "Global Trends in Privacy Protection," *John Marshall Journal of Computer and Information Law* 18, no. 1 (1999): 1–112, 13–14 and 108–111; Robert Gellman, "Does Privacy Law Work?" in *Technology and Privacy: The New Landscrape*, ed. Philip Agre and Marc Rotenberg (Cambridge, MA: MIT Press, 1998); Charles Sykes, *The End of Privacy* (New York: St. Martin's Press, 1999), 74–75.
88. The struggle over adoption of rules on the handling of medical information by private sector organizations is one illustration: Amitai Etzioni, *The Limits of Privacy* (New York: Perseus Books, 1999), 149.
89. Statistics for the United States are not easily obtained. In Canada, almost half of all requests filed under the Access to Information Act are filed by businesses.

8. Remote control

1. The two shopkeepers, Steve Thoburn and Neil Herron, were named Europe's "campaigners of the year" in a 2001 ballot organized by *European Voice* magazine.
2. Bonnie Pfister, "Dolphin-Safe Tuna Debate Returns," *San Antonio Express-News*, April 19, 2003, 1D.
3. Controversy over the project was examined by a 2002 World Bank panel: Inspection Panel, *Investigation Report: Uganda Bujagali Project* (Washington, DC: World Bank Group, 2002). In 2003, a World Bank representative said that it was "in the best interests of the country to develop the project at the earliest opportunity."
4. Larry Rohter, "Argentina Calling Companies to Task," *New York Times*, December 1, 2003, 17; International Monetary Fund, *IMF Country Report 03/392: Argentina – Request for Stand-by Arrangement* (Washington, DC: International Monetary Fund, 2003).
5. G. R. Berridge, *Diplomacy: Theory and Practice* (New York: Palgrave, 2002), 107.
6. J. H. H. Weiler, *The Rule of Lawyers and the Ethos of Diplomats*, Working paper (Cambridge, MA: Harvard Law School, 2000).
7. United States Department of Justice, *Brief for the Petitioners in the Case of U.S. V. Weatherhead* (Washington, DC: United States Department of Justice, 1999).
8. This is an amendment of Theodore Draper's notion of a "bifurcated presidency": Theodore Draper, *A Very Thin Line: The Iran-Contra Affairs*

(New York: Hill and Wang, 1991), 580–598. In a similar vein, Aaron Wildavsky had earlier written about the emergence of "two presidencies." Aaron B. Wildavsky, *The Presidency* (Boston: Little Brown, 1969), 230–245. In the United States, Eric Alterman has complained that foreign policy is "deliberately shielded from the effects of democratic debate, with virtually no institutionalized democratic participation." Alterman, *Who Speaks for America? Why Democracy Matters in Foreign Policy*, 4.

9. E. E. Schattschneider, *The Semisovereign People* (New York: Holt Rinehart and Winston, 1960); Jon Elster, "Strategic Uses of Argument," in *Barriers to the Negotiated Resolution of Conflict*, ed. Kenneth J. Arrow (New York: Norton, 1995); Weiler, *The Rule of Lawyers and the Ethos of Diplomats*.

10. Adam Watson, *Diplomacy: The Dialogue between States* (New York: McGraw-Hill, 1983), 136.

11. Hans Morgenthau, *Politics among Nations*, 2d ed. (New York: Alfred A. Knopf, 1954), 519–521.

12. Alterman, *Who Speaks for America? Why Democracy Matters in Foreign Policy*, 1–19.

13. Watson, *Diplomacy: The Dialogue between States*, 104.

14. Neill Nugent, *The Government and Politics of the European Union*, Fourth ed. (Basingstoke, UK: Palgrave, 1999), 59–61, 76, 97.

15. As it was, the process of ratification by the British parliament was prolonged and difficult, while in Germany ratification was delayed for a year by an unsuccessful court challenge that claimed the delegation of authority to EU institutions violated guarantees of democratic government in German Basic Law.

16. See Article 1 of the Treaty on European Union, and Declaration 17 of the Final Act of the Treaty on European Union.

17. Bill Lamp, "New Poll Says Danes Will Grudgingly Approve Maastricht Treaty," *United Press International*, May 17, 1993; John Palmer, "Danish Plan to Go Public and Lift Plans of Secrecy," *The Guardian*, December 30, 1992, 6.

18. EU leaders promised after the October 1992 Birmingham European Council to "make the Community more open, to ensure a better informed public debate on its activities." Assurances on improved openness were repeated at summits in December 1992 and 1993.

19. The code was implemented by a Council decision of December 1993 and a Commission decision of January 1994. Decision 93/731/EC and Decision 94/90/ECSC, EC, Euratom.

20. The problem of promoting openness in the EU's "complex and fractured" structure is discussed by Deirdre Curtin, "Transparency and Political Participation in EU Governance," *Cultural Values* 3, no. 4 (1999): 445–472.

21. European Ombudsman, *Special Report to the European Parliament Following the Own Initiative Inquiry into Public Access to Documents* (Strasbourg: Office of the European Ombudsman, 1997).

22. See Articles 2 and 4 of Decision 93/731/EC and the comparable provisions of Decision 94/90/ECSC, EC, Euratom.

23. Jürgen Neyer, "Justifying Comitology: The Promise of Deliberation," in *European Integration after Amsterdam*, ed. Karlheinz Neuenreither and Antje Wiener (Oxford: Oxford University Press, 2000).
24. Court of First Instance, *Rothmans International BV v. EC Commission*, Case T-188/97 (1999) ECR-II 2463.
25. European Ombudsman, Decision on complaint 916/2000, July 2001.
26. See the decision of the ombudsman on complaint 1056/96, June 1998.
27. The ombudsman criticized this position in his decision on complaint 1056/96, and the Council abandoned it during investigation of the related complaint 916/2000.
28. *Carvel v. EU Council*, Case T-194/94 (1995) ECR II-2765 (CFI).
29. European Ombudsman Decision on complaint 1087/10.12.96/STATE-WATCH/UK/IJH, 23 November 1998.
30. Court of First Instance, *Tidningen Journalisten v. Council*, Case T-174/95 (1998) ECR II-2289.
31. Court of First Instance, *Hautala v. Council*, Case T-14/98 (1999) ECR II-2489.
32. *Council v. Hautala*, Case C-353/99 P (ECJ), decision rendered December 6, 2001.
33. In addition, many classified documents were automatically excluded from the code. Decision 2000/527/EC, August 14, 2000. Two weeks earlier, the Secretary-General of the European Union, Javier Solana, also amended the Council's rules on security classification, broadening the grounds on which documents could be classified. This was also motivated by the EU's decision to collaborate more closely with NATO (see Chapter 2).
34. Strictly, government representatives voted on appeals against official decisions to deny access to documents. A report by the nongovernmental organization Statewatch tabulated the voting records of member states in 2000: Statewatch, "Survey Shows Which EU Governments Back Openness, Which Do Not," *Statewatch News Online*, 2000. In several instances, the Dutch and Danish governments also began or supported litigation over disclosure disputes.
35. Sverker Gustavsson, "Reconciling Suprastatism and Accountability: A View from Sweden," in *Democratizing the European Union*, ed. Catherine Hoskyns and Michael Newman (Manchester, England: Manchester University Press, 2000), 39; John Carvel, "Sweden Plans Law to Blunt EU Secrecy," *The Guardian*, November 9, 1994, 12. Norwegians rejected EU membership in a 1994 referendum.
36. Reflection Group, *Report on Agenda for the 1996 Intergovernmental Conference* (Brussels: European Council, 1995).
37. Ibid. The 1995 Reflection Group report had observed that "many of us propose that the right of access to information be recognized in the Treaty as a right of the citizens of the Union."
38. Article 45 of the Treaty of Amsterdam, which added Article 191a to the Treaty establishing the European Community (TEC). The Amsterdam Treaty also renumbered articles of the TEC, so that Article 191a became Article 255. The Amsterdam Treaty entered into force in May 1999,

triggering a two-year period within which a disclosure regulation was to be adopted.

39. Declaration 35 of the Final Act of the Treaty of Amsterdam. See also Ulf Öberg, "Public Access to Documents after the Entry into Force of the Amsterdam Treaty," *European Integration Online Papers* 2, no. 8 (1998): http://eiop.or.at/eiop/texte/1998-1008.htm, 17. It was unclear whether this provision of the new disclosure regulation gave member states an absolute veto over disclosure of records. See Ian Harden, "Citizenship and Information," *European Public Law* (2001), 26.

40. The Santer Commission resigned in March 1999.

41. European Commission, *Proposal for a Regulation Regarding Public Access to Documents*, COM(2000) 30 final/2 (Brussels: European Commission, 2000).

42. Söderman, "The EU's Transparent Bid for Opacity."

43. For an illustration of the reaction, see Select Committee on the European Union, *Sixteenth Report, 1999–2000* (London: House of Lords, 2000). The new regulation was adopted by the EU Council in May 2001: Regulation (EC) 1049/2001, May 30, 2001.

44. Strictly, the General Agreement on Tariffs and Trade (GATT) was served by a small secretariat, also referred to by the acronym GATT.

45. Ralph Nader and Lori Wallach, "GATT, NAFTA, and the Subversion of the Democratic Process," in *The Case against the Global Economy*, ed. Jerry Mander and Edward Goldsmith (San Francisco: Sierra Club Books, 1996).

46. Chakravarthi Raghavan, "NGOs Launch "Shrink or Sink" Campaign against WTO," *Third World Network*, April 6, 2000, Web: http://www. twnside.org.sg/title/launch.htm.

47. Oxfam UK, *Discussion Paper: Institutional Reform of the WTO* (Oxford, UK: Oxfam Uk, 2000), 4.

48. World Trade Organization, *Singapore Ministerial Declaration* (Geneva: World Trade Organization, 1996).

49. Marrakesh Agreement Establishing the WTO, Annex III(A). The TPRM was actually begun on an interim basis in 1989 and later included in the 1995 Agreement establishing the WTO.

50. Asif Qureshi, "Some Lessons from 'Developing Countries' Trade Policy Reviews in the GATT Framework: An Enforcement Perspective," *World Economy* 18, no. 3 (1995): 489–503, 493–494.

51. Donald B. Keesing, *Improving Trade Policy Reviews in the World Trade Organization* (Washington, DC: Institute for International Economics, 1998); Joseph F. Francois, *Maximizing the Benefits of the Trade Policy Review Mechanism for Developing Countries* (Tinbergen Institute and CEPR, 1999), 6.

52. General Agreement on Tariffs and Trade, Article X.

53. Sylvia Ostry, "WTO Membership for China," ed. Patrick Grady and Andrew Sharpe (Kingston, Ontario: John Deutsch Institute, 2001).

54. General Agreement on Trade in Services, Articles III and III bis.

55. Agreement on Government Procurement, Articles XVIII and XIX.

56. Reference paper on principles of the regulatory framework for basic telecommunications services, April 1996, Article 4.
57. Agreement on Technical Barriers to Trade, Articles 2.9 and 10.
58. The EU is a member of the WTO, representing all EU member states; hence "Quad."
59. World Trade Organization, *Procedures for the Circulation and Derestriction of WTO Documents*, WT/L/160/Rev.1 (Geneva: World Trade Organization, 1996).
60. The phrase is used in the United Kingdom's new Freedom of Information Act, 2000.
61. For a complaint about the unfairness of this policy, see Oxfam UK, *Discussion Paper: Institutional Reform of the WTO*, 4.
62. WTO Agriculture Committee, *Summary Report of the Meeting Held on 25–26 March 1999*, G/AG/R/18 (Geneva: World Trade Organization, 1999), 9–10.
63. John Weiner and L. Brennan Van Dyke, *A Handbook for Obtaining Documents from the World Trade Organization* (Geneva: International Centre for Trade and Sustainable Development, 1997).
64. See, for example, the following proposal made jointly by Canada and the United States: United States, *Submission Regarding Informal Consultations on External Transparency*, WT/GC/W/413/Rev.1 (Geneva: World Trade Organization, 2000).
65. WTO Secretary General Michael Moore conceded in 2002 that an intensive four-year review of the 1996 policy had produced "little movement" on reform: World Trade Organization, *Press Release: Moore Pledges to Build on Doha Success in 2002* (Geneva: World Trade Organization, 2002).
66. World Trade Organization, *Revised Procedures for the Circulation and Derestriction of WTO Documents*, WT/L/452 (Geneva: World Trade Organization, 2002).
67. World Trade Organization, *Minutes of Meeting of the General Council Held on 13–14 May 2002*, WT/GC/M/74 (Geneva: World Trade Organization, 2002).
68. Comment by Mexico: World Trade Organization, *Minutes of Meeting of the General Council, 26 June 1996*, WT/GC/M/12 (Geneva: World Trade Organization, 1996). Comment by India: World Trade Organization, *Minutes of Meeting of the General Council, 18 July 1996*, WT/GC/M/13 (Geneva: World Trade Organization, 1996).
69. WTO General Council, *Minutes of Meeting Held on 18 and 19 July 2001*, WT/GC/M/66 (Geneva: World Trade Organization, 2001).
70. World Trade Organization, *Report of the Appellate Body: United States – Import Prohibition of Certain Shrimp and Shrimp Products*, WT/DS58/AB/R (Geneva: World Trade Organization, 1998). U.S. environmental groups also leaked a restricted copy of the panel's draft report upholding the complaint.
71. Coalition for Open Trade, "Public Participation Barred Once Again in WTO Dispute Settlement," *Tradewatch Bulletin*, March 6, 2000.

72. United States Trade Representative, *1998 Annual Report of the President of the United States on the Trade Agreements Program* (Washington, DC: Office of the United States Trade Representative, 1998).

73. United States Mission, *Communication to the Working Group on the Interaction between Trade and Competition Policy* (Geneva: United States Permanent Mission to the WTO, 1999).

74. Senator Max Baucus, *Letter to the Honorable Robert B. Zoellick, United States Trade Representative* (Washington: Office of Senator Max Baucus, 2002). For a statement of the Bush administration's position, see United States, *Communication from the United States on the Improvement of the Dispute Settlement Understanding of the WTO Related to Transparency*, TN/DS/W/13 (Geneva: World Trade Organization, 2002).

75. WTO General Council, *Minutes of Meeting of the General Council, 24 April 1998*, WT/GC/M/28 (Geneva: World Trade Organization, 1998). See also Oxfam UK, *Discussion Paper: Institutional Reform of the WTO*, 25.

76. International Centre for Trade and Sustainable Development, "DSU Review: Developing Countries Reject US Proposal on Transparency," *Bridges Weekly Trade News Digest*, September 18, 2002.

77. The Business Times, "Asean Rejects US Call for NGO Access to WTO Dispute," *The Business Times*, September 17, 2002.

78. World Trade Organization, *Report of the Appellate Body: European Communities – Measures Affecting Asbestos and Asbestos-Containing Products*, WT/DS135/AB/R (Geneva: World Trade Organization, 2001).

79. World Trade Organization, *Minutes of Meeting of the General Council Held on 22 November 2000*, WT/GC/M/60 (Geneva: World Trade Organization, 2000).

80. Petros Mvroidis, *Amicus Curiae Briefs before the WTO: Much Ado About Nothing*. Working paper (Cambridge, MA: Harvard Law School, 2001).

81. Chakravarthi Raghavan, "Continuing Conceptual Divides at the WTO," *Third World Network*, March 2, 2000, Web: http://www.twnside.org.sg/title/divides.htm.

82. World Trade Organization, *Report by the Chairman, Special Session on the Dispute Settlement Body*, TN/DS/10 (Geneva: World Trade Organization, 2004).

83. Ian Bowles and Cyril Kormos, "The American Campaign for Environmental Reforms at the World Bank," *Fletcher Forum of World Affairs Journal* 23 (1999): 211–224, 213.

84. Bruce Rich, *Mortgaging the Earth: The World Bank, Environmental Impoverishment, and the Crisis of Development* (Boston: Beacon Press, 1994), 111. Two of these organizations were relatively new: the NRDC was established with Ford Foundation support in 1970, and the EPI in 1972.

85. In the United States, the Environmental Policy Institute attempted to draw attention to the Akosombo Dam: Philip Shabecoff, "Actual Price of High Dams Also Includes Social Costs," *New York Times*, July 10, 1983, 22. However, there were many other comparable cases. For a history of the antidam movement, see Sanjeev Khagram, "Toward Democratic Governance for Sustainable Development: Transnational Civil Society

Organizing around Big Dams," in *The Third Force*, ed. Ann Florini (Washington, DC: Carnegie Endowment for International Peace, 2000); Patrick McCully, *Silenced Rivers* (London: Zed Books, 2001); Rich, *Mortgaging the Earth: The World Bank, Environmental Impoverishment, and the Crisis of Development*.

86. Rich, *Mortgaging the Earth: The World Bank, Environmental Impoverishment, and the Crisis of Development*, 107–108.

87. Khagram, "Toward Democratic Governance for Sustainable Development: Transnational Civil Society Organizing around Big Dams," 97.

88. Ian Bowles and Cyril Kormos, "Environmental Reform at the World Bank," *Virginia Journal of International Law* 35 (1995): 777–839, 837. Summers made the comment in 1994, while Undersecretary of the Treasury for International Affairs.

89. Ibid., 789.

90. Ibid., 790–797. In 1988 and 1989, Congress had also amended the International Financial Institutions Act to emphasize the need for disclosure of project information.

91. General Accounting Office, *Multilateral Development Banks: Public Consultation on Environmental Assessments*, GAO/NSIAD-98-192 (Washington, DC: General Accounting Office, 1998), 52.

92. Rich, *Mortgaging the Earth: The World Bank, Environmental Impoverishment, and the Crisis of Development*, 123.

93. Bowles and Kormos, "Environmental Reform at the World Bank," 789.

94. In 1990, Congress temporarily withheld part of funds requested for a General Capital Increase agreed to by the Bank's Executive Board in 1988. In 1992, an appropriation for the Global Environmental Facility, partly administered by the Bank, was withheld because of noncompliance problems: Ibid., 798 and 801.

95. Ibid., 833. There had also been pressure for improved disclosure during the preceding round of negotiations over replenishment in 1989: Bowles and Kormos, "Environmental Reform at the World Bank," 826.

96. Bowles and Kormos, "The American Campaign for Environmental Reforms at the World Bank," 220.

97. The first center was established in Washington; the next were located in its Paris and Tokyo offices. Today, most World Bank field offices have Public Information Centers.

98. Chris Chamberlain, *Fulfilling the IDA-12 Mandates: Recommendations for Expanding Public Access to Information at the World Bank* (Washington, DC: Bank Information Center, 1999).

99. World Bank, *Addition to IDA Resources: Thirteenth Replenishment* (Washington, DC: World Bank, 2002), vi.

100. World Bank, *The World Bank Policy on Disclosure of Information* (Washington, DC: World Bank, 2002), 2.

101. Graham Saul, *The Ongoing Struggle for World Bank Transparency: The Outcome of the Information Disclosure Policy Review* (Washington, DC: Bank Information Center, 2001).

102. In 2004, the Bank contemplated a pilot project that would allow the release of some draft documents: World Bank, *Memorandum on World Bank Disclosure Policy: Additional Issues* (Washington, DC: World Bank, Office of the Vice President and Corporate Secretary, 2004).

103. Toby McIntosh, *Analysis of Transparency Issues at the World Bank* (Washington, DC: freedominfo.org, September, 2002 [Accessed January 20, 2003]), available from http://www.freedominfo.org/ifti/worldbank/20020900.htm.

104. Toby McIntosh, "World Bank to Release Board Minutes, Make Other Modest Reforms," *freedominfo.org*, March 18, 2005, Web: http://www.freedominfo.org/ifti/worldbank/20050318.htm. The Bank agreed to the release of "limited information" about meetings, such as the list of those attending, the broad subject of briefings, decisions reached, and voting by directors. Board members are given the opportunity to vet the minutes before their release.

105. Alan Beattie, "World Bank Set to Allow Some Public Access," *Financial Times*, August 31, 2001, 7.

106. Saul, *The Ongoing Struggle for World Bank Transparency: The Outcome of the Information Disclosure Policy Review*.

107. Toby McIntosh, *Release of Secret Loan Document in Uruguay Fuels Public Debate* (Washington, DC: September, 2002 [Accessed December 15, 2003]), available from http://www.freedominfo.org/ifti/worldbank/20030100_1.htm.

108. McIntosh, "World Bank to Release Board Minutes, Make Other Modest Reforms." World Bank, *World Bank Disclosure Policy: Additional Issues*, R2003-0112/10 (Washington, DC: World Bank, 2005), 1–3.

109. Saul, *The Ongoing Struggle for World Bank Transparency: The Outcome of the Information Disclosure Policy Review*. In 2002, an Inspection Panel report on Uganda's Bujagali Project found evidence that the intent of disclosure requirements had not been followed; the case is complicated because funding in that case was provided by another arm of the World Bank, the International Finance Corporation: Inspection Panel, *Investigation Report: Uganda Bujagali Project*. An earlier controversy over IFC support of Chile's Bio Bio dam project also involved allegations of inappropriate redactions to a publicly disclosed document: Financial Times, "Chile Dam Row Shows IFC's Problems with Projects," *Financial Times*, August 8, 1997, 4.

110. Nadir Mohammed, *Statement at the Launching Ceremony of the Freedom of Information and Albanian Public Administration Project* (Washington, DC: World Bank Group, 2004).

111. See, for example, Toby Mendel, *Legislation on Freedom of Information: Trends and Standards*, PREM Note 93 (Washington, DC: World Bank, 2004).

112. World Bank, *Program Document for a Proposed Credit in the Amount of SDR 40.54 Million to the Republic of Honduras for a Poverty Reduction Support Credit*, May 26, 2004; World Bank, *Program Document for a Proposed Credit in the Amount of SDR 49 Million to the Republic*

of Nicaragua for a Poverty Reduction Support Credit, December 16, 2003.

113. Leo Van Houtven, *Governance of the IMF*, Pamphlet No. 53 (Washington, DC: International Monetary Fund, 2002), 58–59.

114. International Financial Institution Advisory Commission, *Final Report* (Washington, DC: International Financial Institution Advisory Commission, 2000).

115. "Loan agreements are routinely negotiated in secret between banking and government officials who, for the most part, are not accountable to the people on whose behalf they are obligating the national treasury to foreign lenders." Tony Clarke, "Mechanisms of Corporate Rule," in *The Case against the Global Economy*, ed. Jerry Mander and Edward Goldsmith (San Francisco: Sierra Club Books, 1996), 300.

116. Thomas Dawson, *Transparency and the IMF: Toward Second Generation Reforms* (Washington, DC: International Monetary Fund, 2003).

117. *Wall Street Journal*, "First, Uncloak the IMF," November 21, 1997.

118. Joseph Stiglitz, "What I Learned at the World Economic Crisis," *The New Republic*, April 17–24, 2000, 56–60.

119. Martin Gruenberg, a member of the staff of the U.S. Senate Banking Committee, speaking at an IMF forum in December 2001: International Monetary Fund, *Transparency at the International Monetary Fund: The Road Ahead* (Washington, DC: International Monetary Fund, 2001).

120. In 1983 and 1992 General Accounting Office, *Treasury Maintains Formal Process to Advance U.S. Agenda at the International Monetary Fund*, GAO-03-401R (Washington, DC: General Accounting Office, 2003).

121. HR 3331, 105th Cong.

122. General Accounting Office, *International Monetary Fund: Observations on Its Financial Condition*, GAO/T-NSIAD-98-220 (Washington, DC: International Monetary Fund, 1998).

123. Omnibus Appropriations Act, H.R. 4328 (P.L. 105–277), section 601.

124. Michel Camdessus, *Remarks to the World Affairs Council* (Philadelphia, PA: International Monetary Fund, 1998).

125. Executive Office of the President, *Press Briefing by Treasury Secretary Robert Rubin, National Economic Advisor Gene Sperling, and Deputy Treasury Secretary Larry Summers* (Washington, DC: Office of the Press Secretary, 1998).

126. Joint Economic Committee, *IMF Reform Certification by Treasury and Fed Expected* (Washington, DC: Joint Economic Committee, 1998).

127. International Monetary Fund, *IMF Takes Additional Steps to Enhance Transparency*, PIN 99/36 (Washington, DC: International Monetary Fund, 1999).

128. See, in particular, International Monetary Fund, *IMF Reviews the Experience with Publication of Staff Reports and Takes Decisions to Enhance Transparency*, PIN 01/3 (Washington, DC: International Monetary Fund, 2001).

129. Hans Köhler, "IMF Must Adapt and Reform," *IMF Survey*, August 14, 2000, 258–260.

130. Dawson, *Transparency and the IMF: Toward Second Generation Reforms*.
131. Statistics on the publication of key documents are provided in International Monetary Fund, *The Fund's Transparency Policy – Issues and Next Steps* (Washington, DC: International Monetary Fund, 2003).
132. Bretton Woods Project, *IMF Transparency Still Lagging on Crucial Issues* (Washington, DC: Bretton Woods Project, 2003).
133. International Monetary Fund, *Transcript of Press Briefing by Thomas C. Dawson* (Washington, DC: International Monetary Fund, 2003).
134. International Monetary Fund, *Public Information Notice: IMF Reviews the Fund's Transparency Policy – Issues and Next Steps*, PIN 03/122 (Washington, DC: International Monetary Fund, 2003). In 2003, the IMF also reminded governments that IMF documents could not be released under national disclosure laws without its consent: William Holder, *Publication Policies of the Fund* (Washington, DC: Office of the Deputy General Counsel, International Monetary Fund, 2003), 7.
135. Stanley Fischer, *Farewell to the IMF Board* (Washington, D.C.: International Monetary Fund, 2001).
136. Ydahlia Metzgen, Division Chief of the IMF Policy Development and Review Department International Monetary Fund, *Transparency at the International Monetary Fund: The Road Ahead*.
137. Thomas Dawson, IMF Director of External Relations: Dawson, *Transparency and the IMF: Toward Second Generation Reforms*. On the lack of knowledge about conditions in crisis countries, see Louis Pauly, *Who Elected the Bankers?* (Ithaca, NY: Cornell University Press, 1997), 124; Group of Independent Experts, *External Evaluation of IMF Surveillance* (Washington, DC: International Monetary Fund, 1999), 99; Rachel Glennerster and Yongseok Shin, *Is Transparency Good for You, and Can the IMF Help?* Working Paper 03/132 (Washington, DC: International Monetary Fund, 2004), 2.
138. On the expansion of surveillance following the Mexican crisis, see Pauly, *Who Elected the Bankers?* 127. On the need for expansion following the East Asian crisis, see International Monetary Fund, *Annual Report 1998* (Washington, DC: International Monetary Fund, 1998), 34–38.
139. International Monetary Fund, *Assessing the Implementation of Standards – an IMF Review of Experience and Next Steps*, PIN 01/17 (Washington, DC: International Monetary Fund, 2001).
140. Group of Independent Experts, *External Evaluation of IMF Surveillance*, 41.
141. Paul Blustein, *The Chastening* (New York: PublicAffairs, 2001), 49.
142. Robert Kuttner, "The Role of Governments in the Global Economy," in *On the Edge: Living with Global Capitalism*, ed. Will Hutton and Anthony Giddens (London: Vintage, 2001), 150. See also Blustein, *The Chastening*, 382.
143. Flemming Larsen, "The Global Financial Architecture in Transition," *OECD Observer*, March 11, 2002, 10–12.
144. A 2003 study found that developing countries refused to allow publication of the major surveillance document, the Article IV staff report,

about half the time; publication rates for newer surveillance products were also very low in some regions: International Monetary Fund, *The Fund's Transparency Policy – Issues and Next Steps*, 26–29.

145. International Monetary Fund, *Evaluation Report: IMF and Recent Capital Account Crises* (Washington, DC: Independent Evaluation Office, 2003), 52.

146. International Monetary Fund, *The Fund's Transparency Policy – Issues and Next Steps*, 36. In an earlier report, the Fund observed that major American institutional investors were relying on its reports to guide its investment decisions: International Monetary Fund, *Quarterly Report on the Assessments of Standards and Codes – June 2002* (Washington, DC: International Monetary Fund, Policy Development and Review Department, 2002).

147. Several of these organizations are discussed by Anne Marie Slaughter, *Global Government Networks, Global Information Agencies, and Disaggregated Democracy*, Working Paper 018 (Cambridge, MA: Harvard Law School, 2001).

148. Stephen Gill, borrowing a phrase from Michel Foucault, suggests that the aim of organizations such as the WTO and IMF is "panopticism," designed to advance a project of "disciplinary neoliberalism...a world in which the discipline of capital...would operate along rationalist principles based on full access to relevant public and private information: Stephen Gill, *The Constitution of Global Capitalism*, Paper presented at the International Studies Association Annual Convention, Los Angeles (Toronto, Canada: York University, 2000), 11. See also Ann Florini, *Transparency in the Interests of the Poor* (Washington, DC: World Bank Summer Research Workshop on Poverty, 1999).

9. Liquid paper

1. A wonderful discussion of the role of paper and documents in mid-nineteenth century bureaucracies can be found in David Vincent, *The Culture of Secrecy in Britain, 1832–1998* (New York: Oxford University Press, 1998).

2. For a brief history of the evolution of personal information databases, see Simson Garfinkel, *Database Nation*, 1st ed. (Beijing; Cambridge: O'Reilly, 2000), 13–15.

3. http://www.nicar.org.

4. Matthew Wald, "Link between Tires and Crashes Went Undetected in Federal Data," *New York Times*, September 8, 2000, A1; Josh Barbanel, "Fatal Explorer Accidents Involving Bad Tires Soared in '99," *New York Times*, September 19, 2000, C1.

5. David Barstow, "U.S. Rarely Seeks Charges for Deaths in Workplace," *New York Times*, December 22, 2003, A1.

6. Times reporter Walt Bogdanich wrote several articles on the subject in 2004. The last in the series was Walter Bogdanich, "Questions Raised on Warnings at Rail Crossings," *New York Times*, December 30, 2004, 1.

7. Robert Cohen and J. Scott Orr, "Foreign Objects: The Risky World of Medical Implants," *Newark Star-Ledger*, August 11, 2002.
8. Ken Silverstein, "Unjust Rewards," *Mother Jones*, May–June, 2002, 68.
9. http://trac.syr.edu.
10. Rebecca Carr, "Report Says Terror War Waged Poorly in Court," *Atlanta Journal-Constitution*, December 8, 2003, 3A.
11. David Johnston, "Corporate Risk of a Tax Audit Is Still Shrinking, I.R.S. Data Show," *New York Times*, April 12, 2004, C1.
12. Center for Public Integrity, *Windfalls of War: U.S. Contractors in Iraq and Afghanistan* (Washington, DC: Center for Public Integrity, 2003).
13. Center for Public Integrity, *Incomplete Disclosure: IRS Filings Show Few Penalties for Political Committees That Fail to Meet Requirements* (Washington, DC: Center For Public Integrity, 2004); Internal Revenue Service, *News Release: IRS Acts to Enforce Reporting and Disclosure by Section 527 Political Groups*, IR-2004-110 (Washington, DC: Internal Revenue Service, 2004).
14. A detailed discussion of TRI is provided in Mary Graham, *Democracy by Disclosure: The Rise of Technopopulism* (Washington, DC: Brookings Institution Press, 2002), 21–61.
15. For example, see http://www.scorecard.org, a site maintained by the advocacy group Environmental Defense.
16. The claims were exaggerated, as Graham notes. See also Alasdair Roberts, "Review of Mary Graham, *Democracy by Disclosure*," *Journal of Policy Analysis and Management* 22, no. 4 (2003): 709–712.
17. United States Department of Justice, "Report on 'Electronic Record' FOIA Issues," *FOIA Update* XI, no. 2 (1990).
18. Ibid.
19. Ibid.
20. United States Department of Justice, *Freedom of Information Act Guide*, 79–81.
21. The amendments were contained in the Electronic Freedom of Information Act Amendments of 1996, P.L. 104–231.
22. *Schladetsch v. HUD*, No. 99-0175 (D.D.C. Apr. 4, 2000).
23. *Dayton Newspapers, Inc. v. Dep't of the Air Force*, 35 F. Supp. 2d 1033.
24. Public Citizen brought suit against the Justice Department on behalf of the Clearinghouse in 1998, 2000, and 2002. Their efforts are briefly described at http://www.citizen.org/litigation/briefs/FOIAGovtSec/tracfoialit/.
25. Center for Public Integrity, *Complaint for Declaratory and Injunctive Relief* against the U.S. Department of Justice, July 29, 2004.
26. United States Department of Justice, *Freedom of Information Act Guide*, 82.
27. Kirsti Nilsen, "Government Information Policy in Canada," *Government Information Quarterly* 11, no. 2 (1994): 191–209, 205. Emphasis in original.
28. Bill 2782, Assembly of the State of New Jersey, 211th Legislature, introduced May 10, 2004.

29. Alasdair Roberts, "Less Government, More Secrecy: Reinvention and the Weakening of Freedom of Information Law," *Public Administration Review* 60, no. 4 (2000): 298–310, 315.

30. Jeffrey McCracken, "U.S. Officials Backtrack on Safety Disclosure Amid Suit by Tire Makers," *Detroit Free Press*, September 24, 2004. The data was collected under the Transportation Recall Enhancement, Accountability, and Documentation (TREAD) Act, adopted in Fall 2000.

31. Graham, *Democracy by Disclosure: The Rise of Technopopulism*, 31–34.

32. Peter Fairley and Rick Mullin, "Scorecard Hits Home," *Chemical Week*, June 3, 1998, 24–26.

33. Peter Fairley, "Right-to-Know Knocks: Will the Industry Open Up?" *Chemical Week*, August 20, 1997, 19–21.

34. Andrea Foster, "TRI Expansion Options Shift," *Chemical Week*, May 6, 1998, 33.

35. John Cushman, "EPA Is Pressing Plan to Publicize Pollution Data," *New York Times*, August 12, 1997, A1.

36. The case was *Tozzi et al v. EPA*, (D.D.C. No. 98 CV-00169). See also Graham, *Democracy by Disclosure: The Rise of Technopopulism*, 31–34.

37. The EPA's database of risk management plans was completely removed from the web following the September 11, 2001, attacks: General Accounting Office, *Homeland Security: EPA's Management of Clean Air Act Chemical Facility Data*, GAO-03-509R (Washington, DC: Government Accounting Office, 2003).

38. A survey of the data that might be collected is provided by Daniel J. Solove, "Access and Aggregation: Privacy, Public Records, and the Constitution," *Minnesota Law Review* 86, no. 6 (2002): 1137–1218, 1142–1149.

39. *U.S. Dept. of Justice v. Reporters Committee*, 489 U.S. 749 (1989) at 761.

40. A survey of the dominant firms is provided by Chris Hoofnagle, "Big Brother's Little Helpers: How ChoicePoint and Other Commercial Data Brokers Collect, Process, and Package Your Data for Law Enforcement," *University of North Carolina Journal of International Law and Commercial Regulation* 29 (2004): 595.

41. The acquisitions are reported in ChoicePoint's Form 10-K Annual Report to the Securities and Exchange Commission, filed on March 12, 2004.

42. Shane Harris, "Private Eye," *Government Executive*, March, 2004, 30–36, 32.

43. Hoofnagle, "Big Brother's Little Helpers: How ChoicePoint and Other Commercial Data Brokers Collect, Process, and Package Your Data for Law Enforcement," 600.

44. Robert O'Harrow Jr., "In Age of Security, Firm Mines Wealth of Personal Data," *Washington Post*, January 20, 2005, A1.

45. Hoofnagle, "Big Brother's Little Helpers: How ChoicePoint and Other Commercial Data Brokers Collect, Process, and Package Your Data for Law Enforcement," 600.

46. Solove, "Access and Aggregation: Privacy, Public Records, and the Constitution," 1199.

47. Tom Zeller, Jr., "Release of Consumers' Data Spurs ChoicePoint Inquiries," *New York Times*, March 5, 2005, C2.
48. Hoofnagle, "Big Brother's Little Helpers: How ChoicePoint and Other Commercial Data Brokers Collect, Process, and Package Your Data for Law Enforcement," 623.
49. Solove, "Access and Aggregation: Privacy, Public Records, and the Constitution," 1151.
50. Garfinkel, *Database Nation*, 20–21. The Privacy Act of 1974 introduced specific restrictions on the collection and use of the SSN by federal agencies: Public Law 93–579, section 7.
51. D'Vera Cohn, "Long Forms Returning Slowly," *Washington Post*, April 6, 2000, A15.
52. D'Vera Cohn, "Census Complaints Hit Home," *Washington Post*, May 4, 2000, A09; Rad Sallee, "Texas Democrats Scold Bush over Census Statements," *Houston Chronicle*, April 6, 2000, A28. At the same time, the Republican majority in the U.S. Senate passed a resolution calling on census officials to ensure that nonrespondents would be prosecuted or fined for refusing to answer questions. H.Con.Res. 260, 106th Cong., section 344. Public concern was likely aggravated in 2004 when news reports said that homeland security officials had used specially prepared census reports to identify areas with large numbers of people from Middle Eastern countries.
53. Joan Biskupic, "High Court to Hear Privacy Case," *The Washington Post*, May 18, 1999, A8.
54. *Reno v. Condon* (98–1464) 528 U.S. 141 (2000).
55. Hoofnagle, "Big Brother's Little Helpers: How ChoicePoint and Other Commercial Data Brokers Collect, Process, and Package Your Data for Law Enforcement," Note 184.
56. Government Accountability Office, *Social Security Numbers: Governments Could Do More to Reduce Display in Public Records and on Identity Cards*, GAO-05-59 (Washington, DC: Government Accountability Office, 2004), 24.
57. Solove, "Access and Aggregation: Privacy, Public Records, and the Constitution," 1169–1170.
58. Melissa Brown, "Family Court Files: A Treasure Trove for Identity Thieves?" *South Carolina Law Review* 55, no. 777 (2004).
59. Beth Givens, *Public Records on the Internet: The Privacy Dilemma* (San Diego, CA: Privacy Rights Clearinghouse, 2002), 2–3.
60. George Carpinello, "Public Access to Court Records in New York," *Albany Law Review* 66 (2003): 1089, 1122.
61. The bar on access to criminal court records was temporary, to permit further consideration. The 2002 report of the Judicial Conference Committee on Court Administration and Case Management is discussed in Peter Winn, "Online Court Records: Balancing Judicial Accountability and Privacy in an Age of Electronic Information," *Washington Law Review* 79 (2004): 307; Gregory Silverman, "Justice Information Systems and the

Question of Public Access to Court Records," *Washington Law Review* 79 (2004): 175.

62. The 2002 Model Guidelines of the Conference of Chief Justices and Conference of State Court Administrators are discussed in Silverman, "Justice Information Systems and the Question of Public Access to Court Records."

63. Kristen Blankley, "Are Public Records Too Public?" *Ohio State Law Journal* 65 (2004): 413, 433.

64. Martha Steketee and Alan Carlson, *Developing CCJ/COSCA Guidelines for Public Access to Court Records: A National Project to Assist State Courts.* (National Center for State Courts and the Justice Management Institute, 2002), 9.

65. A survey of state practices is provided in North Dakota Supreme Court, *Requests for Bulk Data from District Court Case Information Systems.* (Court Technology Committee, North Dakota Supreme Court, 2003).

66. One of the central characteristics of bureaucracy, Weber said, was its practice of managing on the basis of "written documents ('the files') which are preserved in their original or draft form." Elsewhere Weber observes that in bureaucracies, "administrative acts, decisions and rules are formulated and recorded in writing. . . . The combination of written documents and a continuous organization of civil functions constitutes the 'office' which is the central focus of all types of modern corporate action." Max Weber, *The Theory of Social and Economic Organization* (New York: The Free Press, 1947).

67. Merrill Lynch & Company, *The Next Software Wave: Intelligently Closing the Loop between EIPs, ERP, CRM and E-Commerce* (New York: Merrill Lynch & Company, 2000).

68. National Archives and Records Administration, *Annual Report 2003* (Washington, DC: National Archives and Records Administration, 2004), 13.

69. Giovanna Patterson and J. Timothy Sprehe, "Principal Challenges Facing Electronic Records Management in Federal Agencies Today," *Government information Quarterly* 19, no. 3 (2002): 307–315.

70. William Matthews, "NARA Seeks Ideas for E-Records Archive," *Federal Computer Week*, August 19, 2002, Web.

71. Michelle d'Auray, *Presentation to CIPS Breakfast: Annual Federal CIO Update* (Ottawa: Office of the Chief Information Officer, 2002).

72. Abigail J. Sellen and Richard Harper, *The Myth of the Paperless Office* (Cambridge, MA: MIT Press, 2002), 1–16.

73. Denise Kersten, "The Paper Paradox," *Government Executive*, April 15, 2005, 42–48, 44.

74. Trent Lott and Ron Wyden, "Hiding the Truth in a Cloud of Black Ink," *New York Times*, August 26, 2004, 27.

75. More detail on original and derivative decisions is provided in the Information Security Oversight Office's annual reports.

76. The statistics are drawn from ISOO annual reports.

77. See the ISOO's comments in its annual reports for 1996, 2000, and 2001.

78. Information Security Oversight Office, *Report to the President 2004*, 4.

79. National Archives of Canada, *The Access to Information Act and Record-Keeping in the Federal Government* (Ottawa, Canada: National Archives of Canada, 2001).

80. Lawrence E. Walsh, *Firewall: The Iran-Contra Conspiracy and Cover-Up* (New York: Norton, 1997), 3–15.

81. John G. Tower, Edmund S. Muskie, and Brent Scowcroft, *The Tower Commission Report on the Iran–Contra Affair* (New York: Bantam Books, 1987).

82. Thomas S. Blanton, *White House E-Mail: The Top Secret Computer Messages the Reagan/Bush White House Tried to Destroy* (New York: New Press, 1995), 4–6.

83. Ibid., 6–11.

84. Peter W. Rodman, "Memos to Cover Your Trail," *The Washington Post*, July 2, 1993, A19. Also quoted in Blanton, *White House E-Mail: The Top Secret Computer Messages the Reagan/Bush White House Tried to Destroy*, 14.

85. Columbia Accident Investigation Board, *Report, Volume 1* (Washington, DC: 2003).

86. Joint Inquiry, *Report of the Joint Inquiry into Intelligence Community Activities before and after the Terrorist Attacks of September 11, 2001*, National Commission On Terrorist Attacks Upon the United States, *Final Report*.

87. Senate Intelligence Committee, *Report on the U.S. Intelligence Community's Prewar Intelligence Assessments on Iraq*, 60.

88. Demetri Sevastopulo, "Air Force Secretary Lobbied for Boeing to Win Deal," *Financial Times*, November 22, 2004, 4.

89. Hutton, *Report of the Inquiry to the Circumstances Surrounding the Death of Dr. David Kelly*.

90. Owen Gibson, "Government Emails To Be Kept on Record," *The Guardian*, September 15, 2003.

91. Financial Times, "Haunted by E-Mail," *Financial Times*, January 24, 2004, 10.

92. Blanton, *White House E-Mail: The Top Secret Computer Messages the Reagan/Bush White House Tried To Destroy*, 5 and 12–13. Emphasis in original.

93. Bob Anez, "Gop Chairman Blasts Cost of Media's E-Mail Request," *Associated Press Wire Service*, May 31, 2002.

94. The requests were submitted to the Canada Revenue Agency.

95. Media reports now talk routinely about the search for "smoking gun" documents; the phrase entered the contemporary lexicon in 1974, during the Watergate investigation.

96. David Walker, *E-Government in the Information Age: The Long View* (Washington, DC: General Accounting Office, 2001).

97. Treasury Board Secretariat, *Media Release: Canada Leads World in E-Government for Third Straight Year* (Ottawa, Canada: Treasury Board Secretariat, 2003).

98. Public Records Office, *E-Government Policy Framework for Electronic Records Management* (Kew, United Kingdom: Public Records Office, 2001), 3.

99. General Accounting Office, *Electronic Records: Management and Preservation Pose Challenges*, GAO-03-936T (Washington, DC: General Accounting Office, 2003).

100. European Commission, *Model Requirements for the Management of Electronic Records* (Brussels: IDA Programme of the European Commission, 2002).

101. Information and Privacy Commissioner of Ontario, *Electronic Records and Document Management Systems: A New Tool for Enhancing the Public's Right to Access Government-Held Information?* (Toronto, Canada: Office of the Information and Privacy Commissioner of Ontario, 2003).

102. Department of Finance and Treasury Board of Canada, *RDIMS Reference Manual* (Ottawa, Canada: Treasury Board Secretariat, 2003), 6.

103. Hans-Gunnar Axberger, *Public Access to Official Documents* (Stockholm: Swedish Institute, 1996).

104. See Chapter 2 of the Freedom of the Press Act.

105. The public statements on priorities are provided in Treasury Board Secretariat, *Backgrounder: The Expenditure Review Committee – a Catalyst for Moderning Management Practices* (Ottawa, Canada: Treasury Board Secretariat, 2004); Treasury Board Secretariat, *News Release: President of the Treasury Board Announces Expenditure and Management Reviews* (Ottawa, Canada: Treasury Board Secretariat, 2004).

106. Request DFO2004000171, received July 26, 2004.

107. Exemption 2 of the U.S. Freedom of Information Act. Among specialists this interpretation is known as a "Low 2" exemption.

108. Athan Theoharis, *Chasing Spies* (Chicago: Ivan R. Dee, 2002), 244–247.

109. Graham, *Democracy by Disclosure: The Rise of Technopopulism*, 58–59.

10. The end of the story?

1. James Ettema and Theodore Glasser, "Narrative Form and Moral Force," *Journal of Communication* 38, no. 3 (1998): 8–27.

2. Alan J. Pakula, *All the President's Men* (Warner Brothers, 1976).

3. Louis D. Brandeis, "Other People's Money," *Harper's Weekly*, December 20, 1913.

4. Washington Post, *Washington Post-ABC News Poll: U.S. Treatment of Iraqi Prisoners* (Washington, DC: Washington Post, 2004 [Accessed May 11, 2005]), available from http://www.washingtonpost.com/wp-srv/politics/polls/polltrend_050704.html.

5. Washington Post, *Washington Post-ABC News Poll: Bush and Iraq* (Washington, DC: Washington Post, May 26, 2004 [Accessed May 11, 2005]), available from http://www.washingtonpost.com/wp-srv/politics/polls/trend_052304_q27_31.html. See also: PIPA/Knowledge Networks, *The PIPA/Knowledge Networks Poll: Americans on Detention, Torture, and the War on Terrorism* (Washington, DC: Program on International

Policy Attitudes, July 22, 2004 [Accessed May 11, 2005]), available from http://www.pipa.org/OnlineReports/Torture/html/new_7_22_04.html.

6. Harris Interactive, *Harris Poll: Two in Five U.S. Adults Believe That Torture of Prisoners Still Prevalent in Iraq and Afghanistan* (Rochester, NY: Harris Interactive, April 20, 2005 [Accessed May 11, 2005]), available from http://www.harrisinteractive.com/harris_poll/printerfriend/index.asp? PID=559.

7. PIPA/Knowledge Networks, *The PIPA/Knowledge Networks Poll: Americans on Detention, Torture, and the War on Terrorism*.

8. NBC News, *NBC News/Wall Street Journal Poll* NBC News, June 25–28, 2004 [Accessed May 11, 2005]), available from http://www.pollingreport.com/iraq3.htm.

9. Washington Post, *Washington Post-ABC News Poll: Bush and Iraq*.

10. Craig R. Whitney, "Introduction," in *The Abu Ghraib Investigations*, ed. Steven Strasser (New York: PublicAffairs, 2004), xxiii.

11. *Washington Post* Daily Tracking Poll, July 25-October 31, 2004. http://www.washingtonpost.com/wp-srv/politics/polls/2004tracking/track110104.html

12. The transcripts, prepared by the Commission on Presidential Debates, can be found at http://www.debates.org.

13. Jane Mayer, "Outsourcing Torture," *The New Yorker*, February 14, 2005.

14. *New York Times*, "Time for an Accounting," February 19, 2005, 14.

15. Anthony Lewis, "More Than Fit To Print," *New York Review of Books* 52, no. 6 (2005).

16. *Washington Post*, "The System Endures," December 5, 2005, B6.

17. Bob Herbert, "Is No One Accountable?" *New York Times*, March 28, 2005, 17.

18. Mark Danner, "We Are All Torturers Now," *New York Times*, January 6, 2005, 27.

19. PIPA/Knowledge Networks, *The PIPA/Knowledge Networks Poll: Americans on Detention, Torture, and the War on Terrorism*.

20. Suppose that you are prepared to concede that in extraordinary circumstances – such as the so-called "ticking time bomb" case – torture by government officials may be justified. Suppose, however, that you believe any formal policy acknowledging this fact would lead to excesses – either because the policy would not be appropriately monitored or because it would erode the stigma that deters torture. Hypocrisy might be the best path: refusing to condone a policy of torture, but tacitly accepting it in extraordinary cases.

21. *NES Guide to Public Opinion and Electoral Behavior*. Table 5C.1. http://www.umich.edu/~nes/nesguide/toptable/tab5c_1.htm. Accessed April 29, 2005.

22. Campbell Public Affairs Institute, *The Maxwell Poll on Civic Engagement and Inequality* (Syracuse, NY: Campbell Public Affairs Institute, 2005).

23. Douglas Kellner, *Media Spectacle* (New York: Routledge, 2003). See also Murray Edelman, *Constructing the Political Spectacle* (Chicago: University of Chicago Press, 1990).

24. Danner, "We Are All Torturers Now."

25. Sunshine Week, *News Release: Survey Finds Public Concerned About Secrecy* (Washington, DC: Sunshine Week Executive Committee, March 11, 2005 [Accessed April 15, 2005]), available from http://www.sunshineweek.org/index.cfm?id=5556.

26. Dorothy Samuels, "Psst. President Bush Is Hard at Work Expanding Government Secrecy," *New York Times*, November 1, 2004, 24.

INDEX

Index

American Bar Association, report on
unchecked power, 12
American Civil Liberties Union
(ACLU)
Joint Terrorism Task Forces and,
143–145
prisoner abuse and, 155
American Society of Newspaper
Editors (ASNE), 13–14, 51
Amsterdam Treaty (1997), 177
Anderson, Charles, 23
Anti-Terrorism Act (Canada), 136,
137
Arar, Maher, 136–138
Arar Inquiry (Canada), 136–138
arcana imperii (secrets of imperial
policy), 10
Argentina, 30, 33, 172, 192
Arizona, prison information access
in, 166–167
Armenia, marred elections in, 120
Article 21, of Universal Declaration
of Human Rights, 12
Article 19 (Great Britain), 109,
114
Ashcroft, John, 64, 66, 78
Asiaweek, 4
atomic secrets (U.S.), 34
Attlee, Clement, 34
Australia
adoption of access-to-information
laws in, 93
attempt to extend FOIA to private
sector in, 169
costs for disclosure law
administration in, 113
FOIA fee increase in, 32
misrepresentation by government
in, 96
obstruction/delays in information
requests in, 96–97
prison contract disclosure in, 153
prison privatization and, 152–153
privatization and, 151
privatization of utilities in,
157–158
recordkeeping in, 111–112

security establishment resilience
in, 35
Security Of Information
Agreement with United
States, 132, 133–134
Aylwin, Patricio, 31
Azerbaijan, media/information
access in, 121

Bangkok, Thailand, school
admissions procedures in, 4
basic civil rights protection,
48–49
basic human right, access to
information as, 165–166
Berkowitz, Bruce, 42
Bernstein, Carl, 231–234
Black Wednesday (Great Britain), 7
Blair, Tony, 46, 83–84. *See also* Blair
government
Blair government
decision-making before Iraq war,
101
delay in implementing disclosure
law, 7, 104–105
FOIA and, 83–84
Iraq intelligence handling by,
82–83
media criticism of, 83
pre-election reform promises,
83
pre-war evidence on Iraq, 46
privatization and, 151
right to information under, 7
Blanton, Tom, 217
Bloc countries, ex-Soviet
disclosure law adoption as
prerequisite to join NATO,
129–130. *See also individual
country*
Blumenthal, Sidney, 102
Bobbit, Phillip, 101–102
Bodin, Jean, 10
Bosnia, whistleblowers on U.S.
military contractor in, 156
Brandeis, Louis, 232
Brazil, 30–31, 34, 183, 184, 193

Index

Etzioni, Amitai, 139
EU Council, 175–176
European Commission, 174, 175, 177
European Court of Justice, 176
European Union
 adoption of EDRM systems in, 219
 transparency in, 173–178
 EU Council actions, 175–176
 new disclosure regulation, 177
 new procedures to access documents, 174–176
 Ombudsman role, 175, 177
 popular resistance to integration and, 174
 U.S. multilateral legal assistance treaties with, 138. *See also individual country*
Executive Order 12958, 35, 38
Executive Order 13292, 35

Falconer, Charles, 105
Fallows, James, 47
Fatality Analysis Reporting System, of U.S. Department of Transportation, 201–202
Fay-Jones report, on prisoner abuse, 154
Federal Advisory Committee Act (FACA; 1972), 15–16, 59, 62–63
Federal Aviation Administration (FAA; U.S.), 37–38
Federal Bureau of Information (FBI)
 data aggregation industry and, 209
 denial of evidence of impending terror attacks, 74–75
 secret support to former Nazi officials, 32
Federal Energy Regulatory Commission (FERC; U.S.), 37, 40, 159
Federal Intelligence Surveillance Court (FISC), 70
Federal Register, 13
federal tax law study, 202

Feith, Douglas, 77
Fianna Fáil government, 84
Filmer, Robert, 10
Financial Times, on World Bank, 187
Finland, *official* documents in, 14
Fischer, Stanley, 192
Fleisher, Ari, 58
Florida, 210, 212
FOIA, *see* Freedom of Information Act (FOIA; U.S.); *individual country*
Ford, Gerald, veto of 1974 amendments to FOIA, 55
Foreign Intelligence Service Act (1978), 59, 72
Foreign Intelligence Service Court, 59, 72
Foreign Policy, 17
Fox, Vicente, 6, 31
France, 9, 151, 176–177, 178, 183
Frank, Barney, 186
Franks, Tommy, 76–77
Freedom of Information Act (FOIA; U.S.), 13–14
 abuse in military facilities and, 78
 administration costs of, 114
 Bush Administration (G. W.) and, 64, 71–72
 classified information and, 35–36
 expanded access to information under, 58
 on files for law enforcement purposes, 13
 forerunner to, 179
 nongovernmental agencies and, 118
 resistance to, 98–99
 Rumsfeld support for 1966 Act, 54–55
 Schlesinger on, 69
 veto of 1974 amendments to, 55
 worldwide trend toward adoption of FOIA-style laws, 14–17
Freedom of Information Act Network, 120
French Revolution, 10

Index

Index